Gate Crashers

Gate Crashers

The Offensive Church

JOE KOHLER

WIPF & STOCK · Eugene, Oregon

GATE CRASHERS
The Offensive Church

Copyright © 2015 Joe Kohler. All rights reserved. Except for brief quotations in critical publications or reviews, no part of this book may be reproduced in any manner without prior written permission from the publisher. Write: Permissions, Wipf and Stock Publishers, 199 W. 8th Ave., Suite 3, Eugene, OR 97401.

Wipf & Stock
An Imprint of Wipf and Stock Publishers
199 W. 8th Ave., Suite 3
Eugene, OR 97401

www.wipfandstock.com

ISBN 13: 978-1-61097-677-0

Manufactured in the U.S.A.   02/16/2015

Scripture quotations taken from the New American Standard Bible®, Copyright © 1960, 1962, 1963, 1968, 1971, 1972, 1973, 1975, 1977, 1995 by The Lockman Foundation. Used by permission. (www.Lockman.org)

For the glory of God.

Contents

Acknowledgments | ix
Introduction | xi

1 The Offensive Church | 1
2 God's Mission | 14
3 Rebels—One and All | 24
4 Jesus Is Lord | 35
5 Ambassadors for Christ | 41
6 The Gospel of Jesus Christ | 56
7 Preachers & Teachers | 71
8 Fruit Inspectors | 92
9 Freedom in Christ | 106
10 We Are the Body | 122
11 A Theological Tapestry of Field-Preaching | 147
12 Afterword | 188

Appendix A: Judgment According to Deeds | 193
Appendix B: Servants & Stewards | 204
Appendix C: Source Discussion | 210

Bibliography | 215

Acknowledgments

As with any book, many influences have contributed to shape the thoughts and content of this one. First and foremost, I must acknowledge that anything good and edifying in these pages is a direct result of studying the Bible. What do we have that we did not receive? My hope is that this book will merely bring some of the amazing truths of Scripture to light and will help connect some dots for the body of Christ.

    I am thankful to two women in particular for their work in leading me to Jesus—my beloved wife, Bethany, and my spiritual mother, Carlene. When I was dead in my trespasses and sins, I was fortunate enough to be engaged to a Christian woman who was praying for me and dragging me to church. Equally important was the influence of my father's widow; who loved a broken, angry, and rebellious sinner enough to tell me the truth of the gospel directly and lovingly—even while I abused her and her faith in Jesus. I am so thankful for both of you. The continuous blessing of a godly wife, for both life and ministry, is more than I can describe.

    After coming to faith, the Lord called me to seminary. I was fortunate to have my formative years in the faith be shaped by godly men who served as professors at Moody Theological Seminary-Michigan. These men all contributed to my growth in the knowledge of the Scriptures and how to accurately handle the word of God. Perhaps even more important than these necessary skills, these men demonstrated to me as a young Christian the importance of dedication to the Lord and living a life worthy of our God. While all of my professors had influence, I am especially thankful to: Dr. John Jelinek—who taught me the importance of knowing *what* the Bible says and *where* it says it; Dr. Eric Moore—who taught me the importance of being a faithful shepherd of God's people; Dr. Paul Wilson—who taught me that there is no excuse for failing to take our calling to learn the Scriptures with all our strength; Dr. Gene Mayhew—who taught me the importance of history in understanding our faith; and Professor Raju Kunjummen—who taught me to greatly respect the written word of God and to pay careful attention to its nuances. Their lives and classes influenced me for the better and for that I am thankful. Without them, this book never would have been written.

I am also thankful for the contribution of Joel Davidson, Karl LaPeer, Aaron Hathaway, and Dr. Eric Moore. Each read portions and/or drafts of the manuscript for this work and offered feedback and suggestions which were beneficial for both clarity and theological accuracy. Any errors, mistakes, or awkward phrasing should be assumed to be my own.

It is a great blessing to have deep and genuine fellowship within the church. As we grow together and make disciples, I am thankful for the men (and their families) who dedicate their lives to serving and growing in Christ with me who have not already been mentioned: Chris Rozek, Tom McClure, Brian Smith, Lawrence Dixon, and Chris Morgan. I am especially thankful for Joel Davidson who has served with me as my evangelist. You men challenge me to grow every day, you never let me get away with being sloppy theologically, and you hold me accountable to actually put into practice (by the power of the Holy Spirit) the things that we read in Scripture. Thank you for pushing me to grow in the grace and knowledge of the Lord, and for serving our king with me, shoulder to shoulder.

Finally, thank you to everyone who supports Fourth Year Ministries and our mission. This book could not have been written if not for your faithful support.

To God alone be the glory. May his kingdom come, may his will be done, on earth as it is in heaven.

Introduction

> The secret things belong to the LORD our God, but the things revealed belong to us and to our sons forever, that we may observe all the words of this law.
> (Deut 29:29)

There is a God and he is not silent. The one who created the universe and all that is in it has chosen to reveal himself and his will throughout history, through the Scriptures, and through the person of Jesus Christ.[1] As those who have received this revelation,[2] we have three choices: we can disagree with and/or ignore it, we can agree with it (and still ignore it), or we can actually live our lives according to it and observe his revealed will and instruction.

God's people throughout history have chosen all three of these options. Abraham,[3] the father of our faith, believed God and his faith was credited to him as righteousness.[4] The thing about Abraham's faith that is most important is that it resulted in him actually *obeying* God and doing what God told him to do. God said, "Move," and Abram *moved*.

God fulfilled his promise to Abraham by making of him a great nation: the nation of Israel. God chose to have a special relationship with Israel and to cause his name to dwell among them. When this nation began to ignore God's revealed will and to wander away from their God, he called them back to himself through his prophets and through divine discipline.[5] One

---

1. E.g., Gen 35:7; Heb 1:1–3.
2. Jude 1:3.
3. Abraham was known as "Abram" when God called him, but God later changed his name to Abraham.
4. Gen 15:6.
5. E.g., Jer 7:1–34.

such prophet whose call to repentance and genuine divine guidance were simply ignored was Jeremiah. God declared his good will towards his people through Jeremiah; yet they spurned this call to return to God through repentance. The people ignored God's will and went their own way.[6]

Perhaps the most interesting response to God's word was illustrated in the response of the people to the prophet Ezekiel:

> But as for you, son of man, your fellow citizens who talk about you by the walls and in the doorways of the houses, speak to one another, each to his brother, saying, "Come now and hear what the message is which comes forth from the LORD." They come to you as people come, and sit before you as My people and hear your words, but they do not do them, for they do the lustful desires expressed by their mouth, and their heart goes after their gain. Behold, you are to them like a sensual song by one who has a beautiful voice and plays well on an instrument; for they hear your words but they do not practice them. (Ezek 33:30–32)

The people gathered to listen to Ezekiel. They believed that God was speaking through this prophet. They identified themselves as God's people. They spoke about the things they heard from Ezekiel in their homes and in public places. Hearing the word of God was like entertainment to them—like a sensual song sung by one with a beautiful voice accompanied by pleasant music. *They hear your words but they do not practice them.*

As a pastor, I know that all three of these categories of responses still exist within the professing church today. Some gather and listen to the word of God and simply do not believe it nor do they consider it relevant. It is foolishness to them; or at best something that only applies if they want it to. Others genuinely humble themselves before their God and heed what he is calling them to do as revealed in his word—enabled by his indwelling Holy Spirit.

The most troubling category exists in the middle. These are the ones who gather to hear the word of the Lord and may even raise their hands in the worship service and give a hearty, "Amen!" or two to acknowledge their agreement with the word of God during the message. They might commend the preacher at the end of the service for speaking an "anointed message" from God. These are the ones who will defend their biblical values and answer all the right ways on the survey. However, these are also the ones who will leave from the presence of God completely *unchanged* each week. They are more concerned about what is for lunch, their stock portfolio, or what team is playing football that day, than they are about the glory of God, the

---

6. E.g., Jer 42:1—43:7.

fate of the lost, or living a life worthy of the calling that they have received in Christ.

It is time for those of us who are called by the name of the Lord to examine ourselves and our practices.[7] If we are genuinely and soundly in the faith, we have nothing to worry about by such an examination. It is likewise time for us to re-identify ourselves as citizens of the kingdom of God. There is a very big difference between being an *American* Christian and being a *Christian* American. Honestly answer this question for yourself: are you more defined by your Christianity and the Lord you claim to serve, or by the American dream, and your right to life, liberty, and the pursuit of happiness?

As a result of "the American Way" influencing everything in our culture—including the forms of what we call "church"—we must re-examine how God has designed his church to work and stop simply examining what "works" according to our cultural ideas and agendas. In God's kingdom, faithfulness is more important than pragmatism.

I believe in the church. I believe that God desires for his name to be glorified and that the church is God's chosen instrument for that very important purpose. I also believe that much of what we call "church" in America is nothing like what the Lord designed. We've strayed from his intention and we've abandoned his design. We've modified and changed it. We've "improved" it. We've taken liberties that were never ours to take. Like many before us, we've gone our own way. This critique extends to every aspect of our current "church" culture—applying from home churches to mega-churches, and everywhere in between.

It is time to humble ourselves before the living God and submit ourselves to his design.[8] If we've strayed, let us repent and return. Upon examination we will once again discover that it is right to praise God for what he has done on behalf of his people and his creation. We will see the beauty of a church that glorifies God and through which God is able to do abundantly more than all we can ask or imagine.[9]

God has designed an *offensive* church. Are you on board?

---

7. 2 Cor 13:5.
8. Isa 66:1–2.
9. Eph 3:20–21.

1

The Offensive Church

> I also say to you that you are Peter, and upon this rock I will build My church; and the gates of Hades will not overpower it. I will give you the keys of the kingdom of heaven; and whatever you bind on earth shall have been bound in heaven, and whatever you loose on earth shall have been loosed in heaven.
> (Matt 16:18–19)

Regardless of what you may think or hear, the church of Jesus Christ is not in a losing position. Jesus himself has promised that he will build his church. Jesus is not worried that the gates of hades will be able to stand up to his advancing kingdom or that they may overpower his church. But what does that really mean?

Many different ideas exist as to what, exactly, "the church" *is* and what it *should be*. Some want the church to be a social club, a place to belong, a place to love and be loved unconditionally. Some want the church to be a place of social and political activism. Others simply want the church to be a place they can take their children to learn good Judeo-Christian morals and hear Bible stories. Some want to meet in a big building with stained glass windows and some want to meet in homes. Some think that "the church" is the building itself. You get the idea.

But is this what *Jesus* wants his church to be? Shouldn't *his* desire be more important than *ours* when it comes to church since it belongs to him and he promised to build it?

Despite these differing notions of what people think the church is, and want the church to be, Jesus made a clear statement recorded in Matthew 16:18–19 about the nature of the church—his church. Jesus' church is built on the recognition of *who* he is.[1] Jesus' church belongs to him and he takes the responsibility for building it. Jesus' church is powerful.

When Jesus declared simply that the gates of hades will not overpower his church, he was making a bold statement. According to the Bible, the present world is currently under the curse of God as a result of our rebellion and sin against him.[2] Part of this curse included God handing the rule and authority of this world over to the devil. This is a missing piece of information for many people today: the world we live in is under control of a tyrannical spiritual dictator who seeks only to steal, kill, and destroy. "We know that we are of God, and that the whole world lies in the power of the evil one" (1 John 5:19). People are enslaved to this tyrant and under his power, many without ever being aware of it. Sometimes, even those who are freed from the domain of darkness desire to become enslaved again: "But now that you have come to know God, or rather to be known by God, how is it that you turn back again to the weak and worthless elemental things, to which you desire to be enslaved all over again?" (Gal 4:9).[3]

Those who are enslaved under this tyrannical spiritual dictator are citizens of the kingdom of darkness and are under the domain of the devil.

---

1. I understand that this is a controversial claim and that different Christian traditions have interpreted this passage differently. I find that the best interpretation of this passage is that Jesus is referring to Peter's confession that Jesus is the Messiah based on the following: (1) Jesus begins this discussion by asking who others identify him to be (Matt 16:13); (2) Upon asking Peter his opinion, Jesus commends his answer because it was divinely revealed to Peter by the Father (Matt 16:17); (3) It is upon this correct identification of Jesus as the Christ by Peter that Jesus then rightly identifies *Peter*, saying, "I also say to you that you are Peter" (Matt 16:18a) thus continuing the theme of proper identification; and (4) When Jesus discusses the foundational "rock" upon which he will build his church, the Greek text records a near demonstrative (upon "this") being employed instead of a relative pronoun (upon "whom"), indicating that Jesus is not referring to Peter himself (which would naturally expect the use of a relative pronoun), but is making a play on words with Peter's name and the "rock" upon *which* (that is, Peter's confession of Jesus as the Christ), not *whom*, more clear. For contextual and grammatical reasons, it appears that the most natural referent to what Jesus will build his church upon is the confession of Jesus as the Christ—an interpretation that fits soundly within the broader scriptural teaching of salvation being by grace through faith alone, applied to all who repent and put their faith in Jesus.

2. E.g., Gen 3:14–19.

3. See also Exod 14:11–12 and Num 14:1–4.

That is heavy. This kingdom of darkness is firmly established upon the earth and those who are under this domain are powerless to escape on their own. Jesus came to set the captives free and to announce that there is a new king and a new kingdom at hand! For those who recognize the king (Jesus) and submit themselves to him, God is willing and able to transfer them from the domain of darkness into the kingdom of light. "For He rescued us from the domain of darkness, and transferred us to the kingdom of His beloved Son, in whom we have redemption, the forgiveness of sins" (Col 1:13–14). When Jesus says that the gates of hades will not overpower his building of his church, he is declaring that the kingdom of darkness is powerless to stop the advance of the kingdom of heaven! Jesus declared war; and not only a war, but a victorious one.[4]

After Jesus ascended into heaven and took his place at the right hand of God the Father in glory, the apostle to the gentiles recognized the truth that the gospel of the kingdom was advancing and bringing forth fruit everywhere:

> We give thanks to God, the Father of our Lord Jesus Christ, praying always for you, since we heard of your faith in Christ Jesus and the love which you have for all the saints; because of the hope laid up for you in heaven, of which you previously heard in the word of truth, the gospel which has come to you, just as in all the world also it is constantly bearing fruit and increasing, even as it has been doing in you also since the day you heard of it and understood the grace of God in truth. (Col 1:3–6)

Nothing has changed today. The gospel is still constantly bearing fruit and increasing in the entire world as people continue to repent and put their faith in Jesus. Jesus knows that his church is on the *offensive* (as opposed to playing *defense*), and that the expansion of the church includes taking ground away from the kingdom of darkness, knocking down its gates, and setting its captives free to go continue the advance of the kingdom of God in the power God provides. The devil, to be sure, does not take this aggression lightly; but he knows his time is short.[5]

Understanding the nature of these warring kingdoms and the *offensive* nature of the genuine church as described by Jesus, we must examine the purpose and calling of God's church in the world. God's people are often lulled into being a *defensive* church. This defensive posture appeals to our flesh and is demanded by this present world in the name of "tolerance" and

---

4. This war is not a physical war, but a spiritual one; see Eph 6:12.
5. Rev 12:12.

"religious pluralism." A *defensive* church is no threat to tear down the gates of the kingdom of hades.

What are some marks of a *defensive* church? A defensive church:

1. Protects its own territory
2. Responds to attacks from without and within
3. Seeks comfort and offers ministry to those who are not "comfortable."

On the surface, all of these things seem good and right. After all, are we not commanded to contend for the faith once for all handed down to the saints as recorded in Jude 1:3? Are we supposed to stand idly by and allow false teachers to bring heresy and false doctrine into the church contrary to the apostolic counsel Paul gave to Timothy in 1 Timothy 1:3? Should the church not address "attacks" on the faith—both from within the ranks of the professing church and from those who are hostile to the faith? Should the church ignore the broken and hurting in this world and shut down all of our ministries to the poor, grieving, and hurting and ignore James 1:27?

While the marks of a defensive church describe many good church activities, they reflect a poor *strategy*. This is true simply because it falls short of Jesus' strategy. A defensive church protects its own territory as if any single particular local church has sole claim to "the kingdom of God" in its area. As a result, a defensive church is often unwilling to participate with other genuine Christians in advancing the kingdom of God and tearing down the gates of hades in unity founded upon their mutual faith in the gospel of Jesus Christ. Heaven forbid that some of "our people" may find a pastor they like more and go sit in his pews instead of ours! How can we grow our "mini-kingdoms" with all this transfer growth happening? Therefore, the defensive mindset convinces us that we must protect what is ours. What we need to understand is that the kingdom doesn't belong to us and it's not *our* church. It's his.

As a result of this defensive attitude, ministry is *hindered*, not benefited; and the body of Christ is divided. Some may object that they cannot partner with other Christians because they are too different—but this is a spirit of divisiveness. It is counter-productive to Jesus' goal for his church. I am the first to agree that the church should not fellowship with the world[6] and that not all who profess to follow Christ actually do follow him.[7] We should not be so inclusive as to elevate "unity" simply for the sake of unity to the neglect of genuine agreement on the gospel. But to get to the place

---

6. 2 Cor 6:14–18.
7. Phil 3:18–19; Titus 1:16, Acts 20:28–31.

where the church is not partnering with *the church* in lovingly reaching the world with the gospel? That is just foolishness.[8]

Due to the predominately defensive posture of the church in the United States, we begin to make a bigger deal about the things that divide us instead of focusing on the one thing that unites us: the gospel of Jesus Christ. Taking this further, we begin to make a big deal about the attacks on our particular pet doctrines and the problems facing the world, and we then trumpet our particular answers and solutions to these real issues. Often, we draw lines in the sand to separate ourselves from anyone who has a different solution than that of our particular denomination. I do not want to diminish the importance of genuine Christians wrestling with the problems in this world or the importance of holding on to true doctrine. I do want to question the *effectiveness* of our defensive strategy.

It doesn't work.

The reason is not because we aren't trying hard enough. The reason is simply because playing defense doesn't bring the gates of hades down.

Playing *offense* does.

So, what are some marks of an *offensive* church? An offensive church:

1. Seeks to take ground from the enemy in expanding the kingdom of God
2. Initiates attacks against the kingdom of darkness
3. Ignores comfort and seeks to release captives as the major ministry and seeks to equip those who have been released to further crash the gates of hades.

The offensive church has many of the same goals as the defensive church but it employs a radically different strategy. The offensive church understands that the best defense is actually a potent offensive attack, relying upon the power of God himself and walking in obedience to his command to make disciples of all nations. The offensive church defends its own territory by aggressively taking ground from the kingdom of darkness and by expanding the borders of the kingdom of God. Want to keep your own gates safe? Expand the frontlines further and further away.

The offensive church does not wait for the attacks against the faith to come. Instead, it initiates attacks against the kingdom of darkness through the bold proclamation of the gospel. It must be stressed that the "attacks" that are being referred to have *nothing* to do with violence in the physical realm: "For our struggle is not against flesh and blood, but against the rulers, against the powers, against the world forces of this darkness, against

---

8. More on this in chap. 9, "Freedom in Christ."

the spiritual forces of wickedness in the heavenly places" (Eph 6:12). The weapons of warfare for the biblical Christian are the proclamation of the gospel, love, prayer, and service; all empowered by the Holy Spirit. Christianity has largely receded from the marketplace of ideas[9] and now tends to only *respond* to attacks from the secular world upon matters relating to the faith. This is a tragedy. Instead, the offensive church seeks to bring the gospel to the world, recognizing that only the gospel has the power to genuinely transform, to make a positive impact on this spiritually dead world, and to bring it back to *life*. Sometimes, when the church *does* try and engage in an offensive attack, it often substitutes the Lord's methods for worldly methods. Here's an example: consider Prohibition.

When trying to rid the country of the "evils of alcohol" an attempt was made to make this change happen through legislation—and not just any legislation, but through a constitutional amendment. The passing of the Eighteenth Amendment to the Constitution of the United States made the manufacture, sale, or transportation of alcohol for drinking purposes illegal in the United States. It also outlawed importing and exporting alcohol to and from other places.[10] If there is no alcohol to drink, then people can't get drunk. Solid logic.

A related and fascinating historical side note: it didn't work. At all.

There is a good case that could be made that it actually made things *worse*. And since it worked so poorly, another constitutional amendment was passed by Congress about fifteen years later repealing Prohibition.[11] By way of comparison, when revival swept through towns as a result of the preaching of the gospel at the hands of the Methodists (most famously George Whitefield and the Wesley brothers) and others like Jonathan Edwards, bars closed down as a result of increased devotion to the Lord. There were towns previously known for drunkenness where a drunken person could not even be found.[12] In contrast to the results of legislated prohibition in the United States, historian Earl Cairns states that in England "the gin traffic was stopped, partially because of the influence of the revival" at the

---

9. For a good survey of this historical movement and the implications, see Moreland, *Love Your God*, 19–40.

10. Reading the Constitution is a good exercise for every citizen of the United States. You can read the full text of the Constitution and the Amendments for free online at http://www.archives.gov.

11. The 18th Amendment was passed by Congress on December 18, 1917, and was repealed by the 21st Amendment, passed by Congress on February 20, 1933. These amendments were ratified on January 16, 1919, and December 5, 1933, respectively.

12. E.g., Kimbrough and Newport, *Manuscript Journal*, 2:518.

hands of the Methodists.[13] As hearts and communities were changed when spiritually dead people were raised to spiritual life through the preaching of the gospel, there was no one left who wanted to live a life of drunkenness and carousing. The market for alcohol dried up without it being legislated by lawmakers. Alcohol was legal and *still* bars closed, drunkards turned sober, and the gin traffic was stopped.

This is a similar problem that the idol-makers encountered in Ephesus when Paul began preaching the gospel there.[14] People were being born-again through repentance and faith in response to the gospel being proclaimed boldly. This was bad for those who profited off of idolatry and sin!

The reason that the offensive strategy is more effective is because preaching the gospel deals with the core problem—the fallen state of human nature—and not the various *symptoms* that result from this core problem. Trying to legislate against the symptoms of fallen humanity without dealing with the cause is like giving pain medicine to someone with a bleeding artery. Stopping the bleeding is much more important to the life of the person than covering the associated pain with medication. When we solve the core problem, the symptoms tend to go away too.

Despite this, many modern members of the church still think that we can eliminate other evils from our land through legislation. They are relying on the defensive church strategy because it is all they know. It's the American way. This strategy wants to take on one symptom at a time without truly dealing with the underlying condition. A prime modern example is the case of abortion. At every election we will begin hearing Christian pundits proclaiming the importance of voting for pro-life candidates. This happens because we are trusting in the legislative process to make abortion illegal.

And, it just might.

But abortion is still a symptom. Even if abortion is made illegal, people will still kill their unborn children. People kill their living children too, even though that is currently illegal. You know who will never kill their baby in the womb? My wife. She's a born-again Christian. If the law of the land *mandated* abortions (like in some other places on the planet) in certain cases . . . still, she would not abort. The law of God transcends the law of the land. This is only true because of what Christ has done in her life. Before Christ, she was pro-choice. Her mind was not changed by persuasive argument or by legislation. Her heart was changed by the gospel. Becoming pro-life was simply part of the transformation. The old is gone, the new has come.[15] The

---

13. Cairns, *Christianity*, 388.
14. Acts 19:23–28.
15. 2 Cor 5:17.

disease was cured. Now the symptoms of the disease are being eliminated one by one from the inside out.

You really want to stop abortion? Go to abortion clinics and preach the gospel. If the Lord is pleased to grant repentance and faith to those who hear you, then they will not murder their babies in the womb—even if it is still legal to do so. The defensive church wants to respond to the evil by making it someone else's problem and protecting their own. In the case of abortion, we want to pass the buck to the state and have them deal with it through legislation. They can't. They can try, but they will fail. It's not their fault (at least, not entirely)—the human heart is too wicked.[16] You can outlaw murder, but people still kill people. You can outlaw thievery, but you should still lock your doors. After a recent school shooting, the solution according to some pundits was to restrict ammunition capacity in certain types of guns as the solution. Wasn't it already illegal to bring guns into a school and kill people?

Do you see how foolish and impotent legislative solutions can be?

To be clear—I'm not arguing that we should abandon just laws or seek after anarchy. On the contrary, just laws are a wonderful thing for any society. Seeking just and true laws *is* a godly thing to do.[17] In the same way, it is a sign that we know God and are members of his kingdom when we plead the cause of the afflicted and needy.[18] I will continue to exercise my right to vote for as long as I have it. I will vote for those who share my values and who I believe will best fulfill the duties of the office. I will do what I can to seek justice, and equity, and to personally help the poor. I will advocate for the protection of unborn children in their mother's wombs.

I will also never put my hope and trust in politicians, our legal system, or my own works of charity. We must understand the *limitations* of politics, legislation, and benevolence. Legislation can only *repress* wickedness, it cannot *cure* it. And while citizens of any country ought to do their civic duty, this does not abdicate *followers of Jesus* from doing their *Christian* duty. The state is not the church, and the church is not the state. When we forget this (and history has plenty of examples), the results are grim.

Finally, the offensive church ignores comfort, understanding that the stakes are too high to merely tend to the wounded and argue over whatever color we want to paint the children's sanctuary. The offensive church knows that going to the frontlines (like to the abortion clinics) is necessary if real change is to be seen in the hearts of people and in our communities. Instead of waiting for those who are wounded to come to the church seeking

---

16. Jer 17:9.
17. E.g., Neh 9:13; Isa 1:16–17.
18. Jer 22:16; Matt 25:31–46; Jas 1:27.

ministry, the offensive church seeks to release captives; to set them free from the domain of darkness as a preemptive strike. Can you imagine if we did not wait until families were broken up before telling them the good news of the gospel and encouraging them to find life in Jesus Christ? The offensive church seeks to give the solution *before* the full extent of the curse is felt in the lives of people.

Will the offensive church stop every hurt? Of course not. There is still plenty of need for ministries to the broken and hurting. The spiritual war is ongoing. No one is immune from getting wounded in this fallen world. However, the offensive church knows that some of the hurt can be avoided by bringing the gospel to the captives even before they realize they need it.

Somewhere along the line the professing church has come to believe a lie that the gospel is only relevant to some people and not to others. *Those who seem to have everything going well for them at the present time, well . . . maybe the gospel is not for them.* This lie has directly contributed to the church transforming into a predominately defensive-oriented posture. *We won't "cram our religion" down your throat, but we'll be here if you need us!* This line of thinking is faulty for at least two major reasons: it fails to properly understand the fundamental nature of the biblical gospel and its implications.

First, it does not truly understand the nature of the gospel proclamation that "Jesus is Lord." Do you know that this is not simply a religious claim? If I were to walk up to you on the street and say, "Barack Obama is the president"—would you shoot back, "Hey! Don't cram your political views down my throat!" I doubt it. If you did, you would be misunderstanding my claim. The fact of the matter is that Barack Obama *is* currently the president of the United States of America. That is not a political view, it is just the truth. To announce this to someone is not cramming anything down their throat—but it is very possible that people still won't want to talk to you about it!

In the same way, Jesus of Nazareth is an historical figure who lived in the first century in Israel. Jesus was crucified under the Roman governor, Pontius Pilate, for claims that he made; specifically, that he was the creator God in the flesh and that he was the Savior of all who will turn to him.[19] To the Jews, this was blasphemy. To the Romans, this was treason, because it would make Jesus king and lord when Caesar was king and lord. As a result, Jesus was executed as a blasphemer and an enemy of the state of Rome.

---

19. For those interested in examining the historical evidence for Jesus, I encourage you to check out William Lane Craig's work at www.reasonablefaith.org. You can find there both scholarly and popular articles that contain evidence for the historical Jesus from Jewish, Roman, and other secular sources, in addition to the Bible.

However, on the third day, Jesus was declared with power to be exactly who he claimed to be when he rose from the dead.[20]

The resurrection proved that this Jesus, whom we crucified, the Father has made both Lord and Christ.[21] This same Jesus ascended into heaven after spending forty days on earth where he took his seat at the right hand of the majesty on high, ruling as King of kings and Lord of lords. He has promised to return and bring judgment upon his creation. And, astoundingly, God has graciously offered forgiveness of sin through repentance and faith in Jesus. On the other hand, God also promises that he will crush all of his adversaries under his feet. This is a terrifying reality for all who persist in their rebellion against God and who die in their sins.[22]

If you believe this, then you should tell people. The implications are huge. If you do not believe it, then you are failing to believe the testimony of God through the Bible. This is who the Bible presents Jesus to be. This is the historical faith that has been passed down from the original eye-witnesses of him and his ministry. Many people are cultural Christians—but are not actually followers of the living Jesus.[23]

We should keep in mind that many people may not like the fact that Jesus is king (just like many people may not like whoever the current president is). We should keep in mind that not everyone will agree that Jesus' policies are "good" and "right" (just like people disagree about the policies of our elected officials). Not everyone will agree that these historical claims are accurate or that Jesus really rose from the dead. In fact, some people scoffed at the resurrection in the first century, too.[24] The response of people to the message, however, has no bearing on the truth of the statement.

Barack Obama is not any *more* or any *less* the president based on how people respond to the statement that he is. Quite frankly, it doesn't matter what people think or how they respond. I know some folks who say things like, "He's not *my* president! I didn't vote for him!" But he is *their* president—unless they move out of the United States. They are citizens of this political system and the governmental domain applies whether they cast a

---

20. Rom 1:4.

21. Acts 2:36.

22. My ministry partner, Joel Davidson, has quipped, "What *other* king would be so gracious as to continue to allow rebels to persist against him so long? Especially when it is well within his power to put down the rebellion and execute his wrath against those in rebellion against him? Only our God is so gracious—continuing to provide breath to those rebels who use that breath to curse his name and live for their own purposes and glory." See also Prov 20:2.

23. E.g., Matt 7:21–29; Luke 14:25–35.

24. Acts 17:30–32.

ballot for the current president or not. Since the jurisdiction of the United States government is limited geographically, moving away to remove yourself from governmental claims is a possibility. However, God's sovereignty extends over all the kingdoms of the earth and there is nowhere in all of creation that we may flee to escape his domain.[25]

The proclamation that "Jesus is Lord" is actually a historical and governmental claim, not simply a religious one. Both the person who agrees and the person who disagrees are expressing some faith that either Jesus did or did not rise from the dead after claiming to be the creator God in the flesh. Neither person's faith changes the historical reality. If this is true, then people are subject to Jesus whether they want to be or not (just like American citizens are subject to the president whether they voted for him or not!), because Jesus' claim of authority is not limited by time or geography.

There is another side to this issue: If Jesus Christ is Lord, and if we are in rebellion against his rule until we repent and put our faith in him to save us from the wrath that is to come,[26] then those who have *not* repented are also subject to the ruler of the domain of darkness—the devil. The person who thinks that the gospel is only relevant to some people (perhaps just the "down and out") simply does not understand the nature of the devil, the curse that is upon this present world and all who live in it, nor the power of the gospel alone to save those who are perishing. Listen to these warnings and admonitions:

1. Be of sober spirit, be on the alert. Your adversary, the devil, prowls around like a roaring lion, seeking someone to devour. (1 Pet 5:8)

2. You are of your father the devil, and you want to do the desires of your father. He was a murderer from the beginning, and does not stand in the truth because there is no truth in him. Whenever he speaks a lie, he speaks from his own nature, for he is a liar and the father of lies. (John 8:44)

If you want to see the clearest picture of the devil's plans for humanity, read Job 1–2. Notice that the devil takes no mercy and grabs every inch that he is allowed. When he is given permission to take life, he takes it. When he is given permission to bring financial ruin, he goes the distance and does not merely cause Job's stock to drop a few points. When he is allowed to bring affliction to the body, he covers the entire body instead of giving minor discomfort here and there. Every inch he is allowed, he takes. Make no mistake: if anything good happens to anyone, it is only because of

---

25. Pss 103:19; 139:7–10.
26. 1 Thess 1:9–10.

the restraining hand of God telling the devil he can go only so far, and not any farther. This is the reason for Paul's stern warnings to those who are no longer under the rule of the devil:

1. And do not give the devil an opportunity. (Eph 4:27)
2. The Lord's bond-servant must not be quarrelsome, but be kind to all, able to teach, patient when wronged, with gentleness correcting those who are in opposition, if perhaps God may grant them repentance leading to the knowledge of the truth, and they may come to their senses and escape from the snare of the devil, having been held captive by him to do his will. (2 Tim 2:24–26)

The enemy is fierce. It is unwise to deal foolishly with him and his forces:

1. And especially those who indulge the flesh in its corrupt desires and despise authority. Daring, self-willed, they do not tremble when they revile angelic majesties, whereas angels who are greater in might and power do not bring a reviling judgment against them before the Lord. (2 Pet 2:10–11)
2. Yet in the same way these men, also by dreaming, defile the flesh, and reject authority, and revile angelic majesties. But Michael the archangel, when he disputed with the devil and argued about the body of Moses, did not dare pronounce against him a railing judgment, but said, "The Lord rebuke you!" (Jude 1:8–9)

Even worse than all of this, those who are still in their rebellion are under the wrath of God: "He who believes in the Son has eternal life; but he who does not obey the Son will not see life, but the wrath of God abides on him" (John 3:36). Although our enemy is fierce and fearsome, he is no match for our Lord who reigns! The devil is not an equal, competing force against God. Instead, the devil is a created being (like we are) who is accountable to God and subject to God's reign. The devil's authority in this world is a result of the curse and rebellion of mankind; it is a portion of the wrath of God being poured out upon this world. God gave the devil authority that was originally given to Adam. The devil's rule is not because the devil has succeeded in gaining power against the living God. It is for this reason that Jesus, the true king, can say with no hesitation that the gates of hades will not overcome the advance of his church. "You are from God, little children, and have overcome them; because greater is He who is in you than he who is in the world" (1 John 4:4).

The church of Jesus Christ must stand in the strength God provides, clothed in him and his power, or else we stand no chance of advancing his kingdom and tearing down the gates of hades. Therefore, followers of Jesus are sternly warned, "do not grieve the Holy Spirit of God, by whom you were sealed for the day of redemption" (Eph 4:30) and "do not quench the Spirit" (1 Thess 5:19). To try and fight against the kingdom of darkness in our *own* strength and with our *own* strategies is a foolish endeavor. Such a plan is doomed to failure.

The living God has called his church to be gate crashers of the kingdom of darkness through proclaiming the good news of the kingdom of God! "But you are *a chosen race*, a royal *priesthood, a holy nation, a people for* God's *own possession*, so that you may proclaim the excellencies of Him who has called you out of darkness into His marvelous light" (1 Pet 2:9). Those who are followers of Christ Jesus are commanded to walk as he walked.[27] Jesus declared to his earliest followers that he was sending them out in the same way that he was sent[28]—as his ambassadors.[29] If we are truly to follow him, Jesus is calling us into the ministry in which he walked:

> And He came to Nazareth, where He had been brought up; and as was His custom, He entered the synagogue on the Sabbath, and stood up to read. And the book of the prophet Isaiah was handed to Him. And He opened the book and found the place where it was written, "The Spirit of the Lord is upon me, because he anointed me to preach the gospel to the poor. He has sent me to proclaim release to the captives, and recovery of sight to the blind, to set free those who are oppressed, to proclaim the favorable year of the Lord." And He closed the book, gave it back to the attendant and sat down; and the eyes of all in the synagogue were fixed on Him. And He began to say to them, "Today this Scripture has been fulfilled in your hearing." (Luke 4:16–21)

The Spirit of the Lord is upon the church that we would preach the good news to the poor. God is sending us to proclaim release to the captives, to demonstrate that the kingdom is at hand, to set free those who are oppressed, and to proclaim the favorable year of the Lord. It is the Father's good will and pleasure to defeat the enemy under the feet of his people. "The God of peace will soon crush Satan under your feet" (Rom 16:20).

We are called to be an *offensive* church, not a *defensive* church.

---

27. 1 John 2:6.
28. John 20:21.
29. John 13:20; 2 Cor 5:17–21.

2

God's Mission

I thank my God in all my remembrance of you, always offering prayer with joy in my every prayer for you all, in view of your participation in the gospel from the first day until now. For I am confident of this very thing, that He who began a good work in you will perfect it until the day of Christ Jesus.
(Phil 1:3–6)

The offensive church understands its mission and takes its marching orders from the living God. As the citizens of the kingdom of Jesus Christ,[1] the church gets its mission from the King of kings and Lord of lords. Our mission is God's mission.[2] It does not change with the seasons. God's mission has endured since the beginning of creation and will continue until the end of time.

You can read about the founding of the church at Philippi by the Apostle Paul and Silas during their missionary journey in Acts 16:11–40.[3] Paul and Silas encountered some persecution as a result of their ministry

---

1. Col 1:13.
2. 2 Chr 15:1–2.
3. I am indebted to Christopher J. H. Wright's excellent book *The Mission of God: Unlocking the Bible's Grand Narrative* for first exposing me to the pervasive and expansive themes discussed in this chapter. Anyone interested in a much more in-depth examination of some of these themes is encouraged to read Wright's book in its entirety.

in Philippi and, shortly after they were released from prison, they went on their way and left the newly-formed church.

A few years later, when Paul writes to this church where he spent a relatively short amount of time,[4] he expresses both his thankfulness for them and his joy in their participation with him in the work of the gospel. The apostle also expresses confidence that the God who began a good work in them will continue to perfect it until the day of Christ Jesus. The word translated as "perfect" in Philippians 1:6 in the NASB comes from the Greek *epiteleō*[5] and is translated as "bring it to completion" (ESV), "perform it" (KJV), "continue to complete it" (NAB), and "carry it on to completion" (NIV) in other prominent English translations of the Bible. The reason for these varied but similar translations of the same word is because it is often difficult to find an exact word in one language that perfectly represents or carries the same connotations from the original language that is being translated.

Despite the slight variance in exact wording chosen by the translators, the idea is clear: God is doing *something*, and God will bring that work to its intended end in fulfillment of his plan. Paul is confident that God will continue to do his work, with the end never being in doubt, until the Day of Christ Jesus. Then it will be finished, and not before. Paul is explicitly declaring his confidence that God is going to finish the work that he (God) has started.

Many interpretations of this passage focus on the *individual* nature of Paul's confidence—that God will complete the *salvation* of each believer in Philippi. By extension, this confidence can then be applied to all believers, in all places. This passage is often used by pastors and teachers to express a certainty of God's work in salvation being brought to completion for all who believe the gospel. The truth of salvation in individuals is a beautiful thing. It is both worthwhile and comforting to dwell on. It has certainly made for many moving sermons, lessons, devotionals, and books!

However, in the context of this letter to the Philippian followers of Jesus, Paul is *not* expressing his confidence in the Lord's work in the *individual*. Paul is discussing something even bigger. He is expressing his confidence in the Lord's work in the *community of believers and in the world*. The confidence of God's continued work in the *individual* can be found

---

4. Especially in contrast to the amount of time spent in places like Corinth and Ephesus.

5. The lexical entry for *epiteleō* includes "1) to finish something begun, *end, bring to an end, finish*, . . . 2) to bring about a result according to a plan or objective, *complete, accomplish, perform, bring about*, . . . 3) to cause something to happen as fulfillment of an objective or purpose, *fulfill*" (BDAG, 383).

elsewhere in Paul's writings (e.g., Rom 8:28–30); but here in Philippians 1:6, Paul is expressing a different and grander truth—a *singular* work amongst the *plurality* of God's people for the benefit of the whole world.

The Bible is really a God-centered book that we often mistakenly read as a man-centered book (or a "*me*"-centered book!). Although it is true that many of the passages in Scripture apply directly to people—both those who are *believers*[6] and those who are not—most of what is written is more directly about God, his activity and work, and how we ought to respond to that work. Our response (the "me" part) is built upon the foundation of his revelation of his glory and his work.

As Paul is writing to this congregation of believers in Philippi, he is expressing his thankfulness that they have been transformed by the gospel of Jesus and have become participants in *God's work* in the gospel. This work, Paul is absolutely certain, will continue until it is brought to completion—*by* God, *through* his people—on the Day of Christ Jesus.

God's work is continuing in the present day, almost two thousand years after Paul originally wrote this letter to the believers in Philippi. Paul wasn't writing to them about his confidence in their *individual* salvation—as glorious as that is!—but instead was pointing to his confidence in the fact that God will continue the work of the gospel and the advance of the kingdom of God until it is completed on the Day of Christ Jesus. A day that—as of the time of my writing these words and your reading them—is still yet future.

Just like Paul, we can be confident that God will complete his work. It's *his* mission and no one can stop him.[7] Yet, the question must be asked: what, *exactly*, is the nature of God's mission? What is God working towards and what can we be confident that he will perfect until the Day of Christ Jesus? What was Paul really pointing the Philippian believers toward? What is the apostle's confidence *really* in?

---

6. The term "Christians" was first applied to believers in the Messiah (Jesus) at Antioch (see Acts 11:26). However, since salvation by grace through faith has been the consistent teaching of Scripture from the beginning (compare Gen 15:6 with Gal 3:6–7 and Rom 4:1–25), and since the gospel has been declared since Adam (Gen 3:15) and Abraham (Gen 12:3; Gal 3:8), with believers all along the line (that is, people who believed that either God *would* send a Savior or that he *has* sent the Savior depending on whether they lived before or after Christ's first coming), the term *believers* is often preferable to the term *Christian* because of the associated connotations that accompany the term *Christian*—especially in a culture that thinks you are Christian because you attend church every once-in-a-while and/or check that box on the surveys. Unfortunately, sitting in a church building doesn't make you a follower of Jesus Christ or a "believer in him" any more than sitting in a tree makes you a banana! Those who belong to Jesus are blessed with Abraham, the believer (cf. Gal 3:9 in the NASB).

7. Deut 32:39; Job 42:2; Dan 4:34–35.

These questions strike at the heart of the gospel. We must remember that the good news of the gospel is first and foremost focused on God. There are certainly implications for us, and for you specifically, but that is only secondary. When we skew our focus and make the gospel about us, we begin to change it.

To modify it.

To add to it and to take away from it.

We make it about "God-shaped holes in *our* hearts." We make it about *our* physical health or *our* bank account(s). We make it about *our* relationships, *our* comfort, *our* will, and *our* desires. And when we make it about us, we make it so much less than it really is. We make it that which is really no gospel at all. These false gospels tend to get people excited because we like to hear about ourselves and what's in it for us. Unfortunately, these false gospels also tend to let us down. Maybe not at first—but eventually, and eternally. The source of these false gospels doesn't matter. They all end in everlasting condemnation.[8]

This point cannot be over-stated. The good news is *not* about proclaiming what *we* get, but about proclaiming *who God is*. The gospel is about the name, glory, and person of the living God. This news has tremendous implications for every man, woman, and child. It demands a response of some sort from us. Even still, the good news is all about God.

If you read the Scriptures carefully, you'll see that the theme of the gospel is tied to the kingdom of heaven. The two are closely related. For example:

1. Jesus was going throughout all Galilee, teaching in their synagogues and proclaiming *the gospel of the kingdom*, and healing every kind of disease and every kind of sickness among the people. (Matt 4:23, emphasis added)

2. Jesus was going through all the cities and villages, teaching in their synagogues and proclaiming *the gospel of the kingdom*, and healing every kind of disease and every kind of sickness. (Matt 9:35, emphasis added)

3. This *gospel of the kingdom* shall be preached in the whole world as a testimony to all the nations, and then the end will come. (Matt 24:14, emphasis added)

4. Now after John had been taken into custody, Jesus came into Galilee, preaching *the gospel of God*, and saying, "The time is fulfilled, and *the*

---

8. Gal 1:8–9.

kingdom of God is at hand; repent and believe in the gospel." (Mark 1:14–15, emphasis added)

5. The Law and the Prophets were proclaimed until John; since that *time the gospel of the kingdom of God* has been preached, and everyone is forcing his way into it. (Luke 16:16, emphasis added)

Throughout the entirety of the Scriptures this is a unifying theme which, sadly, has been almost entirely lost in much contemporary preaching and teaching. Equally as distressing, this theme has been twisted and distorted in some strands of theology that make the kingdom all about *us* again. Throughout the history of God's people revealed in the Scriptures, the God of the Bible has been acting to deliver a people—a kingdom of priests—for himself. His activity in their midst was intended to let the whole world know the glory of his name.[9]

The idea of a kingdom is relatively simple, even for those who have never lived in one. For a kingdom to exist, you need a king, a people, and a territory. When the Bible begins, we see that God creates the heavens and the earth, and all of creation is considered to be part of his domain. He rules sovereignly over all of it.[10] Yet, at the culmination of his creative activity, God created Man—both male and female[11]—in his image and he gave them authority to rule over and subdue the rest of God's good creation.[12]

Essentially, the first human beings (Adam and Eve) were viceroys: they were appointed by the sovereign king to rule God's creation. Sadly, these viceroys rebelled against the rule and authority of the king by violating the one command he gave them after choosing to listen instead to the voice of a creature rather than the voice of the creator.

Demonstrating what it means to be a *believer* begins here. Adam and Eve are tempted to question what God has told them and to decide if they believe that the consequences of their disobedience and rebellion will really be what God has said.[13] In this same sense, Noah stands out as someone who believes God because when God told him to build an ark, he obeyed and actually built it! In the same way, Abram/Abraham believed God and obeyed

---

9. For a short study, read Gen 12:1–3; 18:18–19; 22:18; 26:4; 28:14; Gal 3:7–9, 29; Exod 9:13–16; 19:4–6; Lev 20:26; 1 Pet 2:9–10; Lev 26:3, 11–12; Deut 4:6–9; 28:9–10; Josh 4:21–24; 1 Sam 17:46; 1 Kgs 8:41–43, 54–61; 2 Kgs 19:19; Isa 19:24–25; 42:8; 43:9–12; 45:21–24; Jer 6:18–19; 18:1–11; Ezek 5:7–9; 36:20–26; 38:22–23; Amos 3:1–2; Mic 1:2; Matt 24:14; 28:18–20; and Acts 26:16–18. For an in-depth study, read Wright, *Mission of God*.

10. E.g., Gen 14:22; 24:3; Deut 4:39; 10:14; Ps 103:19.

11. Gen 1:27.

12. Gen 1:26–30; Ps 8.

13. Gen 3:1–7.

what God told him to do.[14] Genuine belief will result in obeying God's word. This is how James and Paul can both cite Abraham as their example when discussing faith[15] without contradicting each other in their discussion about works and deeds. A living, genuine faith will produce deeds appropriate to the confession.[16] Without accompanying deeds, the "faith" is dead—in other words, you don't *really* believe it and your actions are in accord with what you *really* believe. If Noah never built the ark (or if he simply "built it in his heart"—as modern-day professing Christians like to say they are practicing their faith), would that "faith" have saved him when it started to rain and the waters broke forth from the earth? Could we say that Noah really "believed" God if he did not act on what God told him was coming? The scriptural answer is, "No." This same principle is extremely important and relevant when considering the word of God in our own day and the implications of the gospel of Jesus Christ.

The treacherous act of rebellion by the first man and woman against the creator God of the universe could not be ignored. God swiftly responded to this rebellion with curses upon the man, woman, serpent, and creation,[17] and God drove them out of the garden of Eden. In the midst of the curse, God proclaimed the gospel for the first time in Genesis 3:15, prophesying that in the future a seed of the woman (a male child) would come and crush the head of the serpent, destroying the curse.

What follows the expulsion of Adam and Eve from the garden in the Scriptures describes the state of this present world: a condemned and fallen race, sold into bondage to sin and death, under the rule and authority of a spiritual tyrant that we cannot see or touch, and whom many believe does not exist—the devil. Although the Genesis account does not specify directly that part of the curse included handing the dominion and authority once delegated to humans over to the devil and his forces, the New Testament record makes this abundantly clear.

The man Jesus of Nazareth came from God in order to undo the effects of the curse and retake the authority and dominion which was transferred from Adam to Satan.[18] Because the devil was present at the curse[19] and heard God's own promise that a redeemer was coming to take back authority and

---

14. Gen 12:1–4; 15:6.
15. Compare Gal 3:6–29; Rom 4:1–25; and Jas 2:14–26.
16. Jonah 3:10.
17. Gen 3:14–24.
18. Gal 3:13–14; 4:4–5.
19. Rev 12:9.

dominion, look at the strategy employed during the temptation of Jesus in the wilderness:

> And he [Satan] led Him [Jesus] up and showed Him all the kingdoms of the world in a moment of time. And the devil said to Him, "I will give You all this domain and its glory; for it has been handed over to me, and I give it to whomever I wish. Therefore if You worship before me, it shall all be Yours." (Luke 4:5–7)

The domain and glory of all the kingdoms of the world have been handed over to Satan, and he gives them to whomever he wishes. Since the devil knew exactly who Jesus was, and what he came to do, he was offering Jesus a shortcut to claiming the domain and authority over every kingdom of the world, and eliminating the need for going to the cross and enduring the wrath of God on behalf of sinners. All Jesus had to do was bow his knee in worship to Satan. Elsewhere in the Scriptures this same truth is stated regarding the domain and authority of the devil in this present world, the most pointed of which is found in 1 John: "We know that we are of God, and that the whole world lies in the power of the evil one."[20] Thankfully, Jesus did not take the short-cut. Instead, he fulfilled the predetermined plan of God and demonstrates his grace, mercy, and love through dying for those who call on his name.[21]

The evidence of the reality of this present world being under the domain of Satan and the curse of God is abundant. Many who believe in "god" and are regular church attenders have never heard this truth before, yet it is clearly stated in the Bible. For those who are skeptical of the claims of any religion, and for those who reject the idea that there is a God, the evidence of suffering in this world is a weighty argument *against* the existence of a God; particularly a God that claims to be good, kind, and loving.

If we remove this scriptural truth from our understanding (and from our explanation of the gospel to others), it is very difficult to make sense of this fallen world. *Doesn't God care about us? Can't he do something to help the starving children? What about poverty, disease, and natural disasters? Why is God doing such a bad job at running the universe? Is he unable to ease our suffering and pain? Does he just not care?*

Where is he?

The group of believers that I fellowship with participates in evangelism regularly together (at least twice per week). In our experience of having thousands of conversations with people in our community and in other

---

20. 1 John 5:19. See also 2 Cor 4:4 and 1 Pet 5:8. For a survey of the types of things the devil seeks to do, read how he takes every inch he's allowed in Job 1–2.

21. John 3:16; 15:13; Acts 2:23–24; Rom 3:21–26; 5:8; 1 John 3:16; 4:10.

communities to which we've travelled, the reality of God's curse upon his creation—taught explicitly in the events recorded in Genesis 3:14–19—is one of the most disputed items in our conversations. The *false* idea that God is *not* angry with sin presently has so influenced our pulpits across the nation and many of the "Christian" books on the best-seller lists, that people fail to realize God's disposition toward his creation is currently that of wrath. The only way for this disposition of God towards fallen man and woman to be changed is through what Christ did on the cross.[22]

Without understanding the nature of humanity's rebellion against the creator, the reality that his wrath is presently upon his creation as a result of our disobedience to his commandments, and our rejection of him as king, then this present world makes little sense; or, the most sensible position regarding this broken world filled with suffering becomes either that "God" is not as great as some people think or is just a fairy tale. Without understanding that humanity has rebelled against its creator, and that the creator has cursed his creation as a result of our rebellion, the skeptic who claims that religion is just a crutch for the weak who want to cling to fairy tales that make them feel better amidst the cold, dark reality of a world filled with suffering and death is really not that unreasonable.

However, with a proper biblical understanding of a just, holy, and righteous God who has cursed humanity for our rebellion against him, *then* we can see the abundant grace of God everywhere we look! He is the one who created oxygen and provides us with lungs to breathe it, even though we often use those breaths to curse his name. What a gracious God and king! Those who persist in their rebellion against God only do so because he has withheld his full wrath against them because he is patient with them, not desiring any to perish, but for all to come to repentance.[23]

It is God's mission to redeem a people for himself from the curse from every tribe, tongue, and nation. God plans to reconcile them to himself and to establish his kingdom with the redeemed as his people. He plans to do this, not because we deserve it, but to glorify his name. In fact, God will glorify his name through demonstrating both his mercy to the redeemed and through demonstrating his righteous wrath and indignation against sin on those who do not repent and trust in the mediator.[24] To fulfill this mission, God has graciously called (and continues to call) individuals into

---

22. For an excellent discussion of these same themes, see Washer, *Gospel's Power*, 129–65.

23. Prov 20:2; 2 Pet 3:9.

24. 1 Tim 2:5; Rev 16:4–7; 19:1–6.

the service of his kingdom from out of the domain and dominion of the kingdom of darkness.[25]

As God's work has endured from the beginning, his people have always understood this mission. The Apostle Paul was no exception. This is why his confidence never wavered that *God* would complete what *he* had begun in the church at Philippi, until *God* had completed it on the Day of Christ Jesus at a time in the future. Paul is thankful for the Philippians *participation* in God's work and, afterward, Paul turns his attention to that future day a little later in his letter to them as he describes the Day of Christ Jesus:

"For this reason also, God highly exalted Him, and bestowed on Him the name which is above every name, so that at the name of Jesus *every knee will bow*, of those who are in heaven and on earth and under the earth, and that every tongue will confess that Jesus Christ is Lord, to the glory of God the Father" (Phil 2:9–11).[26]

We get to see a glimpse of this future day being fulfilled in the last book of the Bible: Revelation.

1. And they sang a new song, saying, "Worthy are You to take the book and to break its seals; for You were slain, and purchased for God with Your blood men from every tribe and tongue and people and nation. You have made them to be a kingdom and priests to our God; and they will reign upon the earth." (Rev 5:9–10)

2. After these things I looked, and behold, a great multitude which no one could count, from every nation and all tribes and peoples and tongues, standing before the throne and before the Lamb, clothed in white robes, and palm branches were in their hands; and they cry out

---

25. Rom 9:6–33; Col 1:13–14; 1 Pet 2:9–10.

26. Both the NASB and the NET translate this verse differently than virtually every other prominent English translation by translating "will" instead of "should" before every knee bowing and every tongue confessing (either explicitly or implied). The reason for these more common translations is that the verbs are in the subjunctive mood, which is predominantly used "to *represent the verbal action (or state) as uncertain but probable*" (Wallace, *Beyond the Basics*, 461, italics in original). However, to simply translate this particular dependent clause as *probable* yet *uncertain* as to its fulfillment is to miss Paul's original intent. Although the subjunctive is often used in this way, the particular usage reflects a purpose/result clause which takes on a different meaning which "indicates *both the intention and its sure accomplishment*" (Wallace, *Beyond the Basics*, 473, italics in original.) Paul is expressing the divine will and reason for exalting Jesus—for accomplishing the result that every knee *will* bow and every tongue *will* confess that he is lord, to the glory of God the Father. The context strongly suggests that the NASB and the NET have translated this verse properly and all others that mistakenly use "should" have missed the divine intent and rendered the clause with less strength than Paul originally intended. It is not *probable* that every knee will bow and that every tongue will confess. It is certain. Cf. Isa 45:22–23 and Rom 14:11–12.

with a loud voice, saying, "Salvation to our God who sits on the throne, and to the Lamb." (Rev 7:9–10)

The God who knows the beginning and the end will complete his work of instituting his kingdom in its fullness, under the headship of his appointed king, Jesus. He will do so with a people redeemed from the curse from every tribe, tongue, and nation, and with his enemies placed under his feet to the praise and glory of his name. It's his mission. Like Paul, we can rejoice in all whom God has called to participate in the gospel, knowing that he will complete the work he has begun on the Day of Christ Jesus.[27] The end is not in doubt! Jesus has already completed his work of redemption and been appointed king. Accordingly, it is this gospel which must be proclaimed to the ends of the earth and to every creature as a testimony before the end will come.[28]

The offensive church must embrace this mission and walk in accordance with God's revealed will, empowered by his grace, lest we find ourselves disconnected from the head of the church and walking in our own will and power.[29] God is leading his church to seek and save the lost from every tribe, tongue, and nation. God is reaching out to rebels through the church with the glorious gospel of grace in Christ. It is to this reality of humanity's rebellion and the lordship of Christ that we will turn our attention to next.

---

27. Isa 46:10; 1 Cor 15:20–28.
28. Matt 24:14; Mark 16:15.
29. Col 2:18–19; 1 Pet 4:1–2.

3

Rebels—One and All

Why are the nations in an uproar / And the peoples devising a vain thing? / The kings of the earth take their stand / And the rulers take counsel together / Against the LORD and against His Anointed, saying, / "Let us tear their fetters apart / And cast away their cords from us!" / He who sits in the heavens laughs, / The Lord scoffs at them. / Then He will speak to them in His anger / And terrify them in His fury, saying, / "But as for Me, I have installed My King / Upon Zion, My holy mountain." / "I will surely tell of the decree of the LORD: / He said to Me, 'You are My Son, / Today I have begotten You. / 'Ask of Me, and I will surely give the nations as Your inheritance, / And the very ends of the earth as Your possession. / 'You shall break them with a rod of iron, / You shall shatter them like earthenware.'" / Now therefore, O kings, show discernment; / Take warning, O judges of the earth. / Worship the LORD with reverence / And rejoice with trembling. / Do homage to the Son, that He not become angry, and you perish in the way, / For His wrath may soon be kindled. / How blessed are all who take refuge in Him! (Ps 2:1–12)

To genuinely understand why the church must take the message of the gospel to the world as an offensive act—as opposed to waiting for the world to come to the church—we must build off of the foundational truth that the creation has rebelled against its creator. This rebellion is both foolish and futile since the God against whom we have rebelled is more powerful and majestic than we could ever comprehend. According to Psalm 2:4, the one who sits in the heavens looks upon our rebellion and laughs—knowing the futility of our actions.

The creator—the one who stretched out the heavens and who created light with a word, who breathed life into non-living material and made living beings, who set the boundaries for the seas, raised up the mountains, and who numbers the stars, the grains of sand, and each hair on our heads, the one who sustains his creation effortlessly and continuously by the power of his own will—cannot adequately be compared to anyone or anything. There is no one like him. All of the might of our armies and weaponry put together pose no more of a threat to him than a tiny piece of dry paper does to a furnace! Only we are deluded by our rebellion. God is not impressed or worried. It would very literally be easier for any one of us to eat the Sun, than it would be for all of us collectively to defeat the creator of the universe in our rebellion or to thwart his will.

It is God's prerogative *when* and *how* to bring judgment upon his creation for our crimes against him. We are accountable to him and he is accountable to no one.[1] The book of Genesis records God's judgment against his creation through the flood—a judgment which destroyed all human beings (men and women, young and old) except eight persons. After this judgment, God promised never to destroy all flesh with a flood—next time the judgment will be with fire.[2] God would be perfectly just and righteous if he brought his wrath at any moment. We rebelled and he is the judge of all the earth!

Yet, because of God's grace and compassion, he is holding back his wrath because he does not desire for any to perish but for all to come to repentance.[3] It is in this light that we begin to understand God's great love for what he has made.

We rebelled against him, and God was righteous and just to curse us. However, it didn't end with the curse. God has revealed a plan of redemption from the curse—a plan which he himself would accomplish since no one else could. The plan of redemption must demonstrate both God's perfect justice and righteousness, while also demonstrating his mercy, compassion, and grace. It must, because this is who God is—he cannot act in ways that are contrary to his own nature. Otherwise, he would not be God.

Theologians throughout the history of God's people have understood this great theological dilemma: How can a just and righteous God forgive

---

1. 1 Chr 29:11; Dan 4:35; Rom 9:14–24; 14:11–12.
2. Gen 9:11–15; 2 Pet 3:7.
3. 2 Pet 3:8–9.

iniquity, transgression, and sin? The just judge of all the earth will not clear the guilty, will he?[4] A great deception affects many of our fallen race who have believed that God will simply turn his face away from our sins and let most of us into heaven when we die. This deception can be based on a view that God's kindness and mercy will simply cause him to overlook our crimes against him and his law, and that God will treat our rebellion lightly. Or, it simply fails to understand the depth and nature of our rebellion against him. However, when God's attributes are rightly understood, it is precisely the *goodness* of God which will secure the condemnation of every person who has transgressed even the *least* of God's commandments on the Day of Judgment. In his goodness and justice, God cannot leave rebellion unpunished or sin unaccounted for.[5] It is sobering to realize that the "goodness" of God is perhaps his most terrifying characteristic—because what does a good God do with people who are *not* good?[6]

Many are deluded into believing that God grades on a curve and that merely being "no worse than the rest of us" is a safe position to be in. However, there are not degrees of innocence. You are either *innocent* or you are *guilty*. Transgressing even one commandment of God—whether intentionally, through neglect or ignorance, or by mistake—still causes the one who did so to be *guilty*.[7] It may certainly be true that others may be guilty of *more* wickedness, iniquity, transgression, and sin than you are, but guilty criminals are not acquitted because they are less guilty than other criminals. We will all stand individually before the judgment of the Lord and justice will be upheld. The Bible teaches that judgment will be worse for some than for others, but guilty is still *guilty*.[8] Those who believe that they are safe because they are comparing themselves to the people around them are like a person on the Titanic believing they are free from danger because they have reasoned to themselves, "If I'm sinking, then everyone else is sinking, too!" If this world is like a sinking ship, do you see the foolishness of gauging our safety and eternal destiny by comparing ourselves to others who are on board with us? Sometimes the truth is horrifying and the danger is real. Danger is not avoided simply by ignoring it and/or pretending it isn't real.[9]

---

4. E.g., Gen 18:25; Exod 20:5–7; Num 14:18; and Hab 1:13.

5. Exod 34:5–7; Jer 30:11.

6. I first heard this idea about God's goodness being a scary attribute in a message preached by Paul Washer.

7. Jas 2:10.

8. E.g., Matt 10:12–15; 11:21–24.

9. Sometimes people object to this when I am sharing the gospel with them and tell me, "I don't want to be motivated by fear." I understand the sentiment. However, in many cases being motivated to act out of fear is the most reasonable response. For

Another way to attempt to resolve this theological dilemma is to disagree with God's declared judgment in the Bible on the nature of human beings. Many choose to believe that humans are mostly good; or at worst are morally neutral. When people do not understand or agree that they are rebels against God, they often think that their lives are mostly good with only a few mistakes. According to this judgment, they think God would be a monster to send them, their family members, their friends, or their neighbors to hell for an eternity simply because they made a few *mistakes* when they were kids.[10] On the contrary, the Bible teaches that our rebellion is much deeper than this.

To view "sins" merely as *mistakes* is a great error. When this view is believed and taught it often leads people to make superficial declarations of repentance.[11] In reality, our rebellion is pervasive and persistent. It affects every aspect of our being—we have not simply *rebelled*, we *are* rebels to our core. It is our nature as humans. Therefore, to repent of "mistakes" and trust in Christ to forgive only these few naughty things we did in the past is to fundamentally change the biblical teaching of godly repentance and what we *really* need to trust Christ for. We don't need Christ to save us from a few mistakes here and there. We need Jesus for everything. Every moment—past, present, and future. If we are trusting in Christ for our mistakes only, then we are deceived into believing that we are contributing to our salvation through our own good works. We may not be willing to admit this, but it is true nonetheless.

This biblical reality exposes the foolishness of the arguments people make about certain aspects of their personality being "just the way God made me." This is not true. It is the way God's *curse* has made us, but our fallen nature is not something that God will overlook or hold us guiltless

---

instance, fear may motivate you to evacuate a burning house quickly, avoid reaching your hand toward a dog with its teeth bared, or rescue a child that has wandered into the street. In some cases, fear is justified because the danger is real. In these cases, action motivated by fear is perfectly justified and to be commended. In the same way, those who believe they don't "need" Jesus do not understand their present situation. To fail to come to Christ is the same as refusing to evacuate a burning building, saying, "I won't be motivated by fear!" The fear of the Lord is the beginning of wisdom (Job 28:28; Ps 111:10; Prov 1:7; 9:10; 15:33), and *wisdom* in the biblical usage is *acting* in accordance with what is best (e.g., Matt 10:28).

10. While our group was participating in some open-air preaching and evangelism recently, a heckler from the crowd began shouting, "No one deserves hell. No one!" His vocal objections were based on the idea that no human being is wicked enough to deserve everlasting, conscious torment for their sins. He believed in the inherent goodness of humanity. I bet he still locks his doors at night, however.

11. If Christianity is only about morals, what did Saul of Tarsus need to "repent" of? See Phil 3:1–21.

for simply because we were born this way. Yes, we are all by nature a certain way—but unfortunately that *way* is rebellious to God, and to his laws, and is rightly deserving of his wrath and condemnation. Being "human" means being a rebellious criminal against the creator of the universe! This is not what humans were originally created like. It is not what humans *will* be like in the new creation. This is not what God declared "very good" *before* the fall.[12] Jesus serves as the perfect example of what an unfallen human being is supposed to be like. He was drastically different than anyone else who has ever, or will ever, live. Adam and Eve were similar, but they fell. The man, Jesus of Nazareth, is the only example of what human beings are *supposed* to be like that we will ever experience prior to the final judgment. He is the perfect standard against which all other human beings will be measured.

When God looked upon his fallen creation, his judgment of the state of human beings was bleak: "Then the LORD saw that the wickedness of man was great on the earth, and that every intent of the thoughts of his heart was only evil continually" (Gen 6:5).

Every intent. Only Evil. Continually.

It was this judgment that led to the flood. Afterwards, God made a covenant with Noah: "The LORD smelled the soothing aroma; and the LORD said to Himself, 'I will never again curse the ground on account of man, for the intent of man's heart is evil from his youth; and I will never again destroy every living thing, as I have done'" (Gen 8:21).

The creator and judge of the universe is restraining his hand of judgment at the present time, even though, according to his judgment, *every* thought and intention of the human heart is *only* evil from our childhood.[13] God certainly doesn't agree with the cultural ideas about sin that humanity in its fallen state just makes a few "mistakes" here and there, but for the most part are pretty good. Quite the opposite! The only one whose judgment *actually* matters—the one to whom we must all give an account[14]—tells us that human beings are evil. Your personal opinion of this verdict is no more significant than your opinion that the speed limit on the freeway should be higher (or lower). As God's creation, you are accountable to God's moral standard (which is moral perfection[15]); he is not accountable to yours.

---

12. Comparing Gen 1–2 with Rev 21–22 is an interesting exercise to see how God will restore much of his original creation and plan in the end. What takes place between Gen 3 and Rev 20 exposes the fallen reality of our present world.

13. See also Isa 48:9–11. This judgment is upon all who are not hidden from the wrath of God in the Savior, Jesus Christ; see John 3:36.

14. Rom 14:12; 1 Pet 4:4–5; Heb 9:27.

15. Matt 5:20, 48.

His judgment is this: human beings are evil. Every single one of us. No exceptions.[16]

Our rebellion against God is not a product of simple mistakes; it is a product of a fallen nature that has affected every aspect of our being. This rebellion is deeply embedded in our intellect, emotions, and will. This may sound extreme, but it is the revealed judgment of God through his word. For those who think God is being *mean* in telling us this, consider the fact that he did not have to tell us at all! God could have simply brought swift judgment and punishment upon us for our crimes. Instead, God lovingly declares the judgment beforehand and offers salvation for all who heed this warning, repent, and take refuge in the Savior from the wrath that is to come.[17]

To examine how God can make such a judgment against us, consider Jesus' response to this question:

> One of the scribes came and heard them arguing, and recognizing that He had answered them well, asked Him, "What commandment is the foremost of all?" Jesus answered, "The foremost is, 'Hear, O Israel! The Lord our God is One Lord; and you shall love the Lord your God with all your heart, and with all your soul, and with all your mind, and with all your strength.' The second is this, 'You shall love your neighbor as yourself.' There is no other commandment greater than these." (Mark 12:28–31)

According to Jesus, the foremost commandment of the living God is that a person shall love the Lord your God with all your heart, all your soul, all your mind, and all your strength. You've probably heard that before. But have you ever really considered it?

"All" is a little word with big significance. "All" means *all*—as in one hundred percent, and nothing less. The Greek word from which this is translated is *hólos* which carries a lexical range including: "complete, whole, or all." The original Hebrew word used in the commandment which Jesus is quoting from (Deut 6:5) is *col*, which means (you guessed it): "all, the whole." You don't need to be a scholar in the biblical languages to get the point: "all" means *all*.

---

16. John 7:7.

17. The ministry of the Old Testament prophets should be understood in this same context. Although many of these books are hard to read because of the severe judgments recorded in them, consider that God was under no obligation to sound a warning before bringing judgment at any point in human history. Telling of the calamity beforehand so that some may heed the warning to repent and find refuge from the coming wrath is a loving act from a loving God.

The *greatest* and *foremost* commandment from the creator God is that those made in his image would love him with one hundred percent of their heart, one hundred percent of their soul, one hundred percent of their mind, and one hundred percent of their strength simultaneously.

Let that sink in for a second.

One hundred percent. *All*.

What Jesus is saying is pretty intense. He's saying that if you love the Lord your God with anything less than one hundred percent of everything you have and are—*even for a moment*—then you are in violation of the *greatest* and *foremost* commandment the king of the universe has declared![18] That's serious.

Here's the thing: if you are honest with yourself, you can probably admit that you've *never* actually loved God with all of your heart, soul, mind, and strength simultaneously.[19] Not even for one moment of your life. One percent of your heart, one percent of your soul, one percent of your mind, and/or one percent of your strength is an easy thing to give away without even thinking about.[20] Do you see how our rebellion (*your* rebellion) is so much deeper than a few mistakes? Every moment that we fail to love the Lord our God with all of our heart, soul, mind, and strength simultaneously—that is, whenever we put even one percent of our heart, soul, mind, and/or strength into pursuing *anything* other than his glory—we are in violation of God's foremost and greatest commandment.[21]

---

18. See also Exod 20:3–6; 34:14; Deut 4:24; 5:7–10; and 6:13–19.

19. Sometimes I meet people who tell me that they live most of their lives loving God with all their heart, soul, mind, and strength. This is clearly a deception. Every human being is prone to thinking about themselves and their own desires on a regular basis, which is to put at least a portion of our heart, mind, and strength towards pursuing the gratification of these things. If you failed to seek the will of the Lord this morning before putting on your socks, you at least forgot about him with a portion of your mind. No one, except for Jesus, can possibly claim that they have fulfilled this commandment. By comparing our lives to Jesus' we should be able to see how often we fail to embrace this first and foremost commandment of God.

20. I've heard objections along these lines: "But God commands husbands to love their wives, parents to love their children, and Christians to love their neighbors and enemies. Clearly, we're commanded to divide our love accordingly." This is not biblically accurate. Our love for God is primary and results in the rest. The command for Christians to love their enemies would be impossible if our love did not flow through our love for God. Why do we love our enemies? Because we love God. If you love God with all your heart, soul, mind, and strength, your love will overflow to others. This is exactly what John taught in 1 John 4:20–21, saying that if we don't love others, it is proof that we don't love God (see also 1 John 3:10; 4:8–10).

21. 2 Chr 12:14.

If this is true (and it is) then we can all of a sudden see how it is that God can declare such a judgment against us: *every intention and the thoughts of our heart are only evil, all the time*, because we are in violation of his greatest commandment with every breath, every thought, and every beat of our heart . . . since the moment of our conception![22] Every day we are storing up wrath for ourselves in accordance with our multitudes of transgressions against him.[23] We are piling heaps upon heaps of transgressions and sins because even when we appear to be doing "good" our motives and hearts are in the wrong place, failing to be motivated by a commitment to love the Lord with *all* of our heart, soul, mind, and strength.[24]

Admittedly, this is a bleak view of our present state. Even so, the truth has no regard for our feelings—it is true whether we like it or not. A cancer patient is not cured because they ignore the diagnosis of the doctor or because they maintain a positive attitude about their treatment options. A "positive outlook" does not change the reality of the matter. I learned this lesson clearly and painfully while watching my mother battle cancer. She and her doctors all agreed that they would beat cancer and she would be cured. She died anyway. Her doctor had such a positive outlook on the prognosis that he initially refused to sign the death certificate because the treatment was going so well.

She was still dead. It didn't really matter if the doctor refused to do the paperwork.

It would be foolish to ignore the reality of our own sinfulness, and the seriousness of God's judgment against us, simply because it makes us uncomfortable or because we do not like the implications. In contrast, it is this bad news of our miserable and poor condition that makes the good news of the gospel so glorious.

God *fully* understands our current state of rebellion and sin against him (even if we don't). God fully understands the wickedness that dwells in our flesh (even if we don't). And God shows his love for us, despite our rebellion, through Christ. To read the Scriptures and to understand the fallen state of humanity, you can understand the surprise the prophet Daniel must have felt when he received the following vision:

> I kept looking / Until thrones were set up, / And the Ancient of Days took His seat; / His vesture was like white snow / And the hair of His head like pure wool. / His throne was ablaze with flames, / Its wheels were a burning fire. / A river of fire was

22. Ps 51:5.
23. Rom 2:5; Ps 5:10.
24. Prov 16:2; 21:2.

> flowing / And coming out from before Him; / Thousands upon thousands were attending Him, / And myriads upon myriads were standing before Him; / The court sat, / And the books were opened. / Then I kept looking because of the sound of the boastful words which the horn was speaking; I kept looking until the beast was slain, and its body was destroyed and given to the burning fire. As for the rest of the beasts, their dominion was taken away, but an extension of life was granted to them for an appointed period of time. / I kept looking in the night visions, / And behold, with the clouds of heaven / One like a Son of Man was coming, / And He came up to the Ancient of Days / And was presented before Him. / And to Him was given dominion, / Glory and a kingdom, / That all the peoples, nations and men of every language / Might serve Him. / His dominion is an everlasting dominion / Which will not pass away; / And His kingdom is one / Which will not be destroyed. / As for me, Daniel, my spirit was distressed within me, and the visions in my mind kept alarming me. (Dan 7:9–15)

What a picture! The most glorious of earthly thrones is nothing compared to this vision of the majesty and glory of the living God seated upon his—a throne ablaze with flames, with a river of fire flowing before him, with thousands upon thousands of creatures attending to him. From his throne, the king sits to execute judgment, and his decrees are carried out precisely as he declares.

Perhaps the most alarming aspect of this entire vision, which greatly distressed and alarmed the prophet Daniel (see 7:15), was the fact that in the midst of the king of the universe sitting in judgment upon his glorious throne, a human being ("One like a Son of Man") comes before the throne and is presented before the king. The prophet is likely familiar with the passage from Genesis describing the utter sinfulness and depravity of human beings, and he understands the inability for anyone to stand before the king and prevail when they are judged.[25] At the very least, this Son of Man should fall upon his face and declare the glory of the one sitting upon the throne!

But this is not what happens.

Instead of falling upon his face in worship, this Son of Man is given dominion, glory, and a kingdom, that all the peoples, nations, and men of every language might serve *him*—an everlasting dominion which will not pass away and a kingdom which will not be destroyed!

---

25. Isa 6:1–5; Job 42:5–6; Ps 24:3–4; Nah 1:2–6; Rev 20:11–15.

The God of the Bible revealed his character and person to the nation of Israel through the law and the prophets.[26] He revealed himself to be a God that is jealous for the praise and glory of his name, and as a God who would never share his glory with another.[27] God has declared that he is the one to whom every knee will bow and every tongue will swear allegiance.[28] Yet, here the prophet Daniel sees this same God bestowing dominion, authority, and glory upon a *human*! God treats this Son of Man like only God himself should be treated.

The observant reader will immediately notice that the Apostle Paul applied these same truths to the man, Christ Jesus, when making the claim that it is to him (Jesus) that every knee will bow and every tongue will confess that he is Lord, to the glory of God the Father in Philippians 2:9–11.[29] For the people of Israel, who had received this revelation, they knew that the human in this vision needed to be God himself, in the flesh. It is for this reason that the leaders of Israel executed Jesus for blasphemy when he claimed to be the Son of Man from Daniel's prophecy.[30]

The curse that was brought upon humanity by Adam's rebellion and which caused the kingdom to be handed over to the rule of Satan was to be undone by the Christ, Jesus of Nazareth, in fulfillment of God's predetermined plan.[31] "For since by a man came death, by a man also came the resurrection of the dead. For as in Adam all die, so also in Christ all will be made alive" (1 Cor 15:21–22).[32]

If we understand the severity of our rebellion and sin, and the horror of the reality that a Day of Judgment is coming before a just and holy God, it

---

26. E.g., Deut 29:29.

27. Isa 42:8.

28. Isa 45:23.

29. See chap. 2, "God's Mission."

30. Matt 26:63–66.

31. Isa 53:4–12; Gal 3:10–14; 4:4–5; Acts 2:22–28; Rom 3:21–26; 2 Cor 5:18–21.

32. Some have mistakenly taken this passage to teach the doctrine of universal salvation, reasoning that since "all" in Adam have died—which applies to every human being (e.g., Rom 5:12)—that the life in Christ will likewise be applied to "all" in a universal sense. However, this interpretation is contradictory to other explicit passages in Scripture which declare that hell is real and that real people will go there because they will *not* be saved (e.g., Matt 7:13–23; 25:31–46; John 3:16–36; 1 Cor 6:9–10; Rev 21:1–8), and should be rejected on these grounds alone. Instead, this passage points again to the "positional" nature of salvation: all who are *in Adam* (which is the natural state for every human) will die in judgment, and all who are *in Christ* (who are born-again by the Spirit of God through repentance and faith in Jesus) will be made alive. Not every person is born-again, but every person that *is* born-again will be safely hidden *in Christ* on the Day of Judgment.

is natural to ask how God could send his beloved Son, Jesus, to be an atoning sacrifice for the sin of the world. It is sensible to wonder why God would make it possible for rebels to be reconciled to him and even be adopted into his family as children of God with a full right of inheritance in his kingdom. The only answer is that God is not like us. He can demonstrate love for his enemies and he can love us even in our rebellion because God *is* love.[33] At the same time, we must never mistake his love for a *weak* characteristic. God's love will not cause him to simply overlook all sin because he cannot help himself from doing so.

In his righteousness and holiness, God has ordained a singular, very specific way for rebels to receive his love through pardon for their sin.[34] God's offer was purchased with the costly blood of Jesus.[35] This propitiation through the blood of Christ has made it possible for God's disposition of wrath toward sinners to be forever changed to a disposition of favor towards the redeemed in Christ.[36] Salvation is free to receive, it is incredibly gracious, and it is exclusively available by God's grace through repentance and faith. Those who would accept this amazing grace must turn *from* their rebellion (not just from "mistakes") against God *to* Jesus as Lord—an act called repentance—and they must trust fully, completely, and only in Jesus to save them from the wrath that is to come on the Day of Christ Jesus.[37] For those who continue in their rebellion and fail to repent, they can expect nothing but God's fierce wrath and indignation as a response to their multitudes of transgressions, iniquities, and sins against him.

Through his work, Jesus made reconciliation between rebellious humanity and a holy God possible, while also bringing praise and glory to the name of God.[38] The crucifixion of Jesus also demonstrates God's love, justice, righteousness, and holiness for the world to see.[39] The offensive church must take this scandalous message of a crucified Messiah to the ends of the earth in obedience to the command of our risen king. Jesus came to seek and to save the lost, and Jesus' church is called to do the same. It is to the person of Jesus that we will turn our attention to in the next chapter.

---

33. Isa 55:6–11; 1 John 4:8–16.

34. John 14:6; 1 Tim 2:5.

35. 1 Pet 1:18–19.

36. Rom 3:21–26; Heb 2:17; 1 John 2:1–2; 4:9–10. For an excellent discussion on the importance of the doctrine of propitiation, see Washer, *Gospel's Power*, 167–202.

37. E.g., Pss 2:12; 34:22; Isa 55:6–11; John 3:36; 1 Thess 1:9–10; 2 Thess 1:5–10.

38. Isa 43:21–25; 48:9–11; Col 1:19–20; 1 Tim 2:3–5.

39. Rom 3:21–26; 5:8.

4

Jesus Is Lord

> Therefore let all the house of Israel know for certain that God has made Him both Lord and Christ—this Jesus whom you crucified. (Acts 2:36)

Of all the miracles recorded in the Bible, the incarnation is the most astounding. For the infinite, immaterial, uncreated, and eternal God to become a part of his finite, material creation in time is mind-boggling. As a culture, we have lost much of the wonder because we celebrate the "babe wrapped in swaddling clothes" each December, but our familiarity with the story should not take away from the awe-inspiring reality.

God became a man.[1] He dwelt among us.[2]

On its surface, this claim is absurd and virtually impossible to believe. In order to demonstrate the validity of this claim, God prophesied, in advance, details regarding his mission through Christ. God revealed the culminating proof would be his resurrection from the dead.[3] If these audacious claims are not true, the proof would be impossible; death is usually final.

People can hold whatever opinion they'd like, but the fact remains that Jesus of Nazareth was declared to be the Son of God with power when he

---

1. Matt 1:18—2:23; Luke 1:26–38; 2:1–40.
2. John 1:1–4, 14.
3. E.g., Ps 16:10; Isa 53:8–12.

was resurrected from the dead.[4] Death could not hold him; and this powerful declaration from God was given as proof that all men, everywhere, need to repent because a day of judgment is coming, and there is forgiveness of sin and salvation from the wrath that is to come in no other name but the name of Jesus.[5] God has installed his king: Jesus. As king, Jesus will reign until (1) he has gathered his people for himself, and (2) he has put his enemies under his feet.[6]

The culture to which Jesus first came understood the implications of this gospel of the kingdom more immediately than modern Americans do. Since modern Americans live in a republic, we are used to having democratically elected leaders. We do not have a sovereign king presiding over us in our government. Instead, we have elected officials with limited powers through checks and balances. We also have various rights and privileges which allow for us to speak freely about our dissatisfaction with our elected leaders when we disagree with them.

What we need to wrap our heads around is the fact that Jesus is *not* a president. He is not an elected official. He does not have term limits. There are no checks and balances to his power outside of himself. He is bound by his own character and will alone.

Jesus is *Lord*. Jesus is the King of all kings and the Lord of all lords.[7] Before Jesus, every *other* king, and lord, and person of great stature, will fall upon their faces in obeisance. God's kingdom rules over all the kingdoms of the earth.[8]

The Roman government under which Jesus made these claims was very different than modern America. Rome valued peace and it maintained that peace with brutal force. For all citizens living in the Roman world, there was one lord: Caesar. From Caesar was delegated authority and power unlike what citizens of the United States of America see in our modern-day governmental leaders.

Consider the scene leading up to Jesus' execution: the Jewish leaders brought before a Roman governor, Pontius Pilate, a man accused of a crime against Jewish law. The Jewish leaders wanted to execute Jesus because they believed him to be a blasphemer. According to this charge in their law Jesus must die.[9] However, Pilate was not so concerned about disputes regarding

---

4. Rom 1:4.
5. Acts 2:24; 4:10–12; 17:30–31; 1 Thess 1:9–10; John 14:6; Ps 2:10–12.
6. 1 Cor 15:25–28; Heb 10:11–14.
7. 1 Tim 6:13–16; Rev 17:14; 19:16.
8. E.g., Pss 22:27–28; 47:2; 83:18; 103:19.
9. John 19:7.

Jewish law. Therefore, these Jewish leaders explained that Jesus claimed to be a king. This claim from Jesus challenged the authority of Caesar and the Jewish leaders were manipulating Pilate by declaring that if Pilate released Jesus, then Pilate himself was opposing Caesar![10]

Pilate is sometimes viewed sympathetically, but his actions demonstrate a cold, brutal power that is unfamiliar to modern Americans. Pilate believed Jesus to be *innocent*, declaring this fact to the unruly mob in John 19:6. Despite believing in the innocence of the man before him, Pilate was willing to have Jesus viciously beaten and executed by crucifixion simply to pacify the demands of this mob and to keep the peace.

No due process. No justice. No chance for an appeal. Pilate, as a delegated leader in Rome, literally held the power to put anyone to death at any time, no questions asked. Even when they were believed to be innocent.

Unlike our present cultural situation, where "confessing" Christ can be a safe and rather light-hearted thing to do, in the context of the Greco-Roman empire to confess with your mouth that "Jesus is Lord" was to take your life into your hands. To *oppose* Caesar by claiming that Jesus is Lord was to accept a swift death sentence as a real and likely outcome.[11] Similarly, to confess that Jesus is Lord to the Jews was tantamount to blasphemy, since there is one Lord—YHWH—the God of the Hebrew Scriptures (or, the Christian "Old Testament"). To "confess Jesus is Lord" meant something very different in the context of the New Testament authors than it does to those of us who live in a place with elected officials and religious liberty. It is more directly applicable to those who want to profess faith in Jesus in a Muslim or Communist nation where such a profession is illegal and can cost you everything—including your life. Only the powerful demonstration of fulfilled prophecy through the resurrection of Jesus after his death by crucifixion could have proven that Jesus was who he claimed to be—God in the flesh—and that this Jesus, whom we executed, God has made both Lord and Christ.

"Christ" is a title, not a name. "The Christ" can literally be translated as "The Anointed One" and points to the purpose which Jesus came to fulfill. Jesus was anointed for the purpose of dying for the sin of the world, and taking rule and authority over every nation away from the devil so that Jesus can serve as the triumphant Lord over all.

Unlike our American political system, there is not going to be a vote.

Despite the claims that you may hear from many pulpits around the globe and at some evangelistic rallies, Jesus is not campaigning to be Lord

10. John 19:6–16.
11. Prov 20:2; Acts 5:33–39.

of your life or waiting for you to invite him to be. The language employed in the Bible is different than this. The familiar theme of "Jesus knocking at the door of the sinner's heart" waiting for an invitation to come in is often based on Revelation 3:20. Of course, in the context of Revelation, Jesus is not speaking to a lost sinner's heart but to a *church*. This request from Jesus to be "invited in" is being made to a fellowship of professing believers who have neglected to include Jesus in their gathering. Jesus wants those who follow him to invite him into their fellowship and to genuinely fellowship with him, the living Lord and Savior. To use this passage to ask rebellious sinners to "invite Jesus into their hearts" is to twist and abuse the passage. Biblical evangelism instead boldly declares to lost sinners that Jesus *is* Lord, whether they invite him to be or not. The gospel call then invites and urges them to respond to this truth appropriately with genuine repentance and faith. Similarly, biblical evangelism includes a warning of the implications of failing to heed this gospel call.

Human beings are commanded to acknowledge the fact of Jesus' lordship through repentance and to receive his offer of redemption through faith. We do not "make" him Lord of our life; we either *acknowledge* that he is Lord and submit ourselves to his rule, or we persist in rebellion against him. If we *acknowledge* that Jesus is Lord, then we should go the next step and *receive* him as Savior by putting our complete faith in him.[12]

Jesus *is* Lord—of all creation, which includes *you*. Jesus is risen and has been exalted to God's right hand where he presently rules as King of kings and Lord of lords.[13] He does not need permission or an invitation from anyone. As Lord, Jesus is offering pardon for our foolish rebellion through repentance and faith in his completed work.[14] This offer, while incredibly gracious, is also temporary. If his command to all men, everywhere, to repent is not heeded, he will execute his wrath with furious vengeance on all of his adversaries.[15]

If this is not the "Jesus" you know and love, unfortunately you are serving an idol.[16]

Before ascending to heaven, after being raised from the dead, Jesus stood before his disciples and declared: "All authority has been given to Me in heaven and on earth. Go therefore and make disciples of all the nations,

12. Rom 1:28–32; 2 John 1:7.

13. Acts 2:32–36; 7:56; Eph 1:20–23; Phil 2:9–11; Ps 2:6–10.

14. Acts 2:38–39.

15. Ps 2:12; John 3:36; Acts 17:30–31; 2 Thess 1:6–10; Heb 2:1–3; 12:25–29; Rev 19:11–16.

16. See, e.g., 2 Cor 11:4 for the reality that not every "Jesus" is the same. More on this in chap. 6, "The Gospel of Jesus Christ."

baptizing them in the name of the Father and the Son and the Holy Spirit, teaching them to observe all that I commanded you; and lo, I am with you always, even to the end of the age" (Matt 28:18–20).

Jesus completed his work on the cross,[17] and took hold of the prophesied promises of the Son of Man being given authority, dominion, and glory. It is in this authority that Jesus currently stands, and he explains this fact clearly by saying that "all authority has been given to Me in heaven and on earth." You will notice that Jesus does not ask permission from any who are listening to him, nor ask them to invite him to be their Lord, nor request their acceptance of his authority. Jesus merely states the fact plainly: *All authority in both heaven and earth belongs to Me.*

As discussed in chapter 2, God's mission in the world is to bring glory to himself through every knee bowing to his appointed king and every tongue confessing that Jesus is Lord. This will happen in one of two ways:

1. As a response to the proclamation of the gospel by God's people in this life, or

2. As a response to the revelation of God in his majesty and glory on the Day of Christ Jesus.

Unfortunately for those who wait until the revelation of Jesus from heaven in glory, they will have no forgiveness of sin but will perish under his righteous wrath and indignation. Since Jesus is a gracious and compassionate Lord, he does not use his authority to command his people to be silent and to hide the reality that he is Lord from those who are lost in their sin. Instead, Jesus commands his people—the church—to make disciples of all nations, bringing the good news of the kingdom of God to the very ends of the earth. Not only this, but the promise is also given that God's people will not be alone in this task. Jesus himself will be with them until the end[18]— God will bring about the completion of his mission, through his people. His mission is extremely important and he is not willing that any should perish, but that all would come to repentance.[19] He will glorify his name.[20]

---

17. John 17:4–5; 19:30; 1 Cor 2:6–8; Gal 3:13–14; Col 2:13–15.

18. The great commission in Matthew 28 includes a declaration of authority (28:18), a command stemming from this authority (28:19–20a), and a promise to abide with those who will walk in obedience to this command through recognizing his authority (28:20b). Some mistakenly draw a false dichotomy between "obeying Jesus" and "walking with Jesus" as if these two ideas are opposed to each other or mutually exclusive—but here, Jesus indicates that the best way to spend time with him is to walk in obedience to his command.

19. 2 Pet 3:9.

20. John 12:27–28.

The so-called great commission from the Lord Jesus has been covered in great detail through the centuries. It must be understood that Jesus did not command his people to *discuss* this commission, but to *obey* it. The command to "make disciples" has three distinct aspects: *go, baptize,* and *teach*.

The people of God must *go* to the rebels and make them aware that Jesus is king and that he commands them to repent. For those who respond to this proclamation through repentance and make a profession of faith, they are to become initiated into the covenant people of God (the church) through baptism as a testimony of their participation in Christ's death, burial, and resurrection. Baptism is a demonstration of their obedience to him because he commands his people to be baptized as a fruit of their faith in him.[21]

After being initiated into the faith, these professing disciples must be instructed in the faith and taught to *obey*—not simply to believe or acknowledge—everything that Christ commanded. This instruction includes the command to *go*, thus completing the cycle of discipleship that is to endure until Christ returns to be glorified amongst his people.[22]

God has redeemed a people for himself. He has given his people an *offensive* plan and a purpose—to glorify his name. God has commanded the church to proclaim his excellencies throughout the earth.[23] To this *offensive* calling, we will turn our attention to in the next chapter.

---

21. Acts 2:38–41; Rom 6:3–11; Gal 3:27–29.
22. 2 Thess 1:10.
23. 1 Pet 2:9–10.

5

Ambassadors for Christ

Therefore, we are ambassadors for Christ, as though God were making an appeal through us; we beg you on behalf of Christ, be reconciled to God.
(2 Cor 5:20)

If you are a child of God and a disciple of Jesus Christ, then you have been given a new job: ambassador for Christ. Some have tried to make this calling apply only to the apostles, or to a select few. If this mission was only entrusted to the apostles, then God's mission would have died out with them in the first century AD. Our role as ambassadors for Christ in the government of God requires taking on an offensive mentality. The kingdom of heaven is expanding.[1] The offensive church is not called primarily to defend the bunker, but to take the hill—every hill—for our king and his kingdom.[2] The taking of territory from the kingdom of darkness is often perceived to be offensive by members of the domain of darkness.[3] Although it should never be the aim of ambassadors for Christ to be intentionally offensive in their manner and/or person,[4] we must be willing to possibly offend through faithfully sharing the full gospel message, in order that all may have the opportunity to hear and respond to the gospel call. As ambassadors our

1. Matt 13:33.
2. Mark 16:15.
3. Double entendre intended. See also 2 Cor 2:14–16.
4. 1 Cor 10:32–33; 2 Cor 6:3–10.

message is not our own. God's message to rebels is potentially offensive and foolish.[5] It is also the power and wisdom of God to salvation for all who believe.[6]

In the context of the passage quoted from 2 Corinthians at the beginning of this chapter, Paul actually starts his argument in verse 17 saying, "Therefore, if anyone is in Christ, he is a new creature; the old things passed away; behold, new things have come." This is theologically significant. It points to the reality that although all have initially been born into bondage and slavery to sin and death, through repentance and faith they are placed safely "in Christ."[7] As a result, they have become a new creature with a new nature—one that is alive in Christ and cleansed from their rebellion and sin. In fact, those who have turned from their sin to the living God through repentance and faith are actually changed in their status. They are no longer criminals and citizens of the kingdom of darkness. Now, they are adopted into God's family as his children and are, therefore, heirs in the kingdom of light.[8] This is good news indeed! I know of no one who argues strenuously that verse 17 only applied to the apostles or some select few. Even if they did try such an argument, Paul makes it clear that this changed nature is for "anyone who is in Christ," not just for some.

Paul continues into the very next verses (18–19) by describing an important aspect of this "new creation" reality that has come to all who are in Christ: "Now all these things are from God, who reconciled us to Himself through Christ and gave us the ministry of reconciliation, namely, that God was in Christ reconciling the world to Himself, not counting their trespasses against them, and He has committed to us the word of reconciliation."

What justification do we have for believing that Paul has changed the scope of his "us" to limit it only to the apostles? Based on the text, we have none. All of the promises we have *through* and *in* Christ are from God, who has reconciled *us* (all Christians) to himself through Christ and has given *us* (all Christians) the ministry of reconciliation. God has committed to *us* (all Christians) the word of reconciliation, "Therefore, we are ambassadors for

---

5. 1 Cor 1:22–23; 1 Pet 2:7–8.

6. Rom 1:16; 1 Cor 1:18, 24.

7. This is a "positional" understanding of salvation. The Bible describes the work of God in salvation as placing those who repent of their sin and trust in Christ alone for their salvation "in Christ." In the same way, Noah and his family were saved from the flood by being "in the ark." Believing they would have been saved on the ark is not enough—they had to actually get on board and be hidden inside to be safe when the flood came. Likewise, Jesus is the "ark of salvation" and it is only in him that anyone will be saved. To be hidden in Christ is the only refuge when the wrath of God is to be revealed. See, e.g., Pss 2:12; 18:30; 34:22; Nah 1:2–8; Rom 8:1; and 1 Thess 1:9–10.

8. Col 1:13–14; Gal 3:29—4:7.

Christ, as though God were making an appeal through us; we beg you on behalf of Christ, be reconciled to God" (2 Cor 5:20).

It is a mark of a stubborn and rebellious spirit that seeks to deny the call of the living God to walk in the primary ministry that he has entrusted to his people; namely, to be ambassadors for Christ and fervent laborers for him as we seek to walk in the ministry of reconciliation between a righteous God and rebellious sinners. To fail to take this task seriously is to continue to live in rebellion against the king!

Biblical Christianity is *not* moralism, and must never be confused with a simple moral code that declares that Christians follow the list of "Do's" and avoid the list of "Don'ts" or even that this is what Christians are aiming to do (though we keep falling short). This type of thinking is a trap and is preached every week from countless pulpits around the world.

A hugely influential line of false teaching that has abounded since the beginning of the church (and has endured to the present age) is the preaching and teaching of *moralism* instead of the genuine gospel. The reason that this is so dangerous and insidious is that moralism can be preached very easily from the Bible. Even worse, moralism has pervaded much of our language, thinking, and culture to the point that genuine biblical counsel on what is "good" and what is "bad" is completely ignored—often because of ignorance and biblical illiteracy.[9]

Here is an illustration to try and demonstrate the vast difference between biblical Christianity and the false teaching of moralism—imagine that before going to work one morning I give my son the following instructions: "Son, before I return home, I would like for you to clean your room."

Upon returning home from work, I ask my son, "How was your day?" He responds with the following: "Dad, I had a great day today! I cleaned the playroom, my sisters' room, the baby's room, and your room. I swept the floors, took out the garbage, cleaned the cat litter, and even washed all the clothes. After that I folded them and put them away for everyone in the house. I did all my homework, I read my Bible for two hours, and raked the neighbor's leaves for them! After that, I balanced your checkbook and then I made dinner. During all of that, I never once argued with my siblings, or complained to mommy. I didn't hit anybody, I didn't spit on the floor, and I didn't run in the house or jump on the furniture. Like I said, today was a great day!"

Viewed through the lens of moralism, I have the best son in the world! But viewed through the lens of biblical Christianity, I have one question for my son that needs to be asked:

---

9. Jer 8:7.

"Did you clean your room?"

You'll notice that the list of "good things" performed and the list of "evil things" avoided in this example has one conspicuously absent item—*the one thing I actually asked him to do*. Moralism would say this is a "good" child. The reality is that the above scenario paints the picture of a *disobedient* and *rebellious* child.

In the above illustration, the failure to do the one thing that was specifically directed to be done taints everything else. All that the lists of good deeds done and bad deeds avoided really are trying to do is to hide the rebellious nature of the child's day. Regardless of what anyone else might think, the father knows that his son disobeyed his explicit will and *walked in rebellion all day long*.

Many will object to this premise and will defend the practice of preaching and teaching "Judeo-Christian" morals, principles, and values as the plain meaning of the biblical text. However, this interpretation fails to understand the greater context to which our Scriptures came and the overarching theme of personal obedience to the will of God (not simply impersonal adherence to a set of moral laws and standards in some general sense).[10] The first five books in our Bible are Genesis, Exodus, Leviticus, Numbers, and Deuteronomy (otherwise known as the Pentateuch or the books of Moses). Genesis contains history well before the birth of the human author, Moses, and helps to explain how it came to be that God formed a people for himself (the Hebrews) and revealed himself to them through signs, miracles, and his law.

God's mission was already well underway before any of this was written down by Moses, however. God had *already* judged his entire creation through the flood. God had *already* made a promise to Abraham concerning the gospel of salvation and the foundation of salvation by grace through faith (Gen 15:6) more than four hundred years prior to the law being revealed![11] The morals expressed in the law were not meant for anyone to

---

10. A good example of this contrast is found in 1 Sam 15:1–23. In this passage, King Saul disobeys God's command, but covers his disobedience with moralistic language, saying he disobeyed in order to offer sacrifices to God in accordance with the Law of Moses. Samuel rebukes Saul's disobedience, demonstrating clearly the reality that moralism is not the overall theme of either the Old or New Testament. "Samuel said, / 'Has the LORD as much delight in burnt offerings and sacrifices / As in obeying the voice of the LORD? / Behold, to obey is better than sacrifice, / And to heed than the fat of rams. / For rebellion is as the sin of divination, / And insubordination is as iniquity and idolatry. / Because you have rejected the word of the LORD, / He has also rejected you from being king'" (1 Sam 15:22–23). A New Testament example of the same reality is found in Matt 7:21–23.

11. See Gal 3:1–29.

attain salvation, but to make a holy people for himself, to point people to the fulfillment of God's promise in the Christ, and show why God's judgment was just.[12] Therefore, salvation was based on a promise to Abraham (and Adam and Eve in back in Genesis 3:15) and the morals and values were subservient to the main thing, not the main thing themselves. This is why the Sadducees and Pharisees got off track—they became moralists and treated the law as the main thing. In doing so, they failed to see the very person (Jesus) that the law was given to point them to.[13]

The history sections of the Hebrew Bible describe God's dealings with his people, who he raised up for the purpose of declaring his name in all the earth, and the nations through history[14]—often demonstrating God's amazing faithfulness and compassion, despite harsh judgments being poured out. God told his people up-front exactly how to live with him in their midst,[15] what his expectations were, and his promises for blessings if they obeyed, and curses if they disobeyed. Likewise, the prophets were sent by God to call his people back to himself after they went astray, because they were profaning God's name among the nations.[16] If they would not repent, God would fulfill his promises to judge his people severely, for his name's sake.[17]

Similarly, most of the New Testament is written to those who are *already* believers in Christ. They had received the foundational understanding of what it meant to be a follower of Jesus—prior to any of the New Testament documents being written—because they had been confronted with and believed the gospel of Jesus Christ *already*. These Christians had been reconciled to God through Christ as a result of their repentance and faith in the Messiah. They had responded positively to the proclamation of the gospel by the grace of God. As followers of Christ, living and walking in the truth of the gospel, certain issues arose that were secondary to the life of a believer. Important issues to be sure, but still secondary. Sadly, many

---

12. Lev 22:32–33; 23:42–43; 25:55; Luke 7:29; Gal 3:19–24; Rom 7:7.

13. John 5:39–47; see also Gal 3:24 and Col 2:16–17.

14. E.g., Exod 9:16 declares that God sold his people into bondage in Egypt, simply to raise up Pharaoh and demonstrate his power in freeing them from this bondage for the glory of his name in all the earth.

15. Leviticus begins immediately after the narrative of when God's people built the tabernacle in the wilderness and God's glorious presence began to dwell among them. They needed to know how to live with and maintain the presence of God, which is what Leviticus is all about. It was not easy and it required a lot of blood to be shed, which was a foreshadowing of what Christ would do so that Christians could live with, and maintain, the presence of God in their lives.

16. Jer 35:15.

17. Ezek 20:1–32; Amos 4:1–13; Jer 7:23–27; Matt 23:27.

modern believers have made these secondary issues of morals and values the focus.[18] This is failing to understand that "being a nice Christian" isn't the goal of God's grace in their lives! This is why they needed to be told this stuff *after* they were already reconciled to God and had been walking with him for some time. It was not the primary source of instruction, but a corollary to the main thing.[19] The apostolic teaching recorded in the New Testament was subservient to the command Jesus issued to his followers to go into all the world and make disciples—it does not replace that command, but serves to further its expansion in the world to every tribe, tongue, and nation.

To focus on "being kind" while ignoring the main command *to make disciples* is to miss the entirety of Christianity by turning God's work into a system of moral rules and obligations. This is the same type of error and false gospel which was so strongly being taught against by the Apostle Paul in Galatians.[20] It is incredibly dangerous to make this mistake, because if we believe that Christianity is simply moralism, then our nice neighbors, friends, co-workers, and family members who are not born-again may foolishly be neglected because we think the gospel is irrelevant to them because they are *moral*. That is, until they encounter some terrible hardship and need a "forever friend." This is a trap.

Christianity ≠ Moralism.

Of course there are morals involved in Christianity, but they are not the main focus.[21] The glory of God through the gospel of Jesus Christ is

---

18. When Jesus issued the Great Commission, he commanded that his disciples teach the new followers they were going to find to obey everything he commanded them (past tense), not everything he was going to command them in the future (Matt 28:19). Many professing Christians today are seeking a "fresh revelation" from God, yet we are failing to obey what he has *already* commanded. We are not in need of more revelation—we are in need of putting into practice what we have already received (Matt 7:24–27) and which has been handed down once for all (Jude 1:3).

19. Similarly, when the Corinthians wrote to Paul and asked him about some important issues (1 Cor 7:1)—things like marriage, divorce, idolatry, freedom in Christ, spiritual gifts, communion, etc.—he made it abundantly clear as he was winding down his letter that they needed to remember the truth of first and foremost importance: the gospel (1 Cor 15:1–6). Essentially, Paul says, "You asked about *these* things, and here is my answer. What I need you to remember is that *this* truth is much more important than anything else you asked about!" Without the gospel (particularly, the resurrection), Paul said they had believed in vain (1 Cor 15:2, 12–19).

20. See also the contrast that Jesus draws between the "works" (plural) based mentality of those who are questioning him and the "work" (singular) based mentality of faith in Christ in John 6:28–29.

21. As a result of this erroneous focus, some genuine Christians have been led

the main focus. The morality that is involved in following Jesus serves to bolster the witness of his followers because our good deeds are evidence to this dead world that we have been raised to genuine life in Christ.[22] Things like a strong marriage, obedient children, genuine compassion, kindness, generosity, and forgiveness are all platforms from which the glory of God can be proclaimed and demonstrated because it is evidence of God working in the lives of his people. In the same way, if we are living *immorally* then we are providing opportunity for the message of Christ to be discredited.[23] If we are truly changed, our new nature should be evident. Should we expect that spiritually "dead" people and spiritually "living" people are basically the same? Have you ever been to a funeral? It's not usually that hard to tell the dead from the living.

We must never fail to understand the Bible as a whole. The big picture idea that is presented is that God is a righteous king whose kingdom rules over all the kingdoms of the earth. His creation has rebelled against him and God has declared that there is only one way to be forgiven of our crimes against him and be reconciled to himself: through his Son, Jesus Christ.[24] If those who *have been reconciled* fail to understand the nature of the message ("The kingdom of God is at hand. Jesus Christ is Lord. Repent or perish.") and instead go around preaching moralism ("Be good. Be nice. Say you're sorry. Jesus loves you. He understands.") then all we are doing is trying to get *rebels* to be *nice* rebels.[25] And if we continue to misunderstand the big

---

into a fruitless debate with skeptics and atheists about the possibility of being a "moral atheist"—but this debate proves nothing. Those who are not following Jesus do not need to be more "moral," they need to be born-again and receive forgiveness for their sins. Some of the nicest and most moral people I've ever met are still dead in their trespasses and sins. They would never steal from me, kill anyone, or cheat on their spouse. However, they are still guilty of transgressing God's moral law and will face him on Judgment Day. They will not be acquitted of their crimes against God's law and get into heaven by being nicer than their neighbors or even by being nicer than most professing Christians! This issue is not whether one can be "moral" without being "religious." The real issue is how a just and righteous God can forgive iniquity, transgression, and sin—even in people who this world would consider "moral." The answer is found in Christ alone.

22. E.g., Matt 5:16.

23. 2 Cor 6:1–3.

24. John 14:6; 1 Tim 2:5; 1 Thess 1:9–10.

25. Also inherent in these false evangelism tactics is a failure to understand that the hostility that exists between God and man is not one-sided. The Scriptures declare that man has made himself God's enemy through his wicked works (e.g., Rom 5:10)—meaning that man is opposed to God, and God is opposed to sinful man (e.g., Pss 5:5; 7:11–13). If all that happens is that a sinner changes his mind about God, *without God changing his mind about sinful man*, then reconciliation between the two has not occurred. God's disposition is changed through the cross alone, therefore we cannot leave

picture, then it is possible that when we meet *nice* rebels we may think that they are not in any genuine need of hearing the gospel call to repentance and faith. To make this mistake is to fundamentally change the nature of Christianity into something else entirely.

Unfortunately, when the king arrives to render judgment and to recompense people for their deeds, he is bringing furious wrath upon his adversaries.[26] "Nice" rebels will not be saved. They will perish along with the rest of the rebels and criminals.

Only if we understand the difference between moralism and the biblical ideal of obedience to the Father are we able to understand what Jesus was teaching in John 5:28-29 when discussing "good" and "bad" deeds being appealed to on Judgment Day.[27] Consider these additional teachings from Jesus:

1. Not everyone who says to Me, "Lord, Lord," will enter the kingdom of heaven, but *he who does the will of My Father who is in heaven will enter*. Many will say to Me on that day, "Lord, Lord, did we not prophesy in Your name, and in Your name cast out demons, and in Your name perform many miracles?" And then I will declare to them, "I never knew you; *depart from me, you who practice lawlessness.*" Therefore *everyone who hears these words of Mine and acts on them*, may be compared to a wise man who built his house on the rock. And the rain fell, and the floods came, and the winds blew and slammed against that house; and yet it did not fall, for it had been founded on the rock. Everyone who hears these words of Mine and does not act on them, will be like a foolish man who built his house on the sand. The rain fell, and the floods came, and the winds blew and slammed against that house; and it fell—and great was its fall. (Matt 7:21-27, emphasis added)

2. For whoever *does the will of My Father* who is in heaven, he is My brother and sister and mother. (Matt 12:50, emphasis added)

3. Jesus said to them, "My food is *to do the will of Him who sent Me and to accomplish His work.*" (John 4:34, emphasis added)

If God has established his king, and if this king has commanded that his people make disciples of all nations, baptizing them in the name of the Father, Son, and Holy Spirit, and teaching them to obey everything he has

---

out the full biblical command to sinners to repent and trust in Christ. For more on this, see Washer, *Gospel's Power*, 129-45.

26. 2 Cor 5:9-11; 2 Thess 1:6-10; Jude 1:14-15.

27. This passage seems to strongly indicate that Jesus taught a works-based judgment for salvation. See appendix A for a detailed discussion of this passage.

commanded as his ambassadors, then the will of the Father is that we actually walk in that ministry![28] If anyone is in Christ, he is a new creature—the old has gone, the new has come.[29] We no longer live for ourselves, but we now live for Christ and the will of God. He will not be fooled by us covering up our disobedience with "random acts of kindness" or any other such thing. There is nothing "random" about the Christian call. It is systematic and comprehensive.

> Therefore, since Christ has suffered in the flesh, arm yourselves also with the same purpose, because he who has suffered in the flesh has ceased from sin, *so as to live the rest of the time in the flesh no longer for the lusts of men, but for the will of God.* For the time already past is sufficient for you to have carried out the desire of the Gentiles, having pursued a course of sensuality, lusts, drunkenness, carousing, drinking parties and abominable idolatries. In all this, they are surprised that you do not run with them into the same excesses of dissipation, and they malign you; but they will give account to Him who is ready to judge the living and the dead. *For the gospel has for this purpose been preached even to those who are dead, that though they are judged in the flesh as men, they may live in the spirit according to the will of God.* (1 Pet 4:1–6, emphasis added)

The Apostle Paul understood God's mission clearly and the implications of the lordship of Christ.[30] Near the end of his life and ministry, Paul wrote to the believers at Colossae while he was imprisoned for his own ministry in proclaiming the gospel.[31] What is so interesting about this particular letter is that Paul had never met these believers before. He had only heard of their faith through the testimony of other believers.[32] Despite not knowing these believers personally, Paul knew that they had believed the same gospel that he was preaching because they had received it from a faithful laborer, Epaphras.[33] Knowing that these believers are called to participate in the same mission that all believers are called to, under the same Lord, and in the unity of the one Spirit,[34] Paul's prayers for them are instructive:

---

28. 2 Cor 5:6–11; Eph 2:10; 1 Pet 2:9–12.

29. 2 Cor 5:17.

30. Remember Paul's certainty that God will complete his work based on his statements made to the believers at Philippi discussed in chap. 2.

31. Col 4:18.

32. Col 1:4; 2:1.

33. Col 1:3–8.

34. John 17:17–26; Eph 4:1–6.

> For this reason also, since the day we heard of it, we have not ceased to pray for you and to ask that you may be filled with the knowledge of His will in all spiritual wisdom and understanding, so that you will walk in a manner worthy of the Lord, to please Him in all respects, bearing fruit in every good work and increasing in the knowledge of God; strengthened with all power, according to His glorious might, for the attaining of all steadfastness and patience; joyously giving thanks to the Father, who has qualified us to share in the inheritance of the saints in Light. For He rescued us from the domain of darkness, and transferred us to the kingdom of His beloved Son, in whom we have redemption, the forgiveness of sins. (Col 1:9–14)

Notice the content of Paul's prayers for these believers: that they would be filled with the knowledge of his will in all spiritual wisdom and understanding. Paul understood that Christianity ≠ Moralism, so he did not pray that they would "be nice." Instead, Paul prayed that they would understand the *will* of God so that they could then perform God's will in the power that God provides. This prayer was not an end in and of itself, but the reason Paul prayed for these believers to know the will of God was so that they would walk in a manner worthy of the Lord and would please him in all respects; bearing fruit for him and increasing in their knowledge of God.[35] Living in a manner worthy of the Lord includes being "moral" but also goes beyond it. Living immorally would make fulfilling the great commission impossible because our lives would discredit the message. Godly living (more specifically, being conformed to the image of Jesus) is evidence that God's grace is active in the life of the Christian and must be sought for the purpose of glorifying God in addition to actually proclaiming the gospel with our mouths. By uniting our lives and our mouths, we can genuinely preach the gospel in both word and deed. A failure to be more and more conformed to the image of Jesus is evidence that God is not truly at work in that person. Without growth in sanctification, their confession and walk are a work of the flesh. God has ordained that all of his children will be conformed to the image of Jesus.[36]

After explaining *what* he prays for these Colossian believers and *why* he prays it, Paul describes the glory and majesty of Jesus. Paul declares the preeminence of Christ, the reality that Jesus is the one *through* whom and *for* whom all things have been made, and that he is the one who holds all things together by a sovereign act of his own will. Paul then declares the

---

35. Compare this thought to Eph 4:1–6.
36. E.g., Rom 8:28–30.

will of God in Christ to reconcile all things to himself through Christ.[37] As a result of their own reconciliation to God through Christ, and their being transferred from the domain of darkness into God's kingdom of light, Paul declares to them the good news of the gospel: their sins have been forgiven so that they can be presented before the king on Judgment Day, not as rebels and guilty criminals, but as *holy, blameless and beyond reproach*.[38] This is where most preachers of the gospel want to stop. We love to declare the "unconditional" love of God in Christ. Unfortunately for our own comfort, desires, and theological constructs, the Apostle Paul continues with a conditional statement right after this declaration of the grace of God. Paul says that this amazing gospel truth applies to believers, "if indeed you continue in the faith firmly established and steadfast, and not moved away from the hope of the gospel that you have heard, which was proclaimed in all creation under heaven, and of which I, Paul, was made a minister."[39]

If you continue.

If you love Greek grammar (and really, who doesn't?), you know that this is a first class conditional statement. This means that Paul is assuming that the "if" part is true for the sake of the argument that he is making about the "then" part (which in the biblical text comes before the "if" statement). To rewrite this in a way that is more natural to the modern English speaker, we can swap them so it reads as follows: if *you continue in the faith firmly established and steadfast, and not moved away from the hope of the gospel that you have heard*, then *God has now reconciled you in His fleshly body through death, in order to present you before Him holy and blameless and beyond reproach*. Paul is assuming that the evidence of a person continuing in the faith firmly established and steadfast, without being moved, demonstrates that God is actually at work in that person.

Taking this claim at face value, as a theological statement, it does not follow that we can be sure that a person's sins are forgiven if they *fail* to continue in the faith—which a work of the flesh will eventually do. What we *can* know for sure is that Paul is assuming that a genuine conversion will continue until the end, since God is at work in the individual and their nature has been changed.[40] For those who want to ignore the conditional,

---

37. Col 1:15–20.
38. Col 1:21–22.
39. Col 1:23.

40. It is important to acknowledge that "apostasy" is a separate issue from "losing salvation" as a result of sinning as a Christian, and is a deeper work of rejecting salvation to turn back to the world. Genuine Christians can be both biblically assured of their salvation while also being biblically warned to avoid apostasy, without fear of contradiction.

they are assuming that all "confessions of Christ" are the same. Someone who professes to follow Christ and turns away from the faith—both the morality and the command to make disciples and live as an ambassador for Christ—does *not* have good reason to believe that their sins are forgiven.[41] This is true despite the promises of many pastors, evangelists, and seemingly sincere Christians to the contrary.[42]

Paul was much more interested in encouraging those whose lives were being conformed to the image of Christ than he was with those who were living immoral lifestyles and who demonstrated no ongoing evidence of grace, or repentance, or growth in Christ's likeness. Despite this, many professing Christians seem to live today as if the king is okay with a minimal commitment. Many believe that he understands that we would like to *go* and make disciples, theoretically, if and when things slow down a little bit and we get the time. Yet, would such a careless attitude be acceptable in our own earthly government? Imagine an ambassador for the United States that did not consider their work as an ambassador to be primary, but only as something they would accomplish "if and when they get around to it." Would such an ambassador be tolerated?[43]

If such an attitude would be unacceptable to our own government, how much more so is it unacceptable for such a shallow and wishy-washy commitment to the one before whom every ruler and authority will fall upon their face when they stand before him?[44] Without walking in the calling as an ambassador, what separates the "follower of Christ" from the "moral atheist" next door? If both are living their lives in pursuit of worldly

---

41. This remains true for both the apostate Christian (Heb 12:12–17) and the false convert (Titus 1:16).

42. The more logically minded reader may object that this paragraph falls victim to the logical fallacy of denying the antecedent. However, if you are reading closely I am not claiming that Paul's statement here teaches that those who do not continue in the faith are *not* saved. What I am saying is that based on what Paul says in this passage, they have no reason to believe they are saved. Paul is assuming that the evidence of continuing in the faith is proof of the reality that their sins are forgiven. There are other passages that discuss the fate of those who fall away not having salvation (e.g., Luke 8:5–15) or the reality of false professions of Christ by those who similarly do not have salvation (e.g., Titus 1:16). In this particular text, Paul's assumption is that for those who continue in the faith, they will be presented blameless before God on the basis of what Christ did for them. Without the evidence of God's grace *actively* working through the believer in producing endurance, Paul's argument would fall apart because he is assuming the first, before stating the second. To put this another way, without the first, he has no reason to state the second.

43. Luke 9:57–62; Matt 10:32–42.

44. Ps 72:11; Isa 49:7; Mal 1:6–14; Phil 2:9–11.

things[45] and not proclaiming the glory of God in Christ to the ends of the earth, are we to believe that one is saved from the wrath to come because of a magical prayer that may have been prayed and because they sit in a church building most Sunday mornings? Is that what "following Christ" has become?

Following on the heels of Paul's conditional statement to the believers in Colossae, he declares his own ministry in preaching the gospel. This preaching ministry resulted in the salvation of Epaphras, who then preached to his hometown of Colossae resulting in their salvation. In an indirect way, Paul recognizes that his own obedience to the will of God has resulted in the formation of this community of faith in Colossae even though they have never met face to face. Despite their indirect connection, Paul has no problem declaring their shared ministry: "We proclaim Him, admonishing every man and teaching *every man* with all wisdom, so that we may present *every man* complete in Christ. For this purpose also I labor, striving according to His power, which mightily works within me."[46]

Notice the use of pronouns. Since Paul believes that these are genuine believers, he declares that "we" (they just like him, and just like Epaphras) proclaim him (Christ), and that this proclamation includes admonishing[47] *every man* and teaching *every man* with all wisdom, that they may present *every man* complete in Christ. Paul considers himself as one with them, saying it is for this purpose—of declaring Jesus as Lord, warning of the implications of persisting in rebellion against him, and teaching what it means to repent of sin, turn to Christ as Lord, and trust in him as Savior with all wisdom in order to present everyone holy, blameless, and beyond reproach before the king—that he "also" labors. He says "also" because he believes that they do, too. It is not just Paul's work as an apostle. It is not just the pastor's job, or the evangelist's job. It is the labor of *every* Christian to proclaim the gospel to *every* creature under heaven!

Do you see the inclusiveness? No member of the church is excluded from this responsibility and no person on earth is excluded from the scope

---

45. Phil 3:17–21; 2 Tim 4:10; Jas 1:27.

46. Col 1:28–29.

47. "To admonish" means "to warn" or "to put in mind of" and includes a solemn telling of the consequences of persisting in rebellion against God and remaining on the road they are currently travelling, which leads only to destruction. Such admonishment should never be done in a mean-spirited way, but by speaking the truth in love we must never fail to tell the whole truth, either. A doctor must sternly warn a smoker of the danger of continuing to smoke, not because he hates his patient but for their own good. Likewise, the Christian duty and call is to warn sinners of the wrath of God and lovingly point them to the Savior. The failure to include a warning of the consequences of dying in your sinful state is a deficient and unbiblical proclamation of the gospel.

of needing to hear the gospel of the kingdom of God.[48] Remember, it is the Father's good pleasure to reconcile the world to himself through Christ. God is working towards the end of having every knee bow and every tongue confess that Jesus Christ is Lord, to his own glory. He is doing that, whether we participate in his mission or not.[49]

In this same vein, when the Apostle Paul was sharply correcting the immoral conduct that was rampant in the church at Corinth, his rebuke was not primarily so that these Corinthian believers would live morally and, therefore, that God would be more pleased with them. Instead, he pointedly rebuked them because their immoral lives were distracting them from sharing the gospel with everyone in Corinth. "Become sober-minded as you ought, and stop sinning; for some have no knowledge of God. I speak this to your shame" (1 Cor 15:34). Paul thought these followers of Christ should be ashamed of themselves, and that they should become sober-minded in their thinking, because there were still people in their community who *have no knowledge of God*. Who is going to tell them if not the ones who *do* have knowledge of God?[50]

Acts 17:26–27 describes how God arranges to have his people nearby those who do not know him as a means of providing a witness to the gospel so that those who are far from God may hear what must be done to be reconciled to God. As Christ's ambassador, you are responsible for sharing the gospel with those who share your place in history and geography. You are responsible for this, because God has sovereignly arranged it to be so.

It may seem abundantly clear that if God is commanding his people to *go* that when we fail to do so we are in active rebellion against him. Even if the intention to go is present within the Christian, failure to make our calling as ambassadors *primary* is a failure to recognize that we no longer live for ourselves, but we died so that we might live for Christ—for his purposes and glory.[51] Intentions are well and good, but if you are thirsty do you want me to *intend* to give you a cup of water or to *actually* give you a cup of water? The difference between these two things is significant. However, we also must understand that simply *going* is not all that matters.

Imagine an earthly ambassador for the United States who is sent to China on urgent business with a message from the president. This ambassador must take the responsibility seriously and put everything else on hold

---

48. See 2 Cor 5:5–16 and Acts 17:30–31.
49. More on this in chap. 9, "Freedom in Christ."
50. Rom 10:14–15.
51. Rom 6:1–23; Gal 2:19–20.

in order to make the necessary arrangements to discharge his or her duty by travelling to China and meeting with those to whom he is being sent.

Upon arriving in China, how important is it that the ambassador relay the message they were given? Is the ambassador free to simply share whatever is most comfortable for them to deliver? What if the message may possibly upset the recipients—is the ambassador free to edit the message and eliminate any potentially offensive or difficult parts so as to not make anyone upset? Clearly, the manner in which the message is delivered may represent the personality of the particular ambassador. There is nothing wrong with being tactful in the delivery of potentially difficult information. Yet, the *content* of the message cannot be altered. The ambassador simply does not have the authority to make such modifications because it is not their message to change. The content of the message is derived from someone of a higher position.

If an ambassador were to change the message that they received and chose instead to share whatever message they were comfortable sharing, this would be nothing short of treason. Yet today, multitudes of people who call themselves by the name of Jesus either refuse to share the gospel with others or, when they do share, declare a message that is nowhere found in the biblical text and has no historical basis as being the message that Jesus, the apostles, or any of the first Christians preached. Instead, they share *content* that is consistent with their own feelings and that fits with their personality. This is *not* what ambassadors are called to share. Ambassadors are called to represent the message and interests of *another*, not themselves.

God has revealed himself and his gospel to his people.[52] He has entrusted it to us and given us a stewardship of the gospel. As stewards in his kingdom, God requires us to be found trustworthy.[53]

Are you equipped to serve your king faithfully as his ambassador? Are you walking in the offensive mission declared by God for his ambassadors? If not, then get equipped! If you are equipped, then are you being faithful in the ministry of reconciliation through the bold and loving proclamation of his gospel? If not, what are you waiting for?

---

52. 1 Cor 15:1–5; Jude 1:3.

53. 1 Cor 4:1–2. See appendix B for more on this topic of being a steward of the gospel.

6

The Gospel of Jesus Christ

> Now I make known to you, brethren, the gospel which I preached to you, which also you received, in which also you stand, by which also you are saved, if you hold fast the word which I preached to you, unless you believed in vain. For I delivered to you as of first importance what I also received, that Christ died for our sins according to the Scriptures, and that He was buried, and that He was raised on the third day according to the Scriptures, and that He appeared to Cephas, then to the twelve. (1 Cor 15:1–5)

The gospel of Jesus is *the* truth of first importance in Christianity. It is the power of God for salvation to all who believe.[1] As such, it is worthy of your most careful and serious attention.[2] This truth is so important that the Apostle Paul made this declaration in his epistle to the Galatians:

> I am amazed that you are so quickly deserting Him who called you by the grace of Christ, for a different gospel; which is really not another; only there are some who are disturbing you and want to distort the gospel of Christ. But even if we, or an angel from heaven, should preach to you a gospel contrary to what we have preached to you, he is to be accursed! As we have

---

1. Rom 1:16; 1 Cor 1:18.
2. Two excellent books on this topic are Washer, *Gospel's Power and Message* and Gilbert, *What Is the Gospel?* Both are worth a careful read.

THE GOSPEL OF JESUS CHRIST

said before, so I say again now, if any man is preaching to you a gospel contrary to what you received, he is to be accursed! (Gal 1:6–9)

In many teachings on this passage, the reality that any other gospel is worthy of everlasting condemnation is stressed—and rightly so. The source of the deviation makes no difference. Whether through the agency of a human, or even an angel from heaven, all modifications of the gospel result in a distorted gospel that is really no gospel at all.

What is easily missed in this passage is Paul's statement that turning to a different gospel is actually deserting *him* who called you by the grace of Christ. Did you catch that? Turning to a different gospel is an abandoning of the person of God! To discuss the gospel of Jesus is of foremost importance, not only because it is very literally a salvation issue, but also because the gospel message is tied to the very person of God himself.[3]

Paul gave a summary version of the genuine gospel right before stating his amazement at their turning from it, and turning from God, in Galatians 1:3–5: "Grace to you and peace from God our Father and the Lord Jesus Christ, who gave Himself for our sins so that He might rescue us from this present evil age, according to the will of our God and Father, to whom be the glory forevermore. Amen." Notice the declaration of Jesus' mission, fulfilled according to the plan of the Father, for his glory. To turn away from the Jesus who gave his life to rescue us from this present evil age to the glory of God—not to make us more fulfilled or comfortable in this present evil age—is to follow a different Jesus.

False gospels abound. There is a false gospel to appeal to everyone and every situation. False gospels tend to focus on the individual. If you were to close your eyes and envision what you desire most, what would it be?

The answer to that question is very likely the area that you are most susceptible to a false gospel.

Do you desire to be healthy? There's a false gospel for that.

Do you desire to be rich? There's a false gospel for that.

Do you desire to have perfect relationships? There's a false gospel for that.

Do you desire power to overcome all of life's problems? There's a false gospel for that.

---

3. The Apostle Paul chided the believers in Corinth for tolerating the preaching of a different gospel and a different Jesus. The reality that pulpits across America, podcasts, books, etc., proclaim different gospels and different versions of Jesus today should not be surprising. It has been happening from the beginning of the church. See 2 Cor 11:1–4 for Paul's description of his desire to point them back to the genuine Jesus and increase their devotion to him.

You name it, there's a false gospel for it. The true gospel is wrapped up in the person of God; that he is reconciling a people to himself after our foolish and hopeless rebellion against him, adopting us into his family as his children. God himself is the gospel—he has given himself to us through Christ so that we can be reconciled to him. Turning from the true gospel is turning from God. It is all about God and his glory.

Moses understood this truth. When the Israelites had come out of slavery in Egypt and were preparing to go up to the Promised Land—a land flowing with milk and honey—God was displeased with the rebellion and obstinacy of the people and told Moses to go up to the land without him. For many professing believers today, this would not be a bad deal. *Hey, we still get to go to the Promised Land!*

For those who view heaven as simply a better version of this life and world—where they can play golf all the time and where there are always sunny, blue skies, and no chance of rain—there is no problem with this. In fact, many people would love to live in the Promised Land regardless of whether or not God goes with them.

In the same way, if you talk to a lot of people about their view of heaven and what happens after this life, almost everybody wants to go to heaven when they die. Unfortunately, most of them don't really care whether or not God is there when they arrive. In fact, I've heard many people joke about wanting to go to hell when they die because they think hell will be better—simply because it is the place that God is *not*. In these cases, their rebellion and distaste for God are even more apparent than normal.

Go ask some people what they think heaven will be like. Most likely you will hear all sorts of descriptions that leave out the presence of God. I have listened to sermons and read books that described the beauty and glory of heaven and which never once mentioned the presence of God.

Moses was not content with this scenario of paradise without the presence of the living God. "Then he [Moses] said to Him, 'If Your presence does not go with us, do not lead us up from here. For how then can it be known that I have found favor in Your sight, I and Your people? Is it not by Your going with us, so that we, I and Your people, may be distinguished from all the other people who are upon the face of the earth?'" (Exod 33:15–16).

Moses would have rather remained in the wilderness where God's presence was than to enter the Promised Land without him. It is important to understand why God was threatening to send the people without his presence in the first place. God was responding to their idolatry. When someone talks about "idols" what do you think of? Do you think of statues and images that people burn incense to and bow down in front of? Do you think of sports, entertainment, television, success, and things like these?

I've encountered teaching that even "good" things like family and ministry can become "idols" if we are not careful. Is this what you think of?

In Exodus 32, right before Moses begs God not to send them to the Promised Land without accompanying them, the people fall into idolatry in a way that many people today likewise follow after—they made an idol and called it by the name of their God. Read carefully:

> Now when the people saw that Moses delayed to come down from the mountain, the people assembled about Aaron and said to him, "Come, make us a god who will go before us; as for this Moses, the man who brought us up from the land of Egypt, we do not know what has become of him." Aaron said to them, "Tear off the gold rings which are in the ears of your wives, your sons, and your daughters, and bring them to me." Then all the people tore off the gold rings which were in their ears and brought them to Aaron. He took this from their hand, and fashioned it with a graving tool and made it into a molten calf; and they said, "This is your god, O Israel, who brought you up from the land of Egypt." Now when Aaron saw this, he built an altar before it; and Aaron made a proclamation and said, "Tomorrow shall be a feast to the LORD." So the next day they rose early and offered burnt offerings, and brought peace offerings; and the people sat down to eat and to drink, and rose up to play. Then the LORD spoke to Moses, "Go down at once, for your people, whom you brought up from the land of Egypt, have corrupted themselves. They have quickly turned aside from the way which I commanded them. They have made for themselves a molten calf, and have worshiped it and have sacrificed to it and said, 'This is your god, O Israel, who brought you up from the land of Egypt!'" (Exod 32:1–8)

Did you catch it? While Moses is on the mountain right behind them—which is quaking and smoldering because the true and living God is manifesting there—the people want a god whom they can follow that is not as dangerous. When Aaron makes for them an idol in the form of a golden calf, he attributes to this work of his hands the works of the living God: "This is your god, O Israel, who brought you up from the land of Egypt." But this idol did not do that. The God manifesting on the mountain did that. What's more, Aaron tells the people that tomorrow there will be a worship service to YHWH, the LORD. But when the people arose, they did not offer their sacrifices to the true and living God whose name is YHWH, the LORD, but to the golden calf whom they called by the same divine name![4]

---

4. See also Neh 9:18–19.

Do you realize that simply calling your "god" by the name of "Jesus" does not mean that you are actually following the *real* Jesus? Today, millions (perhaps billions) of people worship a golden calf Jesus—a "Jesus" who has virtually nothing in common with the Lord of lords and King of kings whose kingdom rules over all the kingdoms of the earth. I was one of these types of idolaters for nearly twenty years, worshipping a version of Jesus that is not the Jesus revealed in the Bible.

This is not a popular teaching. The unpopularity of it does not mean that it is not true, however. Just like the incident with the golden calf, many church buildings are filled with people that come to make their offering to their golden calf Jesus and then arise to play and do whatever they want to do. Believing that Christianity is moralism makes this idolatry even easier, because while we are out doing whatever *we* want to do (or, in some cases, fulfilling whatever demands the world has placed upon us) we can justify our actions because we are not participating in overt acts of "sin" or living in gross immorality. Unfortunately, this is a failure to recognize that sin is much more than particular acts that are obvious to others or merely listed in the Bible. Sin is walking in our own will and ignoring the will of God. The Apostle Paul wrote under the inspiration of the Holy Spirit that *whatever is not from faith is sin* (Rom 14:23b). If we divide our life into a religious/secular divide, and have activities that correspond to both, then we are acknowledging that everything we do outside of our "religious/faith" section is all sin—living how we want to live and ignoring the will of the Lord, most likely presuming upon his grace that he will forgive us. However, such a view of "grace" is not worthy of the biblical testimony of what God's grace is and does in the life of God's children. The grace of God is not primarily *permissive*. God's genuine grace is *redemptive* and *transformative*. Biblical grace purposefully works toward conforming the child of God more and more into the image of Jesus.

This teaching about idolatry and the golden calf Jesus is not my idea. It is exactly what the Apostle Paul taught. In discussing the reality that not everyone who claims to be a follower of God actually is one,[5] Paul wrote in 1 Corinthians 10:5–8,

> Nevertheless, with most of them God was not well-pleased; for they were laid low in the wilderness. Now these things happened as examples for us, so that we would not crave evil things as they also craved. Do not be idolaters, as some of them were; as it is written, "The people sat down to eat and drink, and stood

---

5. See also Titus 1:16.

up to play." Nor let us act immorally, as some of them did, and twenty-three thousand fell in one day.

Paul is citing the golden calf passage from Exodus 32 and warning those who claim to be Christians not to fall into the same error of idolatry that they did.

Don't worship a golden calf Jesus.

To follow the *real* Jesus means that we believe that he was serious about the great commission and that he will succeed in his mission of expanding his kingdom through the proclamation of the gospel to every tribe, tongue, and nation. Moralism is so dangerous for this very reason: because when we distort the gospel and message of Christ, we begin to turn away from him; even if what we are turning toward seems to be simply be a safer version of "Jesus." To believe that Jesus is more concerned with us being kind to our neighbor than he is about his gospel being proclaimed to the ends of the earth is certainly safer for his ambassadors in the physical realm. Bloodthirsty mobs do not tend to murder people for being *nice* to them. However, the Jesus revealed in the Bible called his people to proclaim a message of the wickedness of humanity and the command of God for all to respond to the gospel with repentance and faith.[6] This is the message Jesus was murdered for. This same message has caused severe persecution to fall upon his followers throughout history in fulfillment of God's word.[7] Understanding the full implications of the gospel leads us to understand that "loving our neighbor" means telling them of their rebellion against God and how to be saved from the penalty for their rebellion. Genuinely loving them does not simply mean smiling at them and talking to them about the weather while they perish under the wrath of God.[8]

I have often heard people object to this form of teaching by asserting that the Bible clearly teaches that Christians *ought* to be kind to people. This is certainly true. The problem is that many professing Christians have confused *kindness* with *evangelism*. These are not the same thing. Followers of Christ are supposed to do *both*. We can do both. We must do both.

When you approach someone on the street, and kindly smile and say, "Hello!" the most common response is that the person will respond in kind. If you demonstrate warmth and kindness, the person to whom you are

---

6. John 7:7; Acts 17:30–31.
7. Luke 6:22.
8. John 3:36.

speaking will often reflect the same.[9] However, if you were to follow up that same cheerful and kind greeting by handing them a gospel tract and asking them about Jesus Christ, it is astounding how quickly their disposition can change! I have several brothers in Christ whom I witness with often who all would testify to the same phenomenon—generally warm people turning immediately cold and hostile as a result of nothing more than the mention of the things of God. This does not only apply to strangers. Coworkers, neighbors, friends, and relatives can all turn cold in a heartbeat when the gospel of Jesus Christ is brought up.

This demonstrates very clearly that there is a difference between *kindness* and *evangelism*. I believe it is also one of the reasons that many sincere Christians want to equate the two.[10] They simply do not have the stomach for genuine evangelism because no matter how kind and compassionate the ambassador for Christ is, the animosity that the unbeliever has toward the living God he or she is in rebellion against often spills out. Obedience to God in evangelism has ruined many "nice" Thanksgiving dinners. As a result, some professing followers of Christ would prefer to "keep the peace" and pray that those who are spiritually dead will spontaneously ask them about how to be saved, despite the lack of biblical teaching that such a strategy is appropriate.[11] Of course, not every evangelistic conversation produces

---

9. Certainly, some people are rude no matter what. Generally speaking this is true.

10. One of the most foolish messages I have ever heard preached included the opinion that making eye-contact with strangers, smiling at them, and opening doors for them was what is most needed in this world and is a form of evangelism. No biblical passage supports such a claim, yet since it was preached from a pulpit, there were those in the congregation who took such foolishness as "gospel truth" on the authority of the person speaking.

11. Sometimes, passages like 1 Peter 3:15 are cited as proof texts that living a moral lifestyle and waiting for people to ask for the "reason for our hope within" is *exactly* what God wants his people to do. Unfortunately, this demonstrates a severe lack in understanding the original context that Peter was addressing. The conclusion that this passage means that we should simply be nice and wait for people to talk to us about Jesus in our present context is a mistake. Certainly, all Christians should be ready and prepared to share the gospel with anyone who asks them, regardless of the reason they are asking. However, Peter was first and foremost writing to a group of Christians who were suffering brutal persecution for their bold identification as followers of Jesus Christ—suffering is mentioned sixteen times in these five chapters—a persecution that could end if they would simply stop calling Jesus their lord and stop being open with their faith! In this context, Peter expects that those who are persecuting these followers of Christ and observing their persecution will ask, "Why do you have hope in Jesus and refuse to be saved from persecution in this life? Why will you continue to endure suffering instead of forsaking allegiance to Jesus?" In the present North American context, the "suffering" and "persecution" that is aimed at Christians is decidedly different than what these believers experienced in Rome (or what our brothers and sisters in Christ

hostility—some produce *life*. Yet, it only takes a few outbreaks of animosity to turn some professing Christians off from ever bringing up the things of God again without a clear invitation to do so.

How can we escape the conclusion that the desire to avoid the persecution associated with proclaiming the gospel of Jesus Christ has choked out the fruitfulness of the one professing faith in Jesus?[12] Is not the will of God that we would bear fruit for him?[13] In fact, it was Timothy's *perseverance* in participating in the work of the gospel alongside Paul which served as *proof* that Timothy was a genuine follower of Jesus Christ.[14] This was in contrast to those who abandoned Paul and the ministry when times got tough and the road got hard to pursue the things of this world.[15]

Since the implications of a failure to obey God are often too much to bear, many in the professing church ignore such conversations and embrace the "Christianity = Moralism" heresy. After all, there are plenty of books and teachers who make such a view seem right and good. This false teaching "resonates" with many people—as if such a test of the truth of claims is ever validated in the Scriptures! The easiest lies to believe are the ones we want to be true, told to us in a way that we want to hear.

Despite the abundance of these false claims and teachings, believers are taught in the Scriptures to be bold with the gospel and to proclaim it

---

are enduring elsewhere around the world). In America, people say "Happy Holidays" instead of "Merry Christmas" and we make a big deal about it. Back then, if you said Jesus was lord, they would torture you, throw you in prison, execute you, or some combination of these things. Since these contexts are so radically different, we should not expect our neighbors to come ask us about our "hope" since our ability to demonstrate our "hope" is decidedly less emphatic, especially when not accompanied by their zeal for evangelizing. I do not mean to diminish the genuine persecution that some face for Christ in our present North American context. However, it is certainly a mistake for us to discount the suffering of those to whom Peter was writing to who were experiencing state sponsored persecution in the Roman Empire and, by extension, the visibility of their "hope in Christ" compared to ours. For this passage to apply directly to us, we must be demonstrating "hope" in the midst of intense personal suffering *for sharing our faith boldly*. This is not usually the context that those who use this passage find themselves in. It is virtually teaching the opposite of the idea that Christians do not have to proclaim the gospel until someone asks them to—instead teaching that if you keep preaching Christ, despite brutal persecution, even more people will get to hear because you won't have to go and tell everyone, but some people will start coming to ask you about your reason for the hope you have.

12. See Matt 13:20-21.

13. E.g., Matt 3:8-10; 7:16-23; John 15:1-10; Rom 7:4; Col 1:9-12.

14. Phil 2:19-22. I am indebted to my ministry partner, Joel Davidson, for first pointing this out to me.

15. Cf. Paul's description of Demas—who is also mentioned as serving with Paul in Col 4:14 and Phlm 1:24—in 2 Tim 4:10.

to every creature under heaven. There is an urgency involved in telling this message. We do not know when our own lives will end. We do not know when the lives of those we are trying to reach will end. We also do not know when Jesus will return. Boldly declaring the gospel has rarely been a popular practice.[16] Nevertheless, proclaiming the gospel has always been the expectation of those who are called by his name despite the practice being socially taboo. The content of the biblical gospel is relatively simple according to Paul in 1 Corinthians 15:3–4. The essential truths are:

1. That Christ died for our sins according to the Scriptures
2. That he was buried
3. That he was raised on the third day according to the Scriptures, and
4. That his resurrection was attested to by eye-witnesses and it is to these truths that we must testify.

What becomes more complicated is an explanation of what these basic elements mean, because the truth and implications of these things are not always immediately apparent to our hearers. Followers of Jesus Christ and ambassadors for his kingdom ought to follow the instruction and example he set.[17] On the day that Jesus rose from the dead, he met two of his followers as they were walking down the road. They were not yet aware that Jesus had risen from the dead (the Bible says "their eyes were prevented from recognizing Him" in Luke 24:16) and Jesus rebuked their failure to understand that the Christ was supposed to suffer, be buried, and rise again (doesn't that sound like the gospel that Paul recounted?): "And He said to them, 'O foolish men and slow of heart to believe in all that the prophets have spoken! Was it not necessary for the Christ to suffer these things and to enter into His glory?' Then beginning with Moses and with all the prophets, He explained to them the things concerning Himself in all the Scriptures."[18]

Jesus relied upon something that is being forgotten in the modern professing church: the power and importance of the "Old Testament" Scriptures. The Hebrew Bible (the Christian "Old Testament") contains the

---

16. It was popular for a little while in the earliest stages of the church; see Acts 2:47. Periods of favor for the gospel are often replaced with persecution in a short period of time; cf. Acts 8:1. Charles Wesley records a time that he was pleasantly surprised to find a place more receptive to the gospel than normal, writing in his journal, "God, as it seems, is turning the heart of this people back again. Nothing but kind salutations, instead of my usual reception with stones and curses" (Kimbrough and Newport, *Manuscript Journal*, 2:381).

17. E.g., Matt 11:1; Luke 20:1; Acts 5:42; 15:35; 28:31; etc.

18. Luke 24:25–27.

Scriptures from which Jesus explained the truth about himself.[19] Likewise, the Apostle Paul spent much of his time in ministry teaching in the synagogues explaining from the Scriptures (the Hebrew Bible) that Jesus is the Christ. If we fail to understand that the Old Testament Scriptures are what Paul is primarily referring to when he says *according to the Scriptures* twice in his explanation of the basic tenets of the gospel in 1 Corinthians 15:3–4, then we will likely rely on a deficient gospel presentation because we will fail to include these powerful scriptural truths. After those two followers recognized Jesus and heard his words, they ran back to tell the other disciples. Jesus again appeared in their midst and ate with them (Luke 24:36–43) and then he spoke to them, saying:

> Now He said to them, "These are My words which I spoke to you while I was still with you, that all things which are written about Me in the Law of Moses and the Prophets and the Psalms must be fulfilled." Then He opened their minds to understand the Scriptures, and He said to them, "Thus it is written, that the Christ would suffer and rise again from the dead the third day, and that repentance for forgiveness of sins would be proclaimed in His name to all the nations, beginning from Jerusalem. You are witnesses of these things. And behold, I am sending forth the promise of My Father upon you; but you are to stay in the city until you are clothed with power from on high." (Luke 24:44–49)

He opened their minds to understand the Scriptures. He spoke to them about things written in Moses, the Prophets, and the Psalms. Jesus told them that they were witnesses to *these* fulfilled Scriptures in him and that they are to testify regarding *these* truths to all nations, beginning at Jerusalem, in the power of the Holy Spirit. If we want to walk in the same ministry and power as the initial ambassadors for Christ, then we must rely on the same Holy Spirit and the same message—a message which is found primarily in the Hebrew Bible. I would never argue that a Christian should *not* use the New Testament Scriptures. Of course we should! However, our gospel message is deficient and lacking if we fail to likewise have our minds opened to the Scriptures and be armed with fulfilled prophecy regarding the person and ministry of Jesus Christ as it pertains to the gospel truth that he died for our sins *according to the Scriptures*, that he was buried, and that he rose on the third day *according to the Scriptures*. We will do well to remember that the early church spread and grew long before the New Testament

---

19. See also John 5:39–40.

was written. The New Testament is God's word and is of amazing value. So is the Old Testament.

Some good places to start in gaining an understanding of the teaching about Jesus in Moses, the Prophets, and the Psalms are as follows: Genesis 3:15; 12:1–3; 15:6; Exodus 12:46; Leviticus 18:5; Numbers 21:6–9; Deuteronomy 18:15; 21:23; 27:26; Psalms 2:1–12; 16:8–11; 22:1–31; 89:3–4; 110:1–7; 132:11; Isaiah 7:14; 9:6–7; 11:1–5; 52:13—53:12; Jeremiah 23:5–8; Ezekiel 37:24–28; Daniel 7:13–14; Joel 2:28–32; Micah 5:2; Nahum 1:2–8; Habakkuk 2:4; and Zechariah 3:8–10; 14:3–11. This list is not meant to be exhaustive. It is, at least, representative of the types of passages that were used by the earliest followers of Christ to proclaim the gospel of Jesus and cover "Moses, the Prophets, and the Psalms" as Jesus indicated on Resurrection Day. To see just two examples of the early preaching of the gospel using some of the texts included in this paragraph, read Acts 2:14–40 and 8:26–35.

There is power in the simple recitation of these gospel truths without explanation or further support; that is certain.[20] If you are confronted with the choice to be faithful to the content *or* to rely upon rhetorical skill and/or human wisdom, then by all means choose faithfulness in reciting these truths without modification every time! However, our call as ambassadors requires us not only to *preach* these truths, but also to *teach* them.

Before proceeding any further we must clarify our terms. *Preaching* does not necessarily imply speaking to large groups from a pulpit or on a street corner. Proclamations are made all the time in wide and varied settings. For our purposes "preaching" means verbally uttering specific things. For a proclamation to be complete it *must* include all of the elements it is supposed to.[21] Various situations, contexts, and other factors may contribute to the necessary components of any particular *proclamation*. "Teaching," on the other hand, is an explanation of the various elements of your proclamation in order to bring about understanding in your hearer(s).

I love coffee and one of the reasons I love living in America is the amount of coffee shops that are available to get a quality cup of coffee at. When I say I love coffee, what I mean is that I love *regular* coffee. Although I have spent a fair amount of time in coffee shops, I must admit that I still sometimes feel like people are speaking a different language inside. When I place my order I say, "I'd like a large coffee." And they understand what I mean. Usually, the person in front of me says something like, "I'd like a tall

---

20. E.g., Rom 1:16 and 1 Cor 1:17–21.
21. E.g., Acts 20:24–27.

mocha latte, no whip, with an extra shot" or something along these lines ... which often I do not understand at all!

Both coffee orders are proclamations. Hopefully, both orders are understood by the person taking the order (there is a good reason I am not employed by a coffee shop). What is being demonstrated in this example, however, is the power of the language of "the initiated." For those coffee-lovers who enjoy other types of beverages, they learn the lingo and speak accordingly. To those who are uninitiated, the "insider" language is weird and scary. It makes no sense. In order to become initiated we must learn by being taught what these things mean. Otherwise, the proclamations that employ this language will be meaningless to us and will sound like foolishness.

To take this example a step further, who the coffee is for makes a difference in the content of the proclamation. More importantly, it makes a difference in who *decides* the content of the proclamation. If I am ordering a coffee for myself, I decide the content of the proclamation. If I am ordering the coffee for my wife, she decides the content of the proclamation. If I fail to proclaim the full list of elements prescribed by my wife, the consequences are minor. As ambassadors for Christ, the content of our proclamation is defined by the Lord Jesus Christ. If we stray too far from his leading and empowering, we risk making a proclamation that carries no power of God for salvation. The consequences of negligence in this area are far more serious.[22]

Teaching is likewise necessary and important for the ambassador for Christ. Just like "tall" means nothing to me when it comes to ordering coffee, "sin" means nothing to those who are not following Christ. For others, they *think* they understand what it means when really they are confused or misguided because they have misconceptions about the terminology for various reasons. This is why *teaching* is important in accompanying our *preaching*. We owe it to those we are addressing to explain what the elements

---

22. It's possible that the more Calvinistic leaning reader may scoff at such a claim thinking this to be overly Arminian in theology and putting too much responsibility on the human element. However, how much liberty and casualness should we allow in our theology regarding the sovereignty of God in bringing about salvation through the foolishness of preaching (1 Cor 1:21)? Should we stray so far to say that God will save sinners through conversations about the weather? There is no biblical precedent or foundation for believing that God is honored through ill prepared ambassadors or that his expectation of his people is to be poorly equipped and to preach whatever is on their hearts or minds. Ironically, it is often those who profess with their mouths a high view of sovereignty that deny such a view through their own casualness and carelessness to heed the commands of the sovereign God. Sticking closely to God's revealed message is based upon the recognition of his sovereignty and power. The power is in the message, not in the messenger; therefore, the messenger ought to take careful steps to ensure that the message is not diluted or changed.

of our proclamation *actually* mean. While we live in a land that has a church on virtually every corner, it is alarming to find the rampant biblical illiteracy that plagues our culture and society. Not too long ago I was witnessing to a man who thought evangelism was unnecessary and stupid because we live in America. He claimed that everyone has already heard the message of Christianity and knows what Christians are all about. I immediately asked him to tell me the gospel, then, since it is so widely known . . . which was met by a good amount of stammering and guffawing before he changed the subject.

Sadly, he had no idea what the gospel really is or what it is about. This is not uncommon. It is exactly why we must obey our king and evangelize for his glory. One well-known evangelist has stated well that our land is not "gospel-hardened" it is "gospel-ignorant."[23] I wish this were not true, but it is. Really, it is shameful.[24]

One of the times I travelled to Ethiopia to preach the gospel and minister at some local churches which our local church at the time supported, I was met by these Ethiopian believers with concern; not for themselves and their well-being, but for me and the status of the church in America! While modern Americans often look with pity at others who are "less fortunate," I was pitied by these third-world brothers and sisters because they are aware of the rampant apostasy in our land and the shallow nature of many "confessions" of Jesus as Lord and Savior. They wanted to know how they could help *me*, because they know how perverted the gospel is becoming in the United States and how rampant the preaching of false gospels and moralism has become. In fact, after preaching the gospel in one of the poorest places I have ever been I watched as, after I sat down, one of the elders of the local church in that area somberly stood up and began to speak to those assembled. He stated how relieved he was that I came preaching the same message and the same gospel as they received and preach. He was relieved because he knows how many Americans come to their land preaching nonsense. His greatest desire was that those offering to "help" by bringing material resources would not even come if they were also bringing a false gospel. How relieved they were to welcome a genuine brother in Christ! Their greatest privilege was not to receive the money I had brought to bless them, but to bless me and my congregation with their on-going prayers for our continued faithfulness in spreading the genuine gospel.

---

23. I heard this in a message preached by Paul Washer.
24. 1 Cor 15:34.

To fully "preach the gospel" means that we must state all of the necessary components.[25] Since we are *heralds* of the gospel and not *editors* we do not have the luxury of picking and choosing which elements to include and which to ignore. Our king has issued a proclamation—we must include all of the elements he has decreed without modification.

However, when I proclaim that *Jesus Christ died for our sins according to the Scriptures*—whether I am proclaiming this from a pulpit to a large gathering or I am proclaiming this in a casual conversation to one friend over a cup of coffee at their house—it is my responsibility as an ambassador to make sure that I explain who *Jesus* is, what *sin* is, and what the Scriptures have to say about these things. These terms are loaded because everyone has different ideas about what they mean, even when they are using the same words. Therefore, we must clarify our terms and *teach* what the Bible truly has to say about these things. Communication is a two-way street. To faithfully communicate the message means we must labor to ensure that our terms are understood how we intend them to be understood.[26]

Fortunately for us, our king has not left us empty-handed. He has provided clear instruction and powerful tools for teaching about the elements of our proclamation in his word. In order to explain what *sin* is, God has given us the Law. Unfortunately, the Law is often misunderstood by professing followers of Christ. You've likely heard the phrase, "We're not under Law, but under grace." But what does that mean? Does it mean that the Law has passed away and is now useless for the Christian? By no means!

"But avoid foolish controversies and genealogies and strife and disputes about the Law, for they are unprofitable and worthless. Reject a factious man after a first and second warning, knowing that such a man is perverted and is sinning, being self-condemned" (Titus 3:9–11).

Paul taught very clearly that the Law is good,[27] that it has not passed away but is for believers to hold up and establish,[28] and to administer to nonbelievers[29] to explain what sin is[30] and lead them to faith in Christ.[31] The Law is

25. For a further discussion, see Washer, *Gospel's Power*, 35–38, and Gilbert, *What Is the Gospel?*, 27–36.

26. Early in my Christian life I spent hours talking with a Jehovah's Witness that I worked with about Jesus. We were talking past each other the entire time because neither of us took the time to explain what we meant when we discussed "Jesus." Even though we were both using the same term, we were not talking about the same person.

27. Rom 7:12; 1 Tim 1:8.

28. Rom 3:31.

29. 1 Tim 1:8–11; Rom 3:31; Gal 3:24.

30. Rom 3:20; 7:7; Gal 3:19.

31. Gal 3:24. Some of the major English translations (e.g., ESV, NET, NLT, NRSV,

not for believers to take upon themselves to attempt to earn their salvation.[32] To quarrel over these things—saying either that the Law is *not* for unbelievers to expose sin and lead them to Christ, or that it *is* for believers to earn their salvation—is unprofitable and worthless, and such activity needs to be warned to stop.[33] According to Paul, failure to heed this warning is worthy of breaking fellowship over!

There exists no more powerful tool for explaining and exposing sin than the Law of God.[34] To proclaim that Christ died for our sins is critical in proclaiming the gospel of our Lord. Even so, teaching what sin is and why Christ died for the sins of the person(s) you are talking to is likewise important.[35] The gospel message itself is a powerful offensive weapon for advancing the church and crashing the gates of hades. Understanding the importance of preaching and teaching the gospel faithfully, the next chapter will focus on some matters of methodology in rightly handling and applying the Law, and in fulfilling our task as stewards of the gospel and as ambassadors for the king.

---

and TNIV) render the Greek prepositional phrase *eis christón* with a temporal idea as *until Christ came* instead of with the directional idea of *lead us to Christ*, as in the NASB and KJV. With the temporal idea, some interpreters object that the Law served as a custodian/guardian/teacher (GK: *paidagōgós*) up until the time that Christ arrived, and now it has been done away with; a position which Douglas Moo argues for in his chapter in Bahnsen, *Law and Gospel*, 319–76. Even if a temporal idea is best for the context (a point that is exegetically arguable), it does not follow that the Law does not still serve the purpose of leading people to faith in Christ even though we are now in the age *after* Christ's incarnation. Everyone is shut up under the Law, whether they realize it or not (Gal 3:22; Rom 3:19). The Jews had the advantage of the Law being their custodian (e.g., Rom 3:1) because the guardianship was purposeful in that it did not merely hold them in bondage until Christ came, but that it allowed the nation of Israel to *know* sin (e.g., Rom 3:19; 7:7) and to look for God's promised Messiah (e.g., Col 2:17). The Law was not merely a babysitter passing the time, but it had a purpose in presenting the nation to Christ *when he arrived*. Now that he has arrived, the Law still serves the same purpose for those who are not yet in Christ. The Galatian error was going back to the Law *after* coming to know Christ (see Gal 3:2–3). It is a logical and interpretive error to assert that because the Galatians were misusing the Law that the Law does not still function in this capacity for those who are not *yet* in Christ.

32. Gal 2:21; 3:1–5; Acts 15:1–11.

33. Titus 3:9–11.

34. The Way of the Master is an evangelism method that teaches these principles clearly and is an excellent first step for anyone desiring to study how these principles can be applied in witnessing for the glory of God. You can learn more about this particular teaching at www.livingwaters.com. A ministry that teaches similar principles and is also worthy of checking out is www.transfired.org.

35. For a review of the depth of sin and the radical depravity of human beings, see chap. 3, "Rebels—One and All."

7

Preachers & Teachers

> And every day, in the temple and from house to house, they kept right on teaching and preaching Jesus as the Christ. (Acts 5:42)

When wrestling with the truth of our calling as followers of Christ it is easy to ask along with the Apostle Paul: who is adequate for these things?[1] We will do well to remember that although the Apostle Paul was highly educated, the Lord chose to call to himself regular people like you and me, too. Our adequacy and competence comes, not from ourselves, but from our God who has made us qualified to speak on his behalf!

"Such confidence we have through Christ toward God. Not that we are adequate in ourselves to consider anything as coming from ourselves, but our adequacy is from God, who also made us adequate as servants of a new covenant, not of the letter but of the Spirit; for the letter kills, but the Spirit gives life" (2 Cor 3:4–6).

It should be our desire to rest in God and in the power he provides. Unfortunately, because we are prone to walking in the flesh, it is easy to look for and desire a methodology that can be easily memorized and recited in our evangelism. Certainly this is not always a bad thing. I serve the church as a church-planter, pastor, and by attempting to raise up and equip evangelists in the local church setting for the equipping of the saints for

---

1. 2 Cor 2:16.

works of service.[2] Working in this capacity has led me to understand the power of teaching a particular methodology for those who have not really studied biblical evangelism and/or who battle fear,[3] because when we are prepared with a standard message it can give us confidence. As a result, our ministry often teaches the Way of the Master[4] as a first step, because this methodology can equip and prepare any Christian to begin sharing their faith according to biblical principles. Another benefit is that this method of evangelism can be learned in a relatively short period of time. We do not teach this methodology as "the" inspired method of evangelism.[5] We would never claim that once someone has memorized this (or any other) methodology that they no longer need to devote themselves to studying the gospel, to studying the Scriptures, and to growing in their ability to preach and teach this truth of first importance to the best of their ability, empowered and led by the Holy Spirit. We all must continue to grow. If you do not know where to begin, and you want to hit the ground running, I have not encountered any materials that are better to get Christians off the pew and into the harvest field more quickly and effectively than this first step of a lifelong pursuit.

Every "method" has a short-coming. Some methods are definitely better than others. You'll notice that as you read through the Gospels and Acts that every time the gospel is recorded as being preached it is not *exactly* the same. Instead, these men and women of faith were equipped with the essential truths and were able to follow the lead of the Holy Spirit in their preaching and teaching. By being saturated in the essential truths of the gospel and being fully confident in the tools God has provided (Law, grace, and fulfilled Scriptures relating to the ministry, work, and person of Christ), then you likewise can follow the lead of the Spirit in your preaching and teaching about the gospel of Christ as his ambassador; custom-tailoring the message to your respective audience without being negligent in your duty to faithfully proclaim the entire message of salvation.[6] By being fully equipped, the ambassador for Christ is ready to share the gospel faithfully

---

2. Eph 4:11–12. For more information about Fourth Year Ministries and why we do what we do visit www.fourthyearministries.com.

3. This is virtually everyone! If you're afraid to evangelize, you're in good company; see 1 Cor 2:3–4.

4. Learn more about the Way of the Master at www.livingwaters.com. A related ministry, www.transfired.org, teaches similar methodology under the leadership of evangelist Andy Lapins.

5. It is, however, virtually identical to the form of evangelism that the Apostle Paul is recorded using in Rom 2:17–24.

6. 1 Cor 9:18–23. For more on this, see Spurgeon, *Lectures*, 336–48.

regardless of the context—to one person in a private conversation or to the gathered multitudes, and everywhere in-between.

In the previous chapter, the purpose of the Law was discussed. While it may be difficult and overwhelming to memorize "the entire Law" it is not altogether difficult to memorize the Ten Commandments (in order) from either Exodus 20:1–17 or Deuteronomy 5:6–21. After this, it is helpful to memorize these (mostly New Testament) Scriptures which correspond or relate to the Ten Commandments. The following Scriptures, which correspond to each of the original commandments, give further insight into how Jesus and the Apostles applied and interpreted the Law:

1. Mark 12:30
2. James 4:4
3. Matthew 12:36
4. Colossians 2:16
5. Colossians 3:20
6. 1 John 3:15; Matthew 5:21–22
7. Matthew 5:27–28
8. 1 Corinthians 6:9–10
9. Proverbs 19:5; Revelation 21:8
10. Proverbs 11:4; Ephesians 5:5

In addition to memorizing these Scriptures that relate to God's Law, it is also helpful to have some passages in mind that will put people in mind of the coming judgment[7] according to God's standard of righteousness revealed in his Law. This, in turn, will help them understand their urgent need for forgiveness of their sins against God:[8]

1. Therefore having overlooked the times of ignorance, God is now declaring to men that all people everywhere should repent, because He has fixed a day in which He will judge the world in righteousness

---

7. Something the Apostle Paul was not shy to do; see Acts 24:25.

8. I've heard plenty of non-believers claim that they "don't need God." This particular response is often based on them thinking that they do not *need* what false gospels have offered to them—they are plenty happy/fulfilled/purposeful (etc.) without him. However, since the gospel is not really about "God-shaped holes" in people's hearts, but about righteousness (e.g., Prov 11:4), then letting people see themselves through the lens of God's Law can awaken them to their genuine need for salvation from the wrath that is rightly coming on all who fail to repent and trust in the Savior. Everyone needs that, whether they know it or not.

through a Man whom He has appointed, having furnished proof to all men by raising Him from the dead. (Acts 17:30-31)

2. And inasmuch as it is appointed for men to die once and after this comes judgment. (Heb 9:27)

3. The conclusion, when all has been heard, is: fear God and keep His commandments, because this applies to every person. For God will bring every act to judgment, everything which is hidden, whether it is good or evil. (Eccl 12:13-14)

4. On the day when, according to my gospel, God will judge the secrets of men through Christ Jesus. (Rom 2:16)

Often, when I am sharing the gospel with people, they will try to take the focus of the conversation off of themselves and start to talk about someone else, or a different group of people, in theoretical terms. They may say something like, "What about people in the jungles of Africa that have never heard of Jesus? Are they going to hell simply because they've never heard of Jesus?" The simple answer to this is, "No. They won't go to hell simply because they've never heard of Jesus. They will go to hell as a result of being judged for their rebellion against their creator."[9] The above passages may also be used to remind them that despite all the theoretical questions they can muster, *they themselves* will die and *they themselves* will be judged. It is also helpful to be prepared to explain that your declaration to them is not "being judgmental" and that *you* are not condemning them—you are not the judge! By appealing to God's righteous standard, you are an ambassador sent to announce to them the judgment of God according to *his* righteous standard. The hope in making this proclamation is that the Holy Spirit will bring conviction to their heart and mind.[10] The hope is to lovingly show them that they are condemned *already* because they have broken multitudes of God's laws.[11]

It is always important for the Christian to remember that we are not judges sitting on the throne. Instead, we are heralds proclaiming the news of the verdict that has been handed down from the judge of all creation.[12] We are watchmen on the wall—declaring danger on the horizon.[13] There's a big difference between these roles. Without the Law, it is easy to come off

---

9. Rom 1:18—2:16.
10. John 16:8-11.
11. John 3:18, 36.
12. 1 Cor 5:12-13.
13. Ezek 3:1-27; 33:1-20; Acts 18:4-6; Rom 1:14; 1 Cor 9:16-23.

as judgmental. With the Law, we are merely exposing sin.[14] And *if* they recognize their need for salvation and *still* burn with compassion for those far away that they have mentioned in theoretical terms who have never heard of Jesus, then by all means encourage them to *go* and proclaim to them the good news of the kingdom of God and salvation through Jesus Christ to them who have never heard so that they may have the opportunity to repent and believe the gospel! More often than not, our theoretical concerns do not lead us to actually do something about it.

The Law can also show people that their sin is not a mistake but is something much deeper. It is something they are a slave to.[15] For example, the Law says, "Thou shall not covet." You can talk with someone about coveting and explain that to covet something means to jealously desire to have it for themselves. They may even agree with you that jealously desiring something that belongs to someone else is wrong. However, the Law can help show the person you are speaking to that they are powerless to stop coveting from occurring in their flesh, heart, and mind. The secret power behind the success of advertising is simple: it is covetousness.

While a person may agree that they do not enjoy being jealous or sad when others have things they do not, it is a fact of life in this fallen world. It is extremely rare for people to be able to be genuinely happy when something good happens to someone else, without secretly wishing it happened to us instead. The idea of "keeping up with the Jones'" is proof. People are often happy with what they have until they see what *others* have. I know of people who love their phones; that is, until the newest release comes out. Is the slavery not evident in people who will stand in lines for hours, even sleep outside in some cases, to be sure they will be the first to get the new gadget or gizmo, all the while using their *old* gadget and gizmo to inform the world that they can't wait to get their hands on the new one? Once the "new" is available, theirs—although it is still perfectly functional—immediately

---

14. One of the most powerful elements of the Way of the Master teaching is that it uses the Law to ask questions of the person you are witnessing to, so that when they acknowledge that they have broken God's commandments it is by their own admission and not by the assertion or accusation of the Christian to whom they are speaking. This method personalizes the use of the Law to the individual and helps them feel the weight of their own violations of God's Law by admitting their own transgressions with their own mouth. When confronted with these violations, it is difficult for the person to claim that the Christian is being judgmental. They were merely asked if they had done these things and they confessed with their own mouth that they are liars, thieves, adulterers, blasphemers, etc. By exposing them to God's word (such as Rev 21:8 and 1 Cor 6:9–10) they can see they are in big trouble if they really have to face God on Judgment Day.

15. John 8:34.

becomes a piece of junk! (You've probably never met anyone like this.) I also know people who simply must have a new vehicle every couple of years, even though each time they trade in their car or sign a new lease, their previous car was still in great shape and was perfectly capable to getting them safely from point A to point B.

That's covetousness. Our economy is built on it. People literally cannot help themselves from being covetous. It can cause people to lose sleep, to go into debt, and to sacrifice relationships. Companies that can harness the power of covetousness can become fabulously successful in selling things no one really needs to people who already had something like it, but simply got tired of the old one. I used to sell vacuum cleaners door-to-door.[16] There was a saying in our office that some of the best customers were previous customers because a lot of them would buy the new model just because it was shiny and had a bright light on it. This was a saying, because it was at least partially true. The saddest part about it all was that a big part of my pitch was that our particular product should have lasted them for the rest of their life and been the last purchase they needed to make for this item—and it could have been, too, if not for covetousness.

Our culture tells us this is *normal*. The Law tells us the truth and exposes that really it is *slavery*. It's dangerous, too, because no covetous person will inherit the kingdom of heaven.[17]

Similarly, the Law of God tells us, "Thou shall not lie," and warns that the consequences of breaking this commandment are to be cast into the Lake of Fire.[18] Yet, human beings cannot help themselves from speaking lies, fibs, "half-truths," and the like. We are often extremely adept at justifying our deception. We are also (if we will be honest with ourselves) capable of surprising ourselves when things that are not true simply fall out of our mouths and roll off our tongues. The circumstances may vary, but people find themselves stretching the truth (or completely fabricating things) in many different situations, often without any form of premeditation or effort. As slaves to deception, it flows out of our mouths as a form of self-preservation. We can try to justify ourselves all we want to, but the truth is that we are slaves to the sinfulness that dwells in our flesh. We are born this way.[19]

---

16. Glamorous, I know.

17. 1 Cor 6:9–10; Eph 5:5. "Covetous" and "greedy" are common translations for the same word in the Greek and, depending on which English translation you are reading, might say one or the other.

18. Rev 21:8.

19. Pss 51:5–6; 58:3.

Even though this is our natural condition, nevertheless, lying lips are an abomination to God and all liars will have their place in the Lake of Fire.[20]

We are commanded not to steal. Most people have never robbed a bank, but does this commandment only apply to stealing of this type? We live in a world that makes theft extremely easy and we are pretty good at justifying ourselves when we take things from people who have "more than enough." If you have ever downloaded a song or movie from the internet without paying for it, that's stealing. You ever take a few extra minutes on your break at work that you weren't supposed to? That's stealing. Ever take a pen from a business without thinking about it (or even on purpose)? That's stealing. Ever take more than one piece of candy from a house on Halloween that had a sign saying, "Please take one." That's stealing. Have you ever failed to bring God his tithe?[21] That's stealing from God.[22] You may not consider it a big deal. It may be true that "everybody does it." Still, according to the righteous standard of God, no thief will enter the kingdom of heaven.[23] Some may think this is petty, and that the punishment doesn't fit the crime. Even still, our judgment is not the one that matters. We don't get to pick where the line is drawn on these matters and what forms of theft are "acceptable"—God has decreed that we should not steal. Period.

At the time of writing this, I have five children and another one on the way. My experience with the first five tells me that I will not have to teach this newest child of mine how to lie, or steal, or any future children of ours for that matter. Without being taught, they will know how to do these things from the very earliest stages of life. When seeing one of its siblings with a toy that they want, they will try to take it. They will protest loudly if their theft is thwarted. Once they are old enough to speak, and understand that they are disciplined for disobedience, they will attempt to shift the blame to others; even when they know that they alone are guilty. Once, my three oldest blamed the (then) baby for breaking an item in our home. At the time the item in question was broken, the baby was sound asleep in his crib on a completely different floor! Nevertheless, these children of mine, whom I never taught how to "twist the truth," colluded together in a way that was

---

20. Prov 12:22; Rev 21:8.

21. The thing about the tithe is that it's not really about your money, but about God being first in your life. The tithe is not just ten percent, but the *first* ten percent. Many people who think they've been tithing have actually never truly tithed, because they tithe off of their *net* income and not their *gross* income—which means that the government took their cut first, and God merely received a portion of what was left over. Good thing we're not saved by works!

22. Mal 3:8.

23. 1 Cor 6:9–10.

consistent, not with their upbringing in a home with "Judeo-Christian values," but with the sinfulness that is inherent in their flesh. I love my children dearly, but they are clearly rebels.

Rebellion that is "cute" in young children and babies, becomes less cute in teenagers, and is downright ugly in adults. The answer to this sinful condition according to much of society is to call it normal or to blame something else. Blame the parents, blame society, blame politics, or the wealthy, or whatever. The biblical answer is redemption and setting the captives free through the gospel.

When Jesus exposed the heart of the commandment not to murder, he told us that being angry with your brother is the same as murder in your heart. "You have heard that the ancients were told, 'You shall not commit murder' and 'Whoever commits murder shall be liable to the court.' But I say to you that everyone who is angry with his brother shall be guilty before the court; and whoever says to his brother, 'You good-for-nothing,' shall be guilty before the supreme court; and whoever says, 'You fool,' shall be guilty enough to go into the fiery hell" (Matt 5:21–22).

Perhaps the best way to expose our slavery to anger is to remind people what happens inside of them when someone cuts them off on the freeway.[24] It is simply amazing how quickly the mood and direction of a person's day can change and how freely we may insult the intelligence of the offender! Often, people will spend the next several hours (or even days) thinking about and cursing the fool who would be so reckless on the road. Of course, when we almost miss our own exit and need to get over in a hurry we expect understanding, compassion, and grace! This further demonstrates our tendency to justify ourselves while seeing the actions and motivations of others as worthy of condemnation—even when their actions and motivations are the same as ours.[25] God does not exercise the same partiality as we do.[26] According to Jesus, God's standard includes calling someone made in his image a "fool" a crime against God severe enough to cause someone guilty of this to go to hell. Have you ever called someone a fool, or worse?

God commanded that his name not be used in vain. He warned that he will not leave them unpunished who take his name in vain.[27] This commandment of God is violated constantly—even by professing Christians! I know of no other person in history whose name is used as a cuss word, other

---

24. Or, perhaps, when their favorite sports team loses.

25. Ray Comfort has accurately stated that sin is like bad breath—it is easier to notice on others, than it is to notice in ourselves!

26. Acts 10:34; Rom 2:11; Gal 2:6; Eph 6:9; Col 3:23–25; 1 Pet 1:17.

27. Exod 20:7; Deut 5:11.

than Jesus Christ. I've never heard anyone shout, "Ghandi!" when they stub their toe. Have you? In the Law of Moses, when the principle of eye for an eye and tooth for a tooth was elucidated, it made sense—the punishment should fit the crime; it should not be too harsh or too lax. In Leviticus, *the penalty for blasphemy was the same as the penalty for murder.* The penalty was death.[28]

In our current culture, blasphemy has lost its shock value. In many cases, it doesn't even need to be bleeped out on television like some of the "worse" curse words. When it comes to blasphemy, God considers not just our words but also our *actions*. It is possible to blaspheme the name of the Lord by calling ourselves Christians and acting like pagans. Our current culture has appropriated symbols relating to Christianity—especially the cross—and uses this symbolism in ways that dishonor the one who died upon it. Countless people wear this imagery on their clothes, jewelry, and bodies (in the form of tattoos), while engaging in behaviors explicitly contrary to God's revealed will. When we take his name upon ourselves, we ought to act in ways that are worthy of the God by whose name we are called.[29] God will not leave him unpunished who uses his name in vain or who defile and slander it among the nations.

Ambassadors for Christ should be fully equipped and willing to go down the entire list of commandments to show people, using the Law, that they are slaves to their own various lusts, impulses, and appetites. We should be prepared to spend as much time as necessary to help whomever we are addressing to understand and feel the weight of their sin against a holy God. An attractive person walking by showing a little too much skin can cause even the most faithful partner to begin down a mental road they may not want to travel. Forgetting and moving on can sometimes prove impossible. God will one day judge the secret things and bring them to light.[30]

We say this is because we're "human." This is true. The part we do not want to admit or acknowledge is that, as humans, we have been sold into bondage to sin as a result of God's curse upon us. We are slaves. The Law is able to show us our slavery and lead us to the solution: freedom in Christ.

---

28. Lev 24:10–23.

29. This is the point of Paul's argument in addressing the Law to Jews in Rom 2:17–24. By boasting in their status as "Jews" and yet breaking the commandments of God, they were blaspheming the name of the Lord to the nations. Likewise, professing Christians who live like the world blaspheme the name of the Lord today. Are we not ashamed that a country that claims to be "Christian" and boasts huge statistics of professing Christians also spends billions of dollars on pornography each year?

30. Luke 12:1–5; Rom 2:16.

That's what the Law is for.[31] Those who think the Law is "bad" have either misunderstood it or misapplied it. God, in his goodness, has given us a perfect diagnostic tool to expose our present miserable condition so that we may search for and cling to the solution: Jesus.

The purpose of our application of the Law as ambassadors for Christ is to help the person(s) we are speaking with see how sinful they really are and how hopelessly enslaved they are to their sinful lusts and passions. Most people will admit that they have made mistakes. *No one's perfect!* However, these same people will almost always profess their own goodness and deny that they are worthy of God's condemnation and an eternity in hell. Modern ideas of "confessing sin" have led us to believe in many cases that this means we admit we have made some mistakes and that covers it. On the contrary, it is the testimony of Scripture that we are wicked to the core of our being. Our nature as rebels against God makes even our most righteous acts *worthless* in his sight. Confession, in a biblical sense, does not mean simply acknowledging that we have made some mistakes; it is a much deeper confession. Confessing our sin means agreeing with God that his judgment is true and that our own eternal condemnation in hell would be just and right. That's much different than the confession of many professing Christians. Many people who are willing to admit they've made mistakes are adamantly opposed to this weightier confession of their deserving the wrath of God and an eternity in hell.

Leprosy is a nasty condition. It literally causes the flesh to decay and rot while the infected person is still alive. The rotting flesh becomes impossible to cover because it will seep through whatever garments are put over it. No matter how expensive or beautiful the clothing may be before it is worn by a leper, once it touches the leper it becomes "unclean" and spoiled. It is not that the garments were unclean on their own, but the "uncleanness" of the person has infected the garment by making contact with it. This is how the prophet Isaiah explains our acts as human beings, saying, "For all of us have become like one who is unclean, / And all our righteous deeds are like a filthy garment; / And all of us wither like a leaf, / And our iniquities, like the wind, take us away" (Isa 64:6). The Law is not primarily meant to expose certain deeds, but to expose the underlying *condition*—we are *sinners* and as a result *everything* we do is unclean before God. Our condition as sinners causes even what acts would *seem* to be righteous to be tainted with sin. As a result, they are actually viewed as sinful in the sight of God. For the person who is not saved by Christ, they can literally not do a single good thing no matter how long they live and no matter how hard they try. This

---

31. Gal 3:23–24; Rom 6:1–23; 7:7–25.

is the testimony of Scripture.³² The only good deeds that can be done are *in Christ*, empowered by the Holy Spirit, and by obedience to the will of God.³³

Because this truth is so hard to believe, and so contrary to modern schools of thought, it is good to memorize passages like these:

1. For those who are according to the flesh set their minds on the things of the flesh, but those who are according to the Spirit, the things of the Spirit. For the mind set on the flesh is death, but the mind set on the Spirit is life and peace, because the mind set on the flesh is hostile toward God; for it does not subject itself to the law of God, for it is not even able to do so, *and those who are in the flesh cannot please God.* (Rom 8:5–8, emphasis added)

2. And without faith it is impossible to please Him, for he who comes to God must believe that He is and that He is a rewarder of those who seek Him. (Heb 11:6)

Armed with such truths, we can administer the Law until our hearer(s) not only confess that they have "made some mistakes" but go even further and confess that they have lived in persistent, pervasive rebellion against the king of heaven and are worthy of God's just wrath and condemnation. The Law has done its work when the person stops trying to justify themselves and their actions and is held accountable to their creator.³⁴

It is easy to lose focus in a discussion of this type, or to wrongly conclude that such a use of the Law is condemning and mean-spirited. Perhaps wrongly applied this is true, but not when rightly used. Our purpose in applying the Law to the conscience of the sinner is to help them see that they are judged *already* by the living God as law-breakers and are rightly deserving of his wrath and condemnation.³⁵ Without the Law, people are often deceived into thinking that they are good in the sight of God. The Law allows them to see themselves as they truly are in God's sight. Once they see their true condition and their true need for salvation, they can appreciate the offer that is being made in the gospel of life and peace with God through Jesus Christ.

It is counterintuitive, but if you want to increase your love and devotion to God, you should dwell on how much he has forgiven you for. Jesus taught this truth in Luke 7:36–50. Those who are self-righteous do not appreciate their need for God's forgiveness and accordingly love God in proportion. I

---

32. Rom 3:12.

33. For a more in-depth discussion of this topic, see appendix A, "Judgment According to Deeds."

34. Rom 3:19.

35. John 3:18–19.

speak to people all the time on the street who profess to be some variation of a Christian, who still boast in their own works as the reason for their right standing before God. In these cases, they believe that Jesus did something for them—maybe saving them from their "mistakes"—while they did their part, too. Depending on the ratio they have in their mind, they may think it is appropriate to give back to God in proportion to his gift. If God did ten percent for them and they did the other ninety percent with "clean living," then it is reasonable to give God ten percent devotion. After all, he earned it.

A healthy dose of the Law can help people to see that they have transgressed multitudes of God's commandments and, in fact, Jesus does one hundred percent or we are hopelessly lost and will be carried away by our iniquities, transgressions, and sins. If, by the grace of God and using the tools he has provided, we can help people to see that they need Jesus for one hundred percent of their salvation (they need to be forgiven *much*), then they will appreciate the amazing grace of God who offers one hundred percent salvation through Jesus Christ. And if they understand their one hundred percent need for Jesus, they will find it reasonable that he demands one hundred percent of our life when we repent and trust in him.

Although it is often difficult for the ambassador for Christ, while evangelizing we must resist the urge to offer God's grace to someone who is still insisting on their own righteousness and who does not confess their need for salvation.[36] To offer grace to a person who is still justifying themselves (for whatever reason) and who has not had their eyes opened to the reality of their own sin, the righteousness of God, and the seriousness of the coming judgment, they will not appreciate the Savior, nor see the need to turn from their rebellion and trust in Jesus. If they refuse to admit they deserve hell as a result of their own sin, then they still believe they will be justified in God's sight by their own righteousness. By trying to give grace too soon to an unrepentant sinner, the ambassador for Christ is casting their pearls before swine and helping them to trample the blood of the Savior under their feet.[37] The opposite of the intended effect can happen, and often the rebel can become more entrenched in their rebellion thinking that God will simply overlook their rebellion and sin because of Jesus, even though they have not taken the necessary steps that God has commanded for receiving

---

36. This is more applicable in one-on-one conversations than it is when proclaiming the gospel to a group of people. When declaring the gospel to a group, the one proclaiming should be faithful to proclaim the whole message if possible. When you are sharing the gospel with an individual, you have more opportunity for specific application of these principles that are not possible when addressing a larger group.

37. Matt 7:6; Heb 10:28–31.

the work of Christ and applying the redemption he purchased to their own account through genuine repentance and faith.[38]

I meet people all the time who have a vague sense that Jesus died for their sin and who believe they will go to heaven when they die, but who demonstrate no evidence of being a new creature, and who still scoff at the idea of living for the will of God instead of pursuing their own desires.[39] In these cases, these unfortunate souls have believed a lie perpetrated against them by someone who claims to speak for Jesus, believing him to simply be a "get out of hell free" card. The Scriptures testify that the gift of everlasting life is a present tense possession—it is both received, and brings forth fruit, in the present.[40]

To presume that salvation is something that we will have in the future, but that we do not currently have, is to base our hope and faith on a non-existent biblical foundation (or on the words of men). Biblical Christianity is unique. It does not fit nicely into the Universalist notion that all religions are merely different paths leading to the top of the mountain where God presumably resides. Instead of a path that ends in heaven, Christianity claims that heaven came down to us in the person of Jesus Christ. The Christian path is not walked *to* God, but *with* God.

Sometimes people will persist in justifying their own actions and will sit in judgment of God, saying that his standards are too strict.[41] Such a statement merely exposes their rebellion further. By making such a statement they are demonstrating their belief that they sit in judgment of God and not the other way around.[42] As an ambassador, you should be willing to tell them so in as loving a way as possible that their rejection of his Law and authority is proof of their need to repent. In these cases it is also helpful to be armed with the principle that the Apostle Paul outlined in Romans 2:1–5. Essentially, Paul allows his readers/hearers to come out from under the Law of God for a moment and be submitted to their own law—without being able to escape condemnation by their own law and standards! Paul wrote, "for in that which you judge another, you condemn yourself; for you who judge practice the same things" (Rom 2:1b). In practice, applying this principle may look something like this:

Ambassador: "So, you think the standards of God are too high?"

---

38. Many modern gospel presentations call for faith without mentioning repentance, which is an anti-biblical gospel call.

39. Phil 3:18–21; Titus 1:16.

40. John 3:36; 10:10; 17:3; 1 John 3:15; 5:11–13, 20.

41. Job 35:1–2.

42. Isa 45:9–12; 64:8; Jer 18:2–10; Rom 9:18–22.

Person: "Yes. My god is much more gracious than that."

Ambassador: "Are you willing to grant that if there is a God, that his standard is higher than yours?"

Person: "Sure, I can agree with that . . . ."

Ambassador: "Okay, well let's assume for a second that God will not judge you by his standard but by your own. Do you like it when people talk about you behind your back?"

Person: "Of course not!"

Ambassador: "Do you ever talk about other people behind *their* backs?"

Person: "Well . . . ."

Ambassador: "By your own standard of judgment, this is wrong. And yet, you've violated your own standard. If God were to use your own standard—which you admit is lower than God's—you've admitted that you've fallen short even of that. How do you plan to escape the judgment of God if you would not even escape your own standard? Because of your failures to meet both God's and your own standard, can you see that you are storing up wrath for yourself on the Day of Judgment?"[43]

Jesus made it clear that we must repent or we will perish.[44] Jesus spoke the truth.[45] If we truly care for people, then we must be this bold when witnessing to the lost. If we are to speak the truth in love, we must be patient and careful to help these people who are made in the image of God to understand the severity of what they must repent *from* and the importance of doing so with haste. We are not guaranteed another breath and God will not be patient forever! In our reaching out to the lost, we who have been redeemed must also remember that *we are no better than they are*. We, too, have suffered from the same disease of sin.[46] We can rejoice that Jesus is able to make the leper clean.[47] In the same way, Jesus is able to wash us from all unrighteousness and present us before the throne of God holy, blameless, and beyond reproach.[48]

Those who point their fingers in the faces of sinners and view them with contempt do not understand their role as ambassadors. Jesus testified

43. Rom 2:5.
44. Luke 13:2–5.
45. John 18:37.
46. 1 Cor 6:11; Eph 2:1–10.
47. Matt 8:2–3.
48. Col 1:21–22.

concerning the wickedness of humanity,[49] but he did so with love and compassion. It is possible to speak the truth *without* love. When we do this, it only makes us a clanging cymbal or a noisy gong.[50] No one needs more noise in their lives. Yes, we need to be bold in relaying the commandment of the Lord to repent. On the other hand, we must do so in a spirit of genuine love and concern. We are pleading with them to turn and be reconciled to God through Christ.[51] Our love and compassion for the lost should drive our boldness, knowing that holding back the full message will result in a diluted proclamation that carries no power of God for salvation.

1. But God demonstrates His own love toward us, in that while we were yet sinners, Christ died for us. (Rom 5:8)

2. Behold then the kindness and severity of God; to those who fell, severity, but to you, God's kindness, if you continue in His kindness; otherwise you also will be cut off. (Rom 11:22)

3. Therefore, since it remains for some to enter it, and those who formerly had good news preached to them failed to enter because of disobedience, He again fixes a certain day, "Today," saying through David after so long a time just as has been said before, "Today if you hear his voice, do not harden your hearts." (Heb 4:6–7)

It is possible to deceive ourselves into thinking that proclaiming this entire message and that teaching the extent and severity of human sin is a "mean-spirited" thing to do. This is especially possible if we are easily swayed by popular opinion. We can take this line of reasoning down a dangerous path and end up believing that it is better to paint a "nicer" picture of who God is than what we see in the Bible. If we do so, we begin treating God as if we are ashamed of him and his nature. We demonstrate that we believe people will only come to God if we do not tell them exactly who he really is. When we do this, we treat God like some drunken uncle who may be a pretty decent guy if you can ignore his drinking problem. Sadly, treating God this way exposes a deficiency in *us*, not in God. Even worse, when we do this, we invite people to come to an idol—a mere caricature of the living God.

It is true that some people will be alarmed, surprised, shocked, and even disgusted when confronted with the character of the God of the Bible. This is especially true of many "churched" people who are not familiar with the Scriptures because they've never been exposed to the whole counsel of

---

49. John 7:7.
50. 1 Cor 13:1–7.
51. Isa 45:18–25; 2 Cor 5:20.

God, nor read the Bible for themselves. But God is not ashamed of who he is. He does not call us to be defenders of his reputation. God can handle himself. When we describe the *true* nature of the God who lives and reigns, what often happens is that people who are in rebellion against him—even some who may claim to be "spiritual" or who are regular church attenders—will begin to manifest their rebellion by objecting to these things and saying, "That's not my god!" They are right. Since they are right, it is loving for us to show them that they are worshipping an idol. Even if they call their idol by the name of Jesus.[52]

Along these same lines, when we try and emphasize certain qualities of God's character that we find to be more appealing, while down-playing other aspects of his character that may be harder to handle, we present a lopsided view of God that may sound good on paper but fails to account for the present reality of this fallen world. I once was witnessing to a young woman who proudly declared to me that she was a worshipper of Satan. She told me she had signed a covenant to him in her own blood, renouncing the God of the Bible, Jesus, and his angels. She declared herself to be the property of Satan. When I asked her what would lead her to do such a thing, her answer was pointed and shocking: "I did this because I grew up in church and all I ever heard was that God loves me. But my life sucks. God doesn't love me. He's a liar. But Satan does love me. He lets me do whatever I want."

I've met other Satanists who make similar claims and offer similar reasons for devoting themselves to the devil.[53] They have fully embraced their rebellion against the living God and seek a master (Satan) who validates their desire to gratify the various lusts and impulses of their flesh which they are enslaved to. The Satanists that I have met while sharing the gospel on the streets are consistent in that they choose Satan over God because they believe he loves them more than God does, evidenced by the fact that Satan lets them do as they please. He encourages them to embrace their fallen state. I have often told people that I believe I learned more about the character of God by becoming a father than I did going to seminary. This is

---

52. See chap. 6, "The Gospel of Jesus Christ."

53. This may not be true of all Satanists, but it is representative of the ones I have met while sharing the gospel. Assumptions can be deadly to communication, so it is often better to ask people *what* they believe and *why* they believe it instead of assuming you know the answers to these questions based on whatever labels we or they may apply. A good resource for how to effectively ask questions and try and lead people to see the faulty foundation of their own positions is Koukl, *Tactics*. Koukl's method assumes that you are already equipped to effectively and faithfully share the gospel with others—the strength of his method is in creating opportunities to share and navigating the conversation.

probably an exaggeration. However, the reality that God chooses to reveal himself as "Father" is both important and telling.

As a father, I know things that my children do not know. As a result, it is part of my parental duty to lovingly keep my children from doing foolish things that may harm them. For example, one of my children thinks it would be fun to eat candy for breakfast, lunch, and dinner. My wife and I do not provide such a diet for him, however. To most reasonable parents, they understand that such restriction is not because we hate our child. It's because we love him. Satan offers to be the "cool" parent who literally lets his children run wild—allowing them to do whatever feels right to them. This is a recipe for disaster. However, there is some fun to be had in the meantime.[54]

"God loves you" is not the gospel. It is true and is part of the gospel, but walking up to someone and saying, "Jesus loves you," is not evangelism. It is just misleading. There is a reason that none of the inspired Scriptures record anyone ever witnessing this way. Romans 5:8 records how God demonstrates (present tense) his love for us: while we were yet sinners, Christ died for us. When I was speaking with that young woman mentioned above, I asked her if she would give me thirty seconds to explain to her what God's love really is and why she is believing a lie when she thinks that Satan loves her because he lets her do "whatever she wants." She gave me the time, and she understood for the first time that she was choosing slavery over freedom and that God's love was not demonstrated in giving her whatever she wants (as if God served her), but in allowing her to breathe at that very moment even though she was using that breath to blaspheme his name. God's love sent his beloved son Jesus to take the curse upon himself so that her blood covenant with Satan could be canceled. The worst part of this entire encounter was that she spent her entire childhood in church *and never heard the genuine gospel of Jesus Christ.*

Once someone is humbled by the fact that they have sinned and deserve hell, then you should freely and lovingly present the grace of God and his mercy.[55] We would never want to withhold the word of life to anyone who is being drawn to the Father through Christ![56]

1. But He was pierced through for our transgressions, / He was crushed for our iniquities; / The chastening for our well-being fell upon Him, / And by His scourging we are healed. / All of us like sheep have gone

---

54. Job 20:4–11; Ps 73:3–20; John 8:44; Heb 11:25; 1 John 3:8–10.
55. Jas 4:6; 1 Pet 5:5.
56. John 6:44; 12:32.

astray, / Each of us has turned to his own way; / But the LORD has caused the iniquity of us all / To fall on Him. (Isa 53:5–6)

2. Seek the LORD while He may be found; / Call upon Him while He is near. / Let the wicked forsake his way / And the unrighteous man his thoughts; / And let him return to the LORD, / And He will have compassion on him, / And to our God, / For He will abundantly pardon. (Isa 55:6–7)

3. But as many as received Him, to them He gave the right to become children of God, even to those who believe in His name, who were born, not of blood nor of the will of the flesh nor of the will of man, but of God. (John 1:12–13)

4. For God so loved the world, that He gave His only begotten Son, that whoever believes in Him shall not perish, but have eternal life. (John 3:16)

5. He who believes in the Son has eternal life; but he who does not obey the Son will not see life, but the wrath of God abides on him. (John 3:36)

6. For by grace you have been saved through faith; and that not of yourselves, it is the gift of God; not as a result of works, so that no one may boast. For we are His workmanship, created in Christ Jesus for good works, which God prepared beforehand so that we would walk in them. (Eph 2:8–10)

7. But when the kindness of God our Savior and His love for mankind appeared, He saved us, not on the basis of deeds which we have done in righteousness, but according to His mercy, by the washing of regeneration and renewing by the Holy Spirit, whom He poured out upon us richly through Jesus Christ our Savior, so that being justified by His grace we would be made heirs according to the hope of eternal life. (Titus 3:4–7)

If we have faithfully done our job as ambassadors for Christ, and have proclaimed all of the elements of the gospel, and taught what these things mean (as necessary), then we are able to declare the implications of this gospel of Christ clearly to our hearer(s): Jesus is Lord and he declares that all people everywhere must repent and believe the gospel. If you do not repent, you will perish under his wrath. All who call on his name and seek refuge in him will be saved. If we are saved by his grace, then we no longer live for ourselves but for the will of God; and we ought to bring forth fruit in keeping with repentance. We no longer live for ourselves—we now live for the will and glory of our God.

We must always remember that our work is faithfulness in stewarding these truths and in delivering this message in love. We are *not* responsible for the results. We are *not* responsible for the response of the hearer(s). What happens in the individual that is born-again is truly miraculous—they are very literally brought to life from death.[57] We can't make this happen. Only God can work in this way.[58] When we forget this, our methodology begins to change in order to bring about the desired results; particularly results that we can see with our own eyes. We must strive to resist the urge to have our message rely on our method, our delivery, the cleverness of our speech, or our rhetorical skill, instead of the power of the Holy Spirit and the gospel message itself. Many well-meaning Christians become editors of the gospel because this message is hard to hear and often is hard to say. When we change the message we also empty the cross of its power.[59] If we believe that God is good, we can trust him. We can trust in his ways, leaning not on our own understanding.[60] We are called to walk by faith, not by sight.[61]

Often, God's ways are counterintuitive. God is not like us. He doesn't operate the way we operate. I have often had people object to this form of teaching simply because it seems that such use of the Law will immediately put people on the defensive and will cause unnecessary harm and conflict. It is much harder to make a biblical case that this is *not* God's intended method—but there is some weight to the reality that such a method seems . . . mean. To this, I can only reply that experience proves the opposite. I've never received this objection from people who actually come out and witness with me on a regular basis. In reality, the Law sheds light that is beneficial and helpful for understanding the implications of the gospel and make it immediately relevant to all—even if they reject it. Does this mean that everyone is excited to hear the gospel when you use the Law? By no means! By its very nature the gospel is foolish and offensive to non-believers. However, when the Law is rightly applied it helps the gospel to make sense—often for the very first time. Even when people don't accept it, they at least know what they are rejecting.

I also find that, often, well-meaning Christians believe the Law could never be used on someone who is already broken because of events in this

---

57. Eph 2:1–10.
58. 1 Cor 1:30—2:5; 3:5–7.
59. 1 Cor 1:17–21.
60. Prov 3:5.
61. 2 Cor 5:7.

fallen world. In many cases, this type of objection is raised by people who believe the gospel is *more* relevant to the broken and hurting than it is for the person who has everything going well. This line of thinking often believes that if a person is broken, they need love and grace, not Law. However, accepting the gospel requires repentance—so the Law is always necessary. People are not called to turn to God because of sadness, loneliness, poverty, sickness, or whatever else. People are called to turn to God for righteousness. My ministry partner and I once met with a woman I'll call Stephanie[62] who was in one of the most broken situations I've ever personally encountered in ministry: Stephanie's friend was dying of cancer, so she decided to show her love to her friend by sharing a meal with her every day.

Her sick friend, however, did not want to die alone. So she began poisoning Stephanie's food so that they could die together. Once Stephanie found out what was happening, it was too late. The poison had done enough damage in her body that she was now terminal. Her friend had betrayed her and taken advantage of the love and compassion Stephanie had shown to murder her slowly and painfully. As we listened to this story, it was impossible for our hearts not to break. Stephanie looked at us with tears in her eyes and declared that she did not understand how this could happen. She had done the right thing. She had tried to be good, kind, and loving. She testified of her belief that good things are supposed to happen to good people.

In my flesh, all I wanted to do was to comfort her and to tell her it would be okay. But that's a lie. It wasn't going to be okay. She was going to die. The only thing I could do was explain that although she may have done what is right in her own eyes, according to the Law of God she had fallen short of God's standard of righteousness. Stephanie admitted that she had violated God's commandments and lived her life for herself and by her own standard of goodness. At the end of our meeting, she expressed gratitude for us telling her the truth and explaining to her for the first time why it was that this world is so broken. Even though she thought she was "good," she now saw that God was being kind to her in allowing her to survive so long even though she had lived every moment in rebellion against him.

Although she did not give her life to Christ at that meeting, she had fully heard the gospel for the first time. The gospel brought forth fruit about a week later when she repented and trusted in Christ. Stephanie was broken by the world, but needed to be broken over her sin. As a result, Stephanie received forgiveness of sin and everlasting life through Jesus. My flesh wanted to lead me and my ministry partner astray. We wanted to comfort Stephanie in this life—a comfort that would only have been temporary. Because we

---

62. Not her real name.

trusted in God's ways, Stephanie will enjoy the blessing of fellowship with God for eternity. We were willing to be *offensive* because that is our call as preachers and teachers of God's glorious gospel. Praise God, that in this case, he was pleased to use our faithfulness to bring forth life from death, and to shine his light in the darkness.

8

Fruit Inspectors

And the one on whom seed was sown on the good soil, this is the man who hears the word and understands it; who indeed bears fruit and brings forth, some a hundredfold, some sixty, and some thirty. (Matt 13:23)

Our culture loves success stories. It is embedded in the American dream. *Anyone can be successful if they work hard enough.* Our entertainment industry thrives on the general public's fascination with success and the stock market provides a way for people to cash in on the success of other people through investing in their success.

This fascination with and love of success has infiltrated the professing church. The cultural idea of what it means to be successful has hi-jacked the biblical picture of success. As a culture, we are obsessed with what we can see, touch, and measure. Therefore, we begin judging the "fruit" of our ministry in these terms. We can measure things like attendance at our services, dollars donated, and the size of our buildings. We can measure things like "baptisms" and "decisions for Christ." We can measure these things because we can see these things.

But is this not, by definition, walking by sight? We are basing our ideas of "success" on what we can see and judging accordingly!

You may be thinking, "Well, of course we measure what we can see! How can we measure what we *can't* see?" That seems reasonable. However, consider two different examples from Acts: Peter's message in Acts 2:14–42 and Stephen's message in Acts 7:2-60. When Peter, filled with the Holy Spirit, stood up and preached the gospel, it says that the hearers were cut to the heart and asked, "What must we do to be saved?" As a result of Peter's faithful proclamation, three thousand souls were saved that day. Praise God!

On the other hand, Stephen likewise was filled with the Holy Spirit and preached the gospel. His hearers turned on him and murdered him in the street where he stood. Even more, after Stephen was ruthlessly killed by the blood-thirsty mob, a great persecution broke out against the church in the city Stephen preached in. This persecution caused many of the earliest followers of Jesus to flee from Jerusalem to the surrounding regions.[1] Praise God?

Based on sight, one of these proclamations was a wild success and the other was a horrifying failure. However, by faith we can see that both were exactly the result that God intended as a result of the faithfulness of his servants. To make sure his readers do not draw any wrong conclusions, Luke (the author of Acts) tells his readers in Acts 7:55 that right before Stephen was martyred, "he gazed intently into heaven and saw the glory of God, and Jesus standing at the right hand of God." What a scene! If your definition of success does not include the reigning king of the universe *standing up from his throne to receive you*, then you have got a faulty definition.

Even more than this, the persecution that broke out against the church was used by God to further his purposes. The people of God have a history of settling down instead of obeying God's commandment to spread over the earth. God has a history of intervening to make it happen anyway.[2] The risen Lord Jesus declared in Acts 1:8 that his people would be his witnesses in Jerusalem, Judea, and Samaria, and even to the ends of the earth. In Acts 2, we read that Jewish believers had gathered in Jerusalem for the feast of Pentecost from the ends of the earth, and Judea, and Samaria. When the three thousand believed on the day of Pentecost, they did not go home (that is, they did not take the message they believed back to Judea, and Samaria, or to the ends of the earth), but they stayed put in Jerusalem and submitted to the teaching of the Apostles. They were getting trained and equipped for living in light of the gospel truth.

When Jesus was pleased to receive his servant Stephen, he was also pleased to allow persecution to drive the church out of their comfort zone in Jerusalem and into fulfilling the task he had given them of being his witnesses; not only in Jerusalem, but also in Judea, and Samaria, and to the remotest parts of the earth. As these earliest believers were scattered, the

---

1. Acts 8:1.
2. E.g., Gen 9:1—11:9.

text tells us, "Therefore, those who had been scattered went about preaching the word" (Acts 8:4). These were mostly *regular* followers of Christ—not just apostles[3] or prophets or deacons or pastors or evangelists or elders—who were baptized into the faith, taught to obey everything that Jesus commanded, and who proclaimed the gospel as they went in obedience to him. Saul of Tarsus was present at the stoning of Stephen and was converted to the faith soon after (Acts 9). Now known as the Apostle Paul, he begins to bring the message of the gospel to the ends of the known earth at the time.

It would be a mistake of the worst sort to think that Stephen's message was a failure and that Peter's was a success simply because we incorrectly judged the "fruit"—three thousand "decisions for Christ" vs. a murdered preacher and great persecution for those claiming to follow Jesus. The real fruit is found in their individual faithfulness to their Lord. Three thousand laborers were added to the kingdom of God through the faithful preaching of Peter and were equipped by submitting themselves to the teaching of the Apostles.[4] Later, these saints were *mobilized* by the persecution that arose from the faithfulness of Stephen. Both men brought forth fruit for the kingdom of God, although the circumstances surrounding their ministries looked very different.

If we are going to judge fruit, we have to judge the right fruit. And Jesus told us how to do that in the parable quoted at the beginning of this chapter. We just have to read all of it:

> Hear then the parable of the sower. When anyone hears the word of the kingdom and does not understand it, the evil one comes and snatches away what has been sown in his heart. This is the one on whom seed was sown beside the road. The one on whom seed was sown on the rocky places, this is the man who hears the word and immediately receives it with joy; yet he has no firm root in himself, but is only temporary, and when affliction or persecution arises because of the word, immediately he falls away. And the one on whom seed was sown among the thorns, this is the man who hears the word, and the worry of the world and the deceitfulness of wealth choke the word, and it becomes unfruitful. And the one on whom seed was sown on the good soil, this is the man who hears the word and understands it; who indeed bears fruit and brings forth, some a hundredfold, some sixty, and some thirty. (Matt 13:18-23)

---

3. In fact, Acts 8:1 records that the Apostles remained in Jerusalem while everyone else was scattered.

4. Acts 2:42.

Not everyone who hears the gospel will respond with repentance and faith. They do not understand the implications of their rebellion and the seriousness of the consequences. They are the ones whom the seed is stolen from.[5]

However, there are three other categories in this parable that make some sort of response. There are those who immediately respond with joy, but fall away because of persecution. These "decisions for Christ" that immediately respond with joy and then fall away because of persecution do not bring forth fruit. They certainly should not be counted as "fruit" in and of themselves! *Profession* is not the fruit that we should be looking for. *Endurance* is.

You will notice that Stephen did not change his message when it became clear that his audience was hostile. He did not try and soften the impact of the gospel. He maintained his stance and further tried to direct them toward the majesty of Jesus, even while they began killing him! Sadly, many professing believers do not share their faith because they are afraid of making people think that they are crazy, stupid, or intolerant (or all three!). Fear of persecution chokes out the life that is in them, even though they get to live a longer life than Stephen did. Stephen brought forth fruit by enduring *despite* persecution. He remained faithful until the end.

Another category of "professing believer" in this parable has the life choked out, failing to bring forth fruit, because of the worries of this world and the deceitfulness of wealth. Uh-oh. That means there are some who will have their spiritual life choked out and will not produce any fruit *by chasing the very measurable things that so many use to define success*! My heart breaks over the countless ministries and churches that have completely sold out for a different gospel,[6] simply because it allows them to put more butts in seats, collect more dollars in their baskets, build bigger facilities, and record more superficial "decisions for Christ." You should mourn over this, too. In the same way, many professing believers have neglected to take their job as an ambassador for Christ seriously because doing so would jeopardize their retirement plans. It is true that being serious about following the Lord may cause you to lose friends, family, your job, and other material comforts. Following Jesus may cause you to lose your life prematurely at the hands of a bloodthirsty mob. He told us this would happen.[7] Did you think Jesus was lying?

---

5. See also 2 Cor 4:3–4.
6. Perhaps most prevalent in our culture is the gospel of "moralism."
7. Matt 19:21–30.

It is important to stress that the life is choked out by the *pursuit* of these things instead of the pursuit of God's glory. Simply having "success" (by the world's terms) does not mean that someone has sold out or embraced a watered-down gospel. Both Peter and Stephen were faithful and filled with the Holy Spirit. The measurable results (by sight) of their ministry were worlds apart. However, the fruit of both was the same because neither man was pursuing anything other than the advance of the kingdom of God through the faithful proclamation of the gospel of Jesus Christ. Both produced fruit that endured into eternity.

Neither was burned out by their fear of persecution or consequences from following Jesus. Neither was distracted by a pursuit of the world or deceived by the allure of wealth. Both followed their Lord and produced fruit for him, well beyond what could be seen and measured by the human eye. The fruit was found in their endurance and their faithfulness, not in the "results." The martyrdom of Stephen is an excellent example of how God works all things together after the counsel of his own will.[8] Jesus wanted his people to be his witnesses in Jerusalem, Judea, and Samaria, even to the ends of the earth—and Peter and Stephen both participated in advancing that purpose by their faithfulness to their king.

This is often how God works. He asks his people to trust him and do what seems silly. Want to escape the Egyptian army? Stretch out your staff over the Red Sea and walk through on dry land.[9] Want to conquer the fortified city of Jericho with no weapons? Walk around the walls a bunch of times. When you're done give a loud shout and blow your horns, and the walls will come crashing down.[10] *Sure.*

Want to save rebels against the king of the universe from their just sentence of an eternity in hell? Preach a crucified Messiah.[11] God became a man in order to redeem us from a curse he put on us as a result of our rebellion and sin against him?[12] *Okay.*

To those who are perishing, the message is foolishness. To those who are being saved, the same message is the power of God.[13]

The "fruit" is measured in not being distracted because of persecution, the worries of this world, or the deceitfulness of riches, from faithfulness in our calling as ambassadors for Christ. "Fruit" is actually living lives that

---

8. Eph 1:11.
9. Exod 14:13–31.
10. Josh 6:1–21.
11. 1 Cor 1:18–25.
12. 2 Cor 5:21; Gal 3:13–14; 4:4–5; 1 Tim 2:5; Titus 3:3–7.
13. 1 Cor 1:18.

are worthy of this calling in obedience to our God who saved us for this very purpose.[14] Sadly, many who profess to be believers in Jesus have either withered or had the life choked out of them by just these very things, because we are so worried that if we tell people about Jesus they will not like us anymore, or we will push them farther away from God. The first excuse is a cop-out and the second is just bad theology. Those who are in their trespasses and sins are *dead* and currently under the wrath of God.[15] You cannot make them be any worse off than they already are. Dead is *dead*. You can merely expose their rebellion with the hope that the kindness of God will lead them to repentance.[16] If the only thing that happens is that they become aware that their "god" is not the God revealed in the Scriptures, then they have gained a valuable piece of information. Only the living God is able to raise them to life. And he has chosen the foolishness of preaching to be his means for saving sinners.[17] Therefore, preaching the gospel to them cannot hurt them spiritually, it can only help them.

It is true that by telling them the truth in love that you might hurt their feelings or offend them. The gospel message is offensive because it declares that we are not good enough to go to heaven on our own, we could *never* be good enough no matter how hard we try, and we are deserving of wrath and indignation for our multitudes of sins against the living God. Considering the stakes it is worth the risk. Would you worry that you were going to hurt the feelings of someone you know who was about to drink poison by telling them that it's a bad idea? What about someone in a burning building or about to be hit by a car—do their feelings cause you to overlook the danger to their well-being? Why is this an acceptable excuse when speaking of people's eternal well-being? On the other hand, the potential offense of the message itself is *never* an excuse for being hostile or hateful in the way we present this message. We are commanded as ambassadors for Christ to not let anything in our own lives be a hindrance to the gospel.[18]

Furthermore, if we truly love people, then we ought to be willing to tell them the truth about their position under the wrath of God and how they can be rescued, even if doing so causes them to hate us. That may seem strange, but many parents are willing to be "hated" by their children by keeping them from doing things that will be harmful to them. How many parents have heard their teenagers scream, "I hate you! You're ruining my

---

14. Col 1:9–12; Eph 2:10; 4:1; 2 Cor 5:11–15; 1 Pet 2:9–10.
15. John 3:36; Rom 1:18–19; Eph 2:1–2. See also Washer, *Gospel's Power*, 129–45.
16. Rom 2:4.
17. 1 Cor 1:21–24.
18. E.g., 2 Cor 6:1–10.

life!" at them, simply because they forbade them from attending a party at which the parents are out of town and there is surely going to be deviant behavior running unchecked? Does the parent "hate" their child through such a prohibition? Surely not! Instead, they love their child enough to be hated for the well-being of the one whom they genuinely love.[19] In the same way, if the Bible is true, then those whom I love that are not *in Christ* are in terrible danger. If I *actually* love them, I am compelled to tell them the remedy to their dreadful state regardless of what they may say or think of me as a result. Love compels me to be scorned if necessary so that they may hear the truth and possibly be saved.[20] The alternative is that they may never hear the message of salvation, and we may simply *use* them as a relationship that brings us joy and happiness in this world with no real care or concern about their eternal well-being. This may sound harsh, but our selfishness must be exposed!

My grandmother once looked me in the eye and asked me, "Joey, do we really have to talk about this every time we are together?" Although it made her uncomfortable, the answer was, "Yes." I knew that she was not trusting in Christ but in her own goodness and her impeccable attendance record in the Presbyterian Church. She told me in no uncertain terms that if anyone ought to go to heaven, she ought to. If human standards were the real measuring stick, she was probably right. I loved my grandmother dearly, and as a result, I could not in good conscience allow her to head into eternity without being confronted with the reality that, while she may be "good" by humans standards, the reality is that *all have sinned and fall short of the glory of God*,[21] which includes her.

The "human standard" is not the standard that matters. We will be judged by the divine standard, which is moral perfection.[22] While my grandmother never fully trusted in Christ (to the best of my knowledge), I can rest assured that she was given plenty of opportunities. I do not need to lose sleep wondering if I could have done more. I could not have. Even though she would have rather talked about her great-grandkids than the things of God, my love for her would not allow me to let her enter into eternity unprepared, unwarned, and unprayed for. There was still plenty of time to talk about the great-grandkids, too.

---

19. E.g., Prov 13:24.

20. George Whitefield wrote, "I always endeavour to speak with the meekness and gentleness of Christ; but if people will account me their enemy, because, out of love, I tell them the truth, I cannot help that" (Whitefield, *Journals*, 171).

21. Rom 3:23.

22. Matt 5:48; Luke 17:7–10; Acts 17:31.

Others have mistakenly changed the grace of God into something that it is not. In doing so, they have provided a way for themselves to actively disobey God while never feeling "convicted" about it. This trick of theological reasoning has redefined God's grace as a "permissive" thing—something that allows them to continue living worldly lives in pursuit of pleasures and/or riches, while believing that God will simply forgive them. Some false gospels even make the kingdom of God all about receiving pleasures and riches in this life. While these appeal to our flesh and often make use of biblical passages, they are false gospels nonetheless.[23]

You have probably heard the cliché, "You can't out sin the grace of God!" It is true that God's grace covers our sins and that no sin is too big to disqualify someone from being able to find salvation in Christ.[24] Yet, often this idea is abused and the entire theology of grace becomes twisted as a result. The grace of God is not primarily a *permissive*-grace, but a *redemptive* and *transformative*-grace. It is a powerful, amazing grace that turns dead sinners into living saints. It is the power of God that raised Jesus to life and works in the heart and flesh of every child of God in conforming them into the image of Jesus until Christ is fully formed in them. God's grace is, in the truest sense of the word, *awesome*.

I once attended a funeral at which the pastor who was officiating continued to stress in no uncertain terms how miserable the deceased person always made everyone. Sadly, those in attendance all chuckled and agreed! Included in this list of things that the pastor stated about the person he was eulogizing was basically what a loud-mouthed, opinionated jerk this particular person was, and how they never left you guessing on what they thought about you, and you always knew when they were around, and how everyone was usually happy that they had left the room. This laundry list of annoyances and character flaws was met with more laughs from those in attendance. At the end of the pastor's talk, during which I was very uncomfortable the entire time, he closed with a solemn declaration, "At least we can be sure that they are now in heaven, with God." Why could we be sure? According to this pastor, we could be sure because they were baptized as a baby, and they sat in church most Sundays (when they did not have

---

23. The devil quoted Scripture when tempting Jesus in the wilderness (Matt 4:1–11). Do not be deceived into thinking that citing scriptural passages is the same thing as adequately handling the word of God and teaching the intended meaning of the passage.

24. For a great sermon that demonstrates boldness, the proper use of Law and grace, and both the stern warnings of refusal to repent and the gracious offer to all no matter how grave of a sinner they may be preached by Charles Wesley, see Newport, *Sermons*, 238–58.

something better to do). For this pastor—and most of the congregation—"grace" was permissive and it allowed someone that virtually everyone present agreed was a real drain to have around, to enter glory without any evidence of "grace" in the life that they lived.

Is this amazing grace? How can it be that this "grace" was so ineffective in changing this particular person progressively more and more into the image and likeness of Christ? How can it be that this person, if they were filled with the Holy Spirit, was so marked by the "deeds of the flesh" and not the "fruit of the Spirit"?[25] How can this be reconciled with the scriptural teaching that eternal life begins, not after death, but at the moment of conversion and is a present tense possession?[26]

Believing that grace is merely permissive, and failing to understand that genuine grace is primarily transformative, is a form of easy-believism, which was taught against by the Apostle Paul in Romans 6:1–23. This form of easy-believism is extremely dangerous. Even worse, it is extremely prevalent throughout the personal theology held by many professing Christians. Listen carefully to the words of Jesus:

> "Be dressed in readiness, and keep your lamps lit. Be like men who are waiting for their master when he returns from the wedding feast, so that they may immediately open the door to him when he comes and knocks. Blessed are those slaves whom the master will find on the alert when he comes; truly I say to you, that he will gird himself to serve, and have them recline at the table, and will come up and wait on them. Whether he comes in the second watch, or even in the third, and finds them so, blessed are those slaves. But be sure of this, that if the head of the house had known at what hour the thief was coming, he would not have allowed his house to be broken into. You too, be ready; for the Son of Man is coming at an hour that you do not expect." *Peter said, "Lord, are You addressing this parable to us, or to everyone else as well?"* And the Lord said, "Who then is the faithful and sensible steward, whom his master will put in charge of his servants, to give them their rations at the proper time? Blessed is that slave whom his master finds so doing when he comes. Truly I say to you that he will put him in charge of all his possessions. But if that slave says in his heart, 'My master will be a long time in coming,' and begins to beat the slaves, both men and women, and to eat and drink and get drunk; *the master of that slave will*

---

25. Gal 5:16–24.

26. Pay careful attention to the verb tenses: John 3:36; 17:3; 1 Cor 15:2; Eph 2:5–6; 1 John 5:11–13.

> *come on a day when he does not expect him and at an hour he does not know, and will cut him in pieces, and assign him a place with the unbelievers*. And that slave who knew his master's will and did not get ready or act in accord with his will, will receive many lashes, but the one who did not know it, and committed deeds worthy of a flogging, will receive but few. From everyone who has been given much, much will be required; and to whom they entrusted much, of him they will ask all the more. I have come to cast fire upon the earth; and how I wish it were already kindled!" (Luke 12:35–49, emphasis added)

Peter's question should reinforce the reality that Jesus' answer is for his followers. We are the ones to whom much has been entrusted! For those who do not live like Jesus is serious about his commandment for his people to make disciples, and who act like he will delay in his return, the parable Jesus tells uses language saying that the Master will cast that wicked servant out and "*assign him a place with the unbelievers.*" Yikes!

There is a huge misunderstanding in the modern professing church about what biblical repentance really is.[27] This misunderstanding is knit closely with the heresy of moralism being preached instead of the genuine gospel. This false idea of repentance is that there are certain deeds that are inherently bad (like getting drunk, cheating on your spouse, and beating your children) and certain deeds that are inherently good (like being kind to your neighbor, giving to charity, reading your Bible, and going to church). As a result of this moralistic worldview, repentance becomes exchanging certain "naughty" behaviors with other "moral" behaviors (often ignoring what we consider to be "neutral" deeds—things like watching television, eating dessert, and going on vacation). But repentance is not turning from evil deeds to *less* evil deeds.

Listen to how the Apostle Paul described the repentance he heard about in the Thessalonian believers: "For they themselves report about us what kind of a reception we had with you, and how you turned to God from idols to serve a living and true God, and to wait for His Son from heaven, whom He raised from the dead, that is Jesus, who rescues us from the wrath to come."[28] They didn't turn from *deeds* to *deeds*, but from *serving idols* to *serving the living God*. Do you see the difference? Surely, genuine repentance will result in a genuine change of deeds[29]—but the deeds that are turned *to* will be acceptable in the sight of God and worked out in obedience to his

---

27. See chaps. 3 and 5.
28. 1 Thess 1:9–10.
29. E.g., Jonah 3:10; Rev 2:5.

will. They will not merely be more acceptable to the people who sit beside us in the pews or live in our neighborhoods.

It may seem subtle, or like nit-picking, but a rebel is still a rebel even if they are polite. If God desires for you to walk across the street and tell your neighbor the gospel, do you realize that you are in rebellion and sin if you stay in your house and read your Bible for two hours? Likewise, if God is desiring for you to show the love of Christ to a homeless person by spending ten dollars to buy them lunch and declare to them the excellencies of the God who has saved you and offered Jesus as an atoning sacrifice for the sins of all who will believe, but you instead donate ten million dollars to your church to build a new facility, that you are still rebelling against the will of your God and king? If you focus on the positive aspect of God's command—that is, the thing he is actually calling you to do—and actually walk in his will, then you will avoid the negative aspect of his command(s) by *not* doing anything else. There are certain deeds that God has prepared in advance for each of his children to do. God intends for us to do them.[30] As we walk with his Spirit, following his lead in fulfilling his will while here on earth, there is no law against our obedience to him![31] We do not need to focus on ourselves. We need to focus on our king and Savior. We need to walk with his Spirit.[32]

Remember, Christianity ≠ Moralism. As a result, biblical repentance is not trading in our "naughty" deeds for more culturally acceptable ones. It is trading in our old life for a new life—a life where we live to glorify our God and king through obeying his commandments and proclaiming his goodness to the ends of the earth. In contrast to the inherent wickedness of humanity, God's goodness is both shocking and terrifying.[33] If anyone is in Christ, they are a new creature—the old is gone, the new has come![34] Of course this will result in a change of deeds, because those who are in Christ are no longer living for themselves! However, the crucial point of turning from dead works (not to other, different, and more acceptable dead works) to the living God cannot be overstated.[35] If this were not true, then how could we account for the "conversion" of Saul of Tarsus? How do we account for Jesus' call for the holiest men of his time, the Pharisees, to repent and turn to him? Those judging the external righteousness of the deeds of

---

30. Eph 2:10.
31. Gal 5:13-25.
32. Col 3:1-4; Rom 8:1-17.
33. See Washer, *Gospel's Power*, 81-93.
34. 2 Cor 5:17.
35. Heb 6:1.

these religious men would have come to the conclusion that they were "better" than anyone I know (myself certainly included)! Yet, they were serving idols. Their moral behavior was still sinful in the sight of the living God because it was lived in rebellion against him and his will. This truth is foundational.[36] Without it, we may find ourselves building upon a foundation of sand and practicing something that looks "Christian" from the outside, but is something else entirely. When building on the wrong foundation, we have no choice but to begin judging the fruit of our ministries by the measurable qualities that are also used to measure success in the secular world.

Do you realize that there are multitudes of "missions" agencies in our professing Christian world that send out missionaries who do *not* preach the gospel? It's true. These missions agencies can boast of their numbers of missionaries in the field and dollars raised, all the while their missionaries are *not* preaching Christ and him crucified. Often the reason for this is because to preach Christ may get these "missionaries" killed.

Do you think Stephen wishes he worked for one of these agencies?

I am not trying to be insensitive. Some may object to this, citing scriptural truths like what we read in James 1:27 and 2:15–16. Yet, such passages do not undermine or contradict the need for evangelizing the world for the glory of God. While fulfilling this task of making disciples of all nations, should Christians ignore the needs of orphans and widows? Should they see people hungry and fail to give them something to eat, or thirsty and not give them something to drink? The Bible consistently calls followers of Jesus to share the message of the gospel and to unite our proclamation with loving, benevolent, and just actions. One does not eliminate the other. These things are designed to go together. If it is important to give someone water when they are thirsty, is it somehow justifiable to withhold from them the living water when they are also in need of salvation?[37] May it never be![38] Somehow, we have forgotten that humanity's greatest need is to be reconciled to the living God and that this need applies to all people, in all places, at all times. Everyone needs a Savior. Not everyone is thirsty. When we encounter someone who is both in need of a Savior *and* thirsty, then by all means we should address *both* of their needs for the glory of God. We cannot use meeting their physical need as an excuse to neglect their more pressing spiritual need, however. At least, we *shouldn't*.

I will admit, if it were up to me, I would like to be able to live a long life and see my kids and grandkids grow up. If it were up to me, I would rather

---

36. Ibid.
37. John 4:13–14.
38. See also appendix A, "Judgment According to Deeds."

not die at the hands of a bloodthirsty mob, but in the comfort of my own bed, preferably while I sleep. Yet, all genuine followers of Christ must be committed to following Jesus *whatever that looks like*. Otherwise, we are not worthy of him and cannot be his disciples.[39] This is what Jesus taught when he foretold to Peter the death that he was going to die for following him in John 21:18–19. Jesus followed up his description of Peter's unpleasant fate by saying plainly, *Follow Me!*[40] Peter responded to this call the same way we often do: he turned around and said, "Well, what about him?" Jesus' answer to Peter is the same as it is to us: "What I want for this other follower of mine has no bearing on what I want for you. Don't worry about everyone else—you, follow me!"[41]

If your Lord and Savior wants you to go and die in a foreign land for him, then you should do that. If Jesus wants you to die in your hometown for him, then you should do that. He may ordain a long life of service for you like the Apostle John or a short ministry term like Stephen. Following Jesus and walking with the Holy Spirit should be your primary focus. Our Lord himself said:

> Therefore do not fear them, for there is nothing concealed that will not be revealed, or hidden that will not be known. What I tell you in the darkness, speak in the light; and what you hear whispered in your ear, proclaim upon the housetops. Do not fear those who kill the body but are unable to kill the soul; but rather fear Him who is able to destroy both soul and body in hell. (Matt 10:26–28)

Jesus told other parables warning about the seriousness of failing to properly steward what was entrusted to his servants.[42] What possible justification could we have for believing that this teaching does not apply to our most valuable possession of truth that we are stewarding for him: the gospel?

Do you think Stephen would have traded in the honor bestowed upon him by the king of the universe, who welcomed him to heaven by standing from his throne, for a longer life because he hid the gospel message in a handkerchief or buried it in the backyard because his intended audience was hostile and "closed" to the message? I doubt it. Talk about walking by sight, not by faith!

---

39. Matt 10:38–39; Luke 14:27.
40. John 21:19.
41. I am paraphrasing John 21:20–23.
42. Matt 25:14–30; Luke 19:12–27.

What about you? Are you living for your God and king, and walking in the good works that he has prepared in advance for *you* to do?[43] Are you equipped as his ambassador? Are you living a life worthy of your calling by submitting yourself to his leading and in the power of his amazing, transformative grace?[44]

Get equipped. Obey your king. Glorify your God.

---

43. Eph 2:10.
44. Eph 2:8–10; 3:14—4:6; Col 1:9–12; Phil 1:27–30.

9

Freedom in Christ

It was for freedom that Christ set us free; therefore keep standing firm and do not be subject again to a yoke of slavery. (Gal 5:1)

Many people who profess to follow Jesus Christ use the phrase "freedom in Christ" to explain how they can do whatever they want because God's grace will bring them to heaven no matter how they live their lives on earth.[1] However, Paul taught in 1 Corinthians and Romans that Christian freedom should be used to live in all things (even trivial matters such as what we eat and drink) in a way that is glorifying to God and brings others closer to him.[2] The call to live "free in Christ" is not a call to anarchy—it is a call to order. Christian freedom means living, not however *we* please, but however *God* pleases. We are free to lay down our rights and our privileges for the benefit of others.[3] We are free to *not* exercise our rights and privileges for

---

1. It has come to my attention that some Christians have never heard this before. I suppose it depends on what circles you run in. The abuse and proper use of Christian liberty was addressed by the Apostle Paul in 1 Cor 5–11, so even if you've never heard these types of claims by professing Christians, these themes have been around for a long time. Charles Wesley also encountered this strain of false teaching, writing "Honest Bell and some others spoke out, and insisted upon their antichristian liberty" (Kimbrough and Newport, *Manuscript Journal*, 1:268).

2. Rom 14:1–23; 1 Cor 9:1–23.

3. 1 Cor 9:12.

our own benefit. We are free to pursue the glory of God instead of the various lusts and impulses of our flesh.

Paul begins 1 Corinthians 11 by saying, "Be imitators of me, just as I also am of Christ" (11:1). Paul is making a transition statement, and linking to what came before it in chapter 10. His command and instruction to the believers in Corinth is to follow his example (as he exemplifies Christ) and not to make the same mistake that Israel made.[4] Paul expressed how he used his own "freedom in Christ"—not to do as he (Paul) pleases but to do as the Lord pleases! Paul is free to do all things; yet he uses his freedom, not to gratify his own desires and ambitions, but to glorify God in all things. In fact, he says just this to end chapter 10: "Whether, then, you eat or drink or whatever you do, do all to the glory of God. Give no offense either to Jews or to Greeks or to the church of God; just as I also please all men in all things, not seeking my own profit but the profit of the many, so that they may be saved."

When we were separated from God we lived how we desired. We were in rebellion against God, his kingdom, and his will. Now that we are Christians, we are free to please God in everything we do. That means using our freedom to *not* do things that may be okay for us to do (since we are not saved by our works, but by the grace of God through faith in Jesus) but that may hinder someone else from coming to a saving knowledge of Jesus. This freedom in Christ is not an end in and of itself. It is a means to the end of advancing the kingdom of God and the salvation of others.

In 1 Corinthians 11, Paul is expressing the reality that Christians are *not* being called to live free from God's design for life and authority (whether in the church, the home, or the world). Christians *are* being called to live free *within the confines of God's design*, no longer as slaves to the world's system, our flesh, or the devil. God's design is in keeping with his mission to redeem a people for himself through the redemptive work of Jesus Christ.

Notice in 1 Corinthians 11:2 that Paul directs our attention to the traditions that have been handed down. For many Christians (Protestants especially), traditions are viewed negatively. Here, Paul is listing this attention to traditions as a good thing. He is saying that the Lord has given his people certain practices and traditions that are valuable, which should be held firmly, and practiced in the church. While we may be free of other cultural traditions and norms, the traditions of the Lord which have been handed down from him should not be discarded in the name of freedom.

---

4. The idea that believers should be imitators of Paul and his ways in Christ was so important to Paul's ministry that he actually taught this *everywhere* in *every* church; see 1 Cor 4:16–17.

There is a negative sense of this freedom that pertains to abstaining from certain things we *can* do—for the benefit of others.[5] On the flip side, there is a positive sense of this freedom in that we are free to do what the Lord pleases, and not what the world, our flesh, or the devil desires and dictates.[6] This freedom is real and not imagined. It presents those who have been born-again by the Spirit of the living God with a genuine choice of whether to submit the members of our body to serve our selves *or* to serve the God who has saved us.[7]

This claim strikes at the heart of a theological paradox that has been the source of much debate and, unfortunately, division throughout the history of the church: divine sovereignty and human responsibility. Due to the sheer volume of ink that has been spilled on this topic, I will not delve fully into an attempt to reproduce those efforts here. Instead, I will merely affirm the same position that Charles Spurgeon stated so eloquently, that we need not reconcile that which are friends.[8] The Bible affirms both the doctrine of divine sovereignty and also that of human responsibility. Therefore, this chapter will assume both doctrines to be true as revealed in the Scriptures.[9]

---

5. This is the entire point of Paul's answer to the Corinthians regarding their question about eating meat sacrificed to idols in 1 Cor 8.

6. For a good treatment of the three enemies the Christian faces (the world, the flesh, and the devil), see Payne, *Spiritual Warfare*.

7. Rom 6:1–23; Gal 5:1–26.

8. Cited in Packer, *Evangelism and Sovereignty*, 35–36.

9. For those interested in a more thorough case being made for this affirmation, see Carson, *Spiritual Reformation*, 146–66, and Packer, *Evangelism and the Sovereignty of God*. The value of Packer's book is in examining the Scriptures to demonstrate the inconsistency in the position that holding a high view of the sovereignty of God would hamper or negate the personal responsibility that Christians have in obeying God through personal evangelism. However, it should be noted that Packer's strength of exegesis does not apply to his opinions on methodological matters pertaining to evangelism. Authors are free to share their opinions, but Packer strays from backing up his methodological arguments (particularly in regards to evangelizing those whom you do not have a relationship with or the appropriateness of waiting long periods of time before sharing the gospel with those you are in relationship with) with anything other than personal opinion and the opinions of others—a shift that should not be missed. Doing so is committing an error of sound reasoning and changes the locus of authority from Scripture to Dr. Packer himself. I agree whole-heartedly that a high view of sovereignty is taught in the Scriptures and should be held by Christians. I agree that the Scriptures do not allow loop-holes for Christians to disobey God's calling and avoid personal evangelism on theological grounds. I could not disagree more with some of the methodological assertions that are made in this otherwise excellent book, because they are directly counter to biblical examples—like Peter in Acts 2 and Paul's entire ministry—which included much (granted, not *exclusively*) straight-forward, "imposing" evangelization of those with whom no relationship was previously had nor maintained afterward. Opinions must be recognized as what they are: opinions. We

Some theologians make these doctrines enemies by assuming that they are in opposition to each other, but they are not.

Instead of delving into a deep theological treatise and attempting to make sense of how these doctrines are in harmony with each other, let us consider the big picture of what we have covered so far and examine some biblical examples of how these themes interact within the pages of the Bible. You can watch a car drive down the road without fully understanding the physics of an internal combustion engine. In the same way, God shows us how these theological themes interact in history, even if he does not seem all that interested in revealing *exactly* how this paradox fits together in a systematic theological treatise. If, for some reason, you are incapable of understanding the internal workings of a car, it does not follow that the car itself will stop working. In the same way, while it is certainly true that we may not be able to understand everything there is to know about God (certainly, if we could, he would be a lot less impressive than he actually is[10]), he has revealed certain truths to us and he intends for us to rightly understand them.[11] With this being the case, it may be beyond our human ability to perfectly understand the full harmonization of divine sovereignty (and the associated doctrines of divine omniscience and predestination) with the doctrine of human responsibility and freedom—just like the doctrine of the Trinity can be rightly understood and communicated without being fully comprehended. We can rightly view some examples that God has revealed which demonstrate how these two strands of theology actually combine together in our world.[12]

Before pressing forward, let's review: God sovereignly created the universe through his own power and for his own glory.[13] His creation rebelled against him and, as a result of this rebellion, God cursed what he had made.[14] Despite the curse, God made a promise that he would redeem a people for himself out from under the curse through the seed of the wom-

---

should be much more interested in biblical counsel than the opinions of men—even godly men like my brother in Christ, Dr. Packer. Likewise, *my* opinions should mean nothing to you. If I could be shown by the Scriptures, I would happily agree with the methodological advice of Dr. Packer and others who teach less "confrontational" forms of evangelism than I read about in every book of the New Testament. Unfortunately for my own comfort, God has a method that he prefers; we ought to submit ourselves to his revealed strategy and methods.

10. D. A. Carson aptly states, "Sometimes it is more important to worship such a God than to understand him" (Carson, *Spiritual Reformation*, 160).

11. E.g., Deut 29:29.

12. For seven more examples, see Carson, *Spiritual Reformation*, 148–56.

13. E.g., Gen 1:1; Col 1:15–20.

14. Gen 3:1–24.

an.[15] In order to fulfill this promise, God chose Abram and made of him a great nation—the nation of Israel.[16] From the nation of Israel, through the line of David, God sent his son, our Savior: Jesus of Nazareth, who was God in the flesh.[17] Until the coming of the John the Baptist—the forerunner of the Messiah, Jesus—all the Law and prophets testified of the fulfillment of God's act of redemption through God's Christ.[18] After the resurrection and exaltation of the Christ, God revealed the mystery that was hidden from the previous ages and generations, which was that God was reconciling to himself both Jew and Gentile in the person of Jesus Christ; tearing down the separation and making for himself one people from every tribe, tongue, and nation—a body of people called the church.[19] God will continue this work through his people until the gospel has been proclaimed to the ends of the earth, and every tribe, tongue, and nation is represented in his work of redemption.[20] Then, the end will come, and the Christ will return. Every eye will see him and he will gather to himself the people who are called by his name. Jesus will crush all of his adversaries under his feet.[21] Those that are redeemed will dwell with him forever—he will be our God and we will be his people. Those that perish will endure an eternity in anguish—cast out from the kingdom of God and perishing under his righteous wrath and indignation as a testimony—both to his righteousness and also his mercy toward all who received pardon for their sin through the blood of Christ.[22]

All of this has either happened already, or it will happen in the future. God is sovereign and no one can thwart his plans. He will be sure to bring about the end result in which every knee will bow to Christ. Every tongue will confess that Jesus is Lord to the glory of God the Father. That is his mission.[23]

Perhaps the most astonishing part of our freedom in Christ is that it is possible to use it to ignore what God has revealed. This is not usually expressed by our words. It is more commonly demonstrated by our actions. Some continue to live as if this present life and world is the one that matters

---

15. Gen 3:15; 12:1–3; Gal 3:1—4:7.

16. Josh 24:1–13; Deut 7:6–11.

17. Ps 89:19–29; Matt 1:1–25; John 1:1–18. See also, e.g., the parallel between Jesus' self-identification with the divine name "I AM" from Exod 3:14 and the reaction of those who heard these claims in John 8:58–59 and 18:4–6.

18. Matt 11:13.

19. Luke 24:44–47; Eph 2:11—4:16; Col 1:25–27.

20. Ps 86:9–10; Matt 24:14; Rev 5:9–10.

21. Pss 2; 110; Zech 14:1–21; Mal 4:1–6; 1 Cor 15:23–28.

22. Rev 14:9–12; 19:1—22:21.

23. See chap. 2, "God's Mission."

the most. Some professing followers of Christ reason that since we get to go to heaven when we die, we ought to try and make this life as much like heaven now as we can—so we pursue the things that bring us pleasure and comfort. But is this what the Scriptures urge us to do?[24] Does Jesus call his followers to live for their own will and comfort, pursuing the gratification of the various lusts of their flesh?[25] Are we not called to live for the glory of our great God and king who loved us and sent his Son to redeem us from the curse?[26] Unlike Hollywood descriptions of heaven as a place of fulfillment of our greatest physical desires without end, the Bible describes the reality of heaven as a place where God and man have restored fellowship. Heaven is where God and humans dwell together in harmony.[27] Therefore, for a Christian to try and genuinely produce heaven on earth would be to live in fellowship with God, seeking his face and presence, and not the gratification of our various lusts and impulses.

It is in this sense that we are reminded in the New Testament to live lives that are worthy of our calling as followers of Christ and to spend our time here on earth as "aliens and strangers," abstaining from the fleshly lusts we were once enslaved to, which wage war against our souls.[28] The freedom that Christ purchased for his people was a freedom from living for anything else other than him and his glory! We get to have fellowship with the living God *now*, in this life, and we get to participate *with him* in his mission. This is truly amazing. No call is greater. Nothing could be more serious.

It is humbling to realize that God does not actually need us for anything. Throughout the history of God's people we see that God will fulfill his promises and plan regardless of whether or not his people choose to participate. When God said that he would bring his people out of Egypt and into the Promised Land, it did not matter that the first generation rejected the land and wanted to return to Egypt. Since God very literally has all the time in the world, he merely killed off that sinful generation and brought in the next generation to fulfill his promise.[29]

Problem solved.

Divine sovereignty and human responsibility affirmed.

Furthermore, Moses warned the generation that *did* survive that if they likewise persisted in rebellion against God's command, then God

---

24. Cf. Paul's description of Demas in 2 Tim 4:10.
25. Matt 16:23–26; Mark 8:33–38; Luke 9:23–26.
26. 2 Cor 5:14–15.
27. E.g., Exod 6:7; Jer 7:23; 11:4; 30:22; Ezek 36:28; Rev 7:15–17; 21:3–7.
28. Eph 4:1; Phil 1:27; Col 1:10; 1 Pet 2:11.
29. Num 13:1—14:38; 26:1–65.

would simply abandon them in the wilderness, kill them off, and raise up a *new* generation to take *their* place.[30]

Both the Apostle Paul and the author of Hebrews make use of examples in the history of God's dealing with the nation of Israel to be an example and a warning to New Testament followers of Christ to not fail to take hold of the promises of God through disobedience like they did.[31] God will achieve his desired end. God is sovereign. Every human being who has ever existed will glorify him in some way; either through perishing under his wrath, or through serving as an example of his great mercy through Christ. For those who have tasted of his grace, we ought not toy with his grace and treat it with contempt, thinking that the freedom he has purchased should be used for us to pursue our own lusts, kingdom, or whatever else, and ignoring his call to participate with him in his mission of making his glory known to the ends of the earth.[32] This is a great responsibility. Failing to take this responsibility seriously is nothing less than idolatry and committing treason against the kingdom of heaven.

Are we so confident in our theological constructs, creeds, and denominational mantras, that we are willing to test the word of God? Are we bold enough to declare to God that we need not heed these apostolic warnings and admonitions because we are "under grace"? In many ways, this so-called "grace" resembles wishful thinking more than the biblical reality.

The kingdom of Judah was slow to believe that Jerusalem and the temple could ever be destroyed, despite the preaching of repentance through God's prophets. When the kingdom was divided after Solomon, the northern kingdom of Israel quickly went apostate and never turned back. They were judged for their apostasy through the nation of Assyria and destroyed in 722 BC. The southern kingdom of Judah marched on, perhaps thinking they were immune from the judgment of God,[33] even though they too were wandering away from keeping God's covenant. They had convinced themselves that nothing could happen to them because of the temple. It is easy to conclude that since God had caused his name to dwell in the temple, he would not allow anything bad to happen to Jerusalem or his temple because such events would diminish his own name and glory.[34]

Despite sounding good, this theology was wrong. The prophet Ezekiel saw a vision of the glory of the Lord departing from the temple, clearing the

---

30. Num 32:6–15.
31. Rom 11:17–24; 1 Cor 10:1–14; Heb 4:1–11.
32. Heb 2:1–4; 6:1–8.
33. E.g., Lam 4:12.
34. E.g., Mic 3:11–12.

way for judgment to come. Ezekiel was already in exile when receiving this vision (Ezek 10), but this vision further explained how God's temple could have been destroyed and how the God of Israel was "unable to deliver" them from the hands of the Babylonians. When the northern kingdom of Israel fell to the hands of the Assyrians previously, Sennacherib was able to conquer Israel and besiege Jerusalem—but the Lord delivered the southern kingdom from the hands of Assyria in miraculous fashion.[35] In fact, the God of Israel did not *fail* to protect his people or his temple from the Babylonians; God withdrew his presence and handed them over for judgment for their sin and for blaspheming his name among the nations.[36] The apostasy of Jerusalem was met with severe judgment at the hands of the Babylonians in accordance with everything God declared he would do if they forsook his commandments and neglected to walk in obedience to him.[37] They were judged for failing to be adequately responsible with their task under God's sovereignly appointed domain.

Are we so confident today that our own theological constructions will save us from being cut off from God's promises if we, too, persist to ignore his will and walk according to our *own* will?[38] Will God hold back judgment forever simply because we are *Americans* and citizens of that "shining city on a hill"? Are we so sure that America is a Christian nation? It sure does not seem like one to me.[39] Even if we are a "Christian nation"—does that mean we are immune from God's judgment if, as a nation, we dishonor him and cause his name to be blasphemed throughout the earth by failing to exercise our duties as ambassadors for Christ?[40]

At the same time, we should never make the mistake of believing that our disobedience somehow threatens God's plans or in any way could prevent them from being accomplished without us. His sovereignty will assure

---

35. See Isa 37:21–38.

36. E.g., Jer 25; Ezek 5; 2 Chr 7:19–22; Hab 1:1—3:19.

37. Cf. Lev 26:14-45 and Deut 28:15-68 with the book of Lamentations.

38. Rom 11:17-24.

39. For more on this, see Brown, *Rude Awakening*.

40. I am not a replacement theologian who believes that the church has taken the place of Israel in God's plan. As a result, I understand that many may object to the idea that America could be judged by God in such a fashion. However, in the New Testament we see warnings about God's people being judged and I do not have confidence that we are immune from God's judgment simply because of "grace." God is more serious about the glory of his name being proclaimed to the ends of the earth than he is about the glory of democracy and freedom being spread to everyone who wants it. God's sovereignty rules over all the kingdoms of the earth (Ps 103:19), including the United States of America. The ideals of the kingdom of God, therefore, supersede the ideals of democracy.

that God's desired end will be accomplished because he works all things together according to the counsel of his will.[41] God does not need us; but he chooses to use us. If we persist in our refusal to partner with God in his mission, God will use someone else.[42]

Consider the disobedient prophet Jonah. Although Jonah is probably most talked about in children's church, and while the major focus of the attention seems to be on the "great fish," the book of Jonah proclaims a distinctly profound message that demonstrates the interaction between human freedom and divine sovereignty. In the book of Jonah, we see the sovereign God command Jonah to participate in the very mission of God that has been described throughout this book and throughout the entirety of the Scriptures. Jonah is being sent to Nineveh, the capitol of the pagan nation of Assyria, brutal enemies of Jonah and his people, to proclaim to them repentance and faith in the God of the Bible. If these Assyrians will repent, they will be saved from the wrath of God despite their great wickedness.

Jonah demonstrates his human freedom in that he rejects God's sovereign command and instead goes the opposite way. What should be very interesting to the person who believes that the God of the Old Testament and the God of the New Testament are different—or that the God of the Old is a big "meany-head" and the God of the New is amazingly gracious and compassionate—is the reason that Jonah initially disobeys this command to go and preach repentance: Jonah believes this God of the Old Testament to be *too gracious*. Jonah knows that if he obeys God's call, then the Assyrians will repent. He knows this because of God's sovereignty in calling to himself a people from every tribe, tongue, and nation—including those people that Jonah hated! Jonah refused to participate initially in the hope that in his rebellion and sin, somehow the Assyrians will miss out on God's grace and will not be represented around God's throne when his kingdom comes in its fullness.

However, God's will cannot be thwarted. God demonstrates his sovereignty over all of creation through the events that led to Jonah eventually doing exactly what God asked him to do in the first place. God shows his power over the plants, wind, waves, and sun. God demonstrates his power to command creatures both great and small. God works all of these circumstances to get Jonah to do exactly what he desires him to do, all while Jonah is free to exercise his own will within the parameters of God's sovereignty. There will be representatives around God's throne from the Assyrians, and

---

41. Eph 1:11.

42. God chose King Saul (1 Sam 9:15—10:24), then rejected him for his unfaithfulness (1 Sam 15:10–29). God handed over the kingdom to David as a result (1 Sam 16:1–23). This is just one example. See also 2 Chr 15:1–7; Esth 4:14; and Rom 11:17–24.

God called Jonah to proclaim the message of repentance and faith in the God of Israel.

Had Jonah exercised his freedom responsibly, the book of Jonah could have been two chapters instead of four. Better still, Jonah could have preached to the Ninevites without stinking of fish vomit. Had Jonah been even *more* disobedient, the book could have been longer . . . perhaps six or eight chapters, with no shortage of God demonstrating his sovereignty over all of creation and continuing to call his child towards obedience to his revealed will. Eventually, like the Israelites in the desert, God could have killed off the disobedient prophet and spoken to another, telling them to, "Arise, go to Nineveh the great city and proclaim to it the proclamation which I am going to tell you."[43] God did raise up another prophet, Nahum, who proclaimed a judgment against Assyria which God would not relent of about 150 years later without the opportunity to be saved through repentance. Before wiping this nation off the map, God saved a group of them through his grace by sending one of his people to proclaim repentance to them. God's mission was a success.

Do you see how the sovereignty of God and the freedom/responsibility of humanity interacted here? Theologians and philosophers can argue all they want to about which doctrine has preeminence, or can wrongly conclude that one doctrine makes the other irrelevant or impossible, but in the life of Jonah we see an amazing example of God sovereignly arranging the parameters and allowing for freedom and responsibility of human beings to play out; all the while never having any doubt on the outcome. This is not "open theism" in which God's omniscience is questioned and the freedom of human beings somehow leads to "openness" in the possible outcome of human history. This is a God who sovereignly interacts with his creation's freedom (a freedom which we could only have if he sovereignly declared us to be this way when he created us), always working toward the end that every knee will bow and every tongue will confess that Jesus Christ is Lord to the glory of God the Father.

God fully knows the plan for whether we obey or disobey and he often lays out in Scripture the two options as such, indicating what he will do in either case.[44] We do not need to seek theological constructions that "ex-

---

43. Jonah 1:2; 3:2.

44. E.g., Exod 19:5; Lev 26:3–46; Deut 28:1–68; 30:8–20; Judg 3:4; Isa 1:19–20; Jer 22:4–5; Amos 4:1–13; Zech 6:15; Matt 23:37. God also demonstrates his omniscience through declaring his knowledge of future human actions in advance in places like Deut 17:14–17 and 1 Sam 10:17–19; Judg 4:9, 21–22; and Josh 6:26 and 1 Kgs 16:34. Many more examples could be cited. Romans 6:1–23 teaches the reality of human responsibility to consistently choose to exercise our freedom to present ourselves to God

plain these passages away." Instead, we should seek to rightly understand exactly what God is showing us about how he sovereignly directs the events of human history for the praise and glory of his name. God demonstrates his omniscience and sovereignty while also affirming human responsibility and freedom to make genuine decisions. Ultimately, the decisions we make will have no impact on the end goal of God being accomplished. God sovereignly works all things according to the counsel of his will. Yet, we will be held responsible for our actions nonetheless. Clearly, it is better to participate with God than to try and foolishly resist his will.

Some will object to this saying that this view does not represent genuine "freedom." Really, it is no more limiting than our laws of physics. Our world is governed by physical laws that set parameters on actions. I am able to sit, walk, run, jump, and stand, but not fly. Do these parameters mean that I am not free? I don't think so. I am free *within the parameters*. Even more than this, the realm of *possibility* is far wider than the realm of *actuality*. While it is theoretically possible at any given moment that I could run, because the laws of physics allow for such a possibility, the reality is that I will run in very limited circumstances only (which, to be honest, virtually never arise). In many ways, human beings are more "bound" by their personality and character than they are by physics. I can theoretically throw myself out of a second story window or pound on my own toe with a hammer, but I am not going to do that—at least, not on purpose. I can theoretically drive myself to a bar and use my money to purchase alcohol—I'm old enough and have sufficient means to make this a theoretical possibility. However, you won't find me frequenting bars. In these cases, my character and personality bind my actions far more than the laws of our land or physics do.

Some philosophers speak of "determinism"—a view that makes human action a product of circumstances that began at the beginning of time. They claim that although we may feel free, we are really slaves to our nature and our surroundings. Determinism teaches that our "freedom" is merely perceived. It is difficult to avoid this conclusion if we are simply material beings. If the physical world is all there is, and the law of cause and effect holds true, it becomes difficult to escape the conclusion of determinism. However, the Christian notion of a "spirit" and/or "soul" adds an immaterial element to our composition as human beings that is not necessarily so slavishly tied to material factors and would not need to be a slave of material determinism.[45]

---

as servants of his will.

45. The fact that human beings are not simply "meat machines" is proven by the fact that often doctors cannot explain why we die, especially in cases where it seems like we should be able to get hearts to start beating again and they simply will not. The

However, as argued previously, in a very real sense we are slaves to various forces; natural and supernatural, material and immaterial. The genuine Christian, who has been born-again by the Spirit of God, is freed from slavery to their flesh, the world, and the devil, and can begin submitting themselves to God as his servant. The Christian often bounces back and forth between serving God and serving their flesh as they exercise this freedom in reality.[46] All the while, this "freedom" is really choosing which master to serve. Never does this freedom make it possible for the Christian to avoid slavish obedience to physical forces such as the law of gravity! This is how God can allow freedom and can hold us responsible. We genuinely act in accordance with our nature. This is also how we can avoid the erroneous extreme of open theism. This is how such offers as were made in Deuteronomy 30:15–20 can be extended in earnest, without challenging the sovereignty of God or making a mockery of human freedom and responsibility. Our freedom is a genuine freedom—a freedom within parameters that are divinely set by the sovereignty of God.

If this view is accurate, then the end that God intends is never in doubt. The only thing that changes is how quickly we get there. Like with Jonah, if God's people obey him and his will, then the end should conceivably come faster because God does not need to do so much extra work in sovereignly arranging events to bring his people back into conformity with his will, nor does he need to wait while he brings judgment upon his own people and raises up a new generation that will faithfully obey him and walk according to his will.

In fact, this seems to be exactly how the Apostle Peter understood God's sovereignty and human freedom. In 2 Peter 3:3–10, Peter describes how people are exercising their human freedom to persist in rebellion against the sovereign, just, and righteous judge of the universe. Since God does not desire for any to perish under his wrath, but for all to receive forgiveness of sin through accepting the gift of everlasting life purchased by the blood of the Savior, he is holding back his judgment in patience. Since this is what God is doing, what then ought his people to do? The Apostle Peter continues:

Scriptures make it clear that our life comes from God and when our spirit returns to him, the physical body is dead (Pss 104:29; 146:4; Ecc 12:7). When our spirit departs from the flesh, no amount of heroics in keeping our hearts beating or our lungs breathing can thwart this. This immaterial aspect of human beings does not "die"—it is separated from the body when we die in this world, and it will be reunited to our resurrected bodies at the final judgment (Rev 20:1—21:8).

46. Rom 6:1–23.

Since all these things are to be destroyed in this way, what sort of people ought you to be in holy conduct and godliness, *looking for and hastening the coming of the day of God*, because of which the heavens will be destroyed by burning, and the elements will melt with intense heat! But according to His promise we are looking for new heavens and a new earth, in which righteousness dwells. Therefore, beloved, since you look for these things, *be diligent* to be found by Him in peace, spotless and blameless, and regard the patience of our Lord as salvation; just as also our beloved brother Paul, according to the wisdom given him, wrote to you, as also in all his letters, speaking in them of these things, in which are some things hard to understand, which the untaught and unstable distort, as they do also the rest of the Scriptures, to their own destruction. You therefore, beloved, knowing this beforehand, *be on your guard* so that you are not carried away by the error of unprincipled men and fall from your own steadfastness, but grow in the grace and knowledge of our Lord and Savior Jesus Christ. To Him be the glory, both now and to the day of eternity. Amen. (2 Pet 3:11–18, emphasis added)

Notice this amazing statement from Peter: "looking for and *hastening* the coming day of God." Hastening here in the NASB (and so in the ESV, KJV, NKJV, NAB, and NET) is translated as "speed its coming" in the NIV.

Amazing!

But, is it really that surprising? Are we astounded that *obeying* God would lead to the best and fastest completion of his purposes? Is that really such a profound statement? What do you think would happen if God's people began to *obey* our God and king instead of arguing with each other over which doctrine we should emphasize more: divine sovereignty or human responsibility? What if God's people humbled themselves before the living God and stopped trying to prove that they are right, and instead simply obeyed the commandment of Jesus to go, and make disciples of all nations . . . what would happen? What would happen if we exercised our freedom in Christ to lay down all other pursuits, and actually sought first the kingdom of God and its righteousness, and walked with Jesus in obedience to his great commission?

According to Peter, the end would come sooner. This may challenge our theological constructs, but where do we read that God commands us to follow rigorous manmade theological constructs and neglect obedience to his revealed will? Are we immune from making mistakes in our theologizing? We must never put obedience to God's specific commands on hold because our theological constructions have explained them away.

Jesus prayed for laborers to enter the harvest field in Matthew 9:37–38. If God's people would heed this call to live as ambassadors for Christ and would begin to steward the gospel message faithfully, instead of concealing it because "people don't like to talk about religion," would you be surprised that the end would come sooner?

Perhaps Jesus was kidding when he said, "This gospel of the kingdom shall be preached in the whole world as a testimony to all the nations, and then the end will come" (Matt 24:14). But, what if Jesus wasn't kidding? It is sad but true that many people who claim to follow Jesus live as if many of his statements were followed by, "just kidding!" Of course, you won't find this anywhere in the written text.

We will all stand before God on the Day of Judgment. Many of us are hoping that he will understand why we spent most of our time building our own kingdoms instead of building his. We are hoping that God will understand why we spent most of our time pursuing our own interests instead of his fame and glory. We are hoping that God will understand why we prioritized ourselves over him. At least, that is what our present actions demonstrate.

If we really believed, as the people of God, that this gospel must be preached in the whole world as a testimony to all the nations, then why are we not pursuing this more seriously? With all of the technology and resources that we have today, and with our ability to travel the globe so quickly and safely, how is it that we have not yet succeeded in bringing the gospel to every nation? If we really took this seriously, and if all who profess to know and follow Christ were willing to do whatever it takes, we could preach this gospel in the whole world in just a few years. One hundred years, tops. Instead of spreading the gospel of Jesus Christ, the reverse is actually true. We have been so careless with our stewardship of the gospel that in our own country, many people who profess to follow Jesus don't actually have any idea of what the biblical gospel truly is, or what it means to follow him. Many people have believed and held to a false gospel, which is really no gospel at all. Obedience to Jesus in the great commission and preaching the biblical gospel boldly has become so strange *within the ranks of the professing church* that often those most hostile to followers of Christ evangelizing are those who profess to be Christians themselves!

I listened to a sermon from a prominent pastor in my area who described witnessing someone preaching the gospel on a street corner at an event he attended. This pastor said during his message that he watched this street preacher intently from a distance, because he wanted to find out what on earth would possess someone to do such a thing. I was interested to hear if the criticisms of this particular street preacher would be based on the content of his message (was he preaching falsehood?) or his demeanor (was he being mean-spirited, hateful, rude, or vulgar?). But his criticisms did not mention any of these things. This pastor's conclusion, to the delight of his large congregation, was that such activity is foolishness of the worst sort *simply by virtue of the fact that he was preaching on the streets.* Sadly, the bombing during the Boston marathon happened shortly after I listened to this message. Do you think that anyone who participated in that event would have been worse off by having someone preach the genuine gospel to all as they passed by? We truly do not know when our last day on earth will be. We do not know when Christ will return. As a result, we must be faithful with the time we have.

How many nations could be reached with the billions of dollars that we spend on gratifying our own lusts and desires? How many missionaries could be equipped and sent out with the billions of dollars we waste each year celebrating covetousness in the name of the incarnation at Christmas time or buying candy on Halloween? How many millions of people could hear the gospel of salvation with the resources we waste on buying candy for Easter? *What do jelly beans have to do with the resurrection and exaltation of Jesus?*

It is sad that many professing Christians spend more money investing in whatever company pumps television channels into their households than they do investing in the advancement of the gospel.[47] Freedom in Christ means that you *can* pay to have cable TV. Freedom in Christ also requires that we answer why we would do so when we are free to lay down our own comfort and entertainment for the benefit of those who are perishing under God's wrath. On Judgment Day, will we be happy to see our neighbors perishing under the wrath of God because we were too busy entertaining ourselves to have told them the message of salvation? Those who are staunchly Calvinistic in their theological persuasion may scoff at such a statement thinking that their neighbor's status as the "elect" of God has no bearing on whether or not we preach to them, but what justification do we have for *withholding* the word of life from them while we pursue our own interests? On the heels of the Apostle Paul's strongest teaching on election

---

47. Two organizations that I am aware of that are attempting to bring the Bible to unreached people groups in every language on earth through different means are World Mission (www.worldmission.cc) and Wycliffe Bible Translators (www.wycliffe.org). World Mission makes use of solar powered technology to provide the Bible and other resources in an audio format in native languages, while Wycliffe seeks to translate the written word into every language on earth. Both ministries are worth checking out.

and predestination in Romans 9 comes the urgent need for preaching the gospel to all in Romans 10. Paul wasn't a Calvinist or an Arminian. Paul was a Christian. Paul had no problem living under the sovereignty of God and understanding his own responsibility in exercising his freedom to participate with God's revealed will.

When we stand before our God and king someday, will our actions demonstrate that we are hoping that he will understand why we thought it was more important to invest our time, energy, and resources into entertaining ourselves than it was to proclaim his name and glory to the ends of the earth?[48] By his grace and compassion, God is calling us out from such foolishness. He is patient with us and with those who are still in rebellion against him. God is calling us to that which is truly life.

The good news is we are not alone.

---

48. Jas 5:1–6.

10

We Are the Body

> Now to Him who is able to do far more abundantly beyond all that we ask or think, according to the power that works within us, to Him be the glory in the church and in Christ Jesus to all generations forever and ever. Amen.
> (Eph 3:20–21)

I remember early in my pastoral ministry when an elder looked me in the face with a look that was a mix between exasperation and pity and said, "You really believe that this stuff can change the world, don't you?"

"Yes, I do," I replied.

"Well, you're still young." And then he looked out the window and changed the subject. The clear implication was that my idealism about the church and the power of the gospel to positively change the world would wear off as I got older. Not too long after this I began a mentoring relationship with another pastor whom I respected for a number of reasons—and still do—who had been pastoring what seemed to be a successful local church for many years. I'll never forget a piece of advice that he gave to me which forever changed our relationship.

"If you want to succeed in ministry," he told me, "lower your expectations."

Lower my expectations?

I certainly do not doubt the effectiveness of such a strategy. I am confident that many pastors and church leaders have been able to endure in ministry only through such an exercise of lowering their expectations. Nevertheless, is this a biblical strategy?

The Apostle Paul wrote that God is "able to do far more abundantly beyond all that we ask or think, according to the power that works within us, to Him be the glory in the church and in Christ Jesus to all generations forever and ever" (Eph 3:20–21). A statement like this does not seem to indicate that we should *lower* our expectations, but instead that we ought to *raise* them! Paul's expectation was *not* that this amazing work of God would die out in the first century. Instead, his expectation was that this abundant power of God which is at work in the church for God's own glory would extend to all generations, forever and ever, which certainly sounds like it includes us. At least it *should*.

So why does the church in America look so unlike the church in Acts? Why does the powerful force that rolled through the Roman Empire exist so impotently in the United States today?[1] How can it be that genuine followers of Christ who have been called to be leaders in the church can actually give counsel to the next generation of pastors to lower their expectations? What is it about the present state of the American church that leads those who have been involved for years to begin to doubt the power of God and believe that the gospel won't (or can't) make much of a difference anymore? How have we fallen so far?

I think the answer is simpler than we may initially think. However, a different question is whether or not we are willing to do anything about it. We must be careful to note that Jesus' church is alive and well and is composed of all believers in the Messiah. Unfortunately, much of what is called the "church" is not really the church. Jesus' church exists independently of our forms and systems. If you think it is impossible to have a "church" without Jesus, then read Revelation 3:14–22, especially verse 20, to see that God's people can exclude Jesus and his plans from their local congregations. Denial is not the solution. The solution is to invite Jesus back in if we find that our forms have excluded him.

We are experiencing a systemic failure in the American church because we have done what Americans love to do with everything: tried to improve

---

1. The "force" with which Christianity spread in the first century AD was not a violent force. Instead, it changed communities and nations despite brutal violence being used *against* it. When I say the church should be a "force" again, it would be a mistake of the worst sort to think that this is in any way a call for violence to be employed by Christians in spreading it. The tools of spreading Christianity are the faithful proclamation of the gospel, love, service, and prayer—all empowered by the presence of the Holy Spirit within believers. Violence is *not* a valid Christian mission strategy. For a good study on the prayers of the Apostle Paul as a model for personal spiritual reformation and edification of the church, see Carson, *Call to Spiritual Reformation*.

upon what came before. This may be shocking to some, but Jesus does not need us to improve upon his organization. He got it right the first time. Every modification we make to God's design is not an *improvement*. It's really a *hindrance*. Unfortunately, we have tried to make so many *improvements* and *tweaks* along the way that much of what we call "church" today has nothing to do with what God revealed the church to be in the Scriptures.

What you may be expecting now is a critique on the "mega-church" movement, or perhaps the "seeker-sensitive movement," or maybe even a strong endorsement of the "home church movement" or something else. But what I am suggesting is different than this.

Bigger. Systemic.

In practice, we have dismembered the body of Christ and are losing connection with the head of the church.[2] It shows in our expressed theology of spiritual gifts, unity, and the church. Sometimes people ask me, "When you emphasize the spiritual gift of evangelism, aren't you neglecting the other gifts which are just as valid and important?" This is a great and important question. I know that many people who are familiar with the ministry I lead have asked this question out loud or in their mind. It is good to be able to address it for mutual edification and in the hopes of bringing clarity to this particular issue of spiritual gifts and the purpose/unity of the body.

Before diving in, it is important to state without qualification that every spiritual gift which is given by the Lord is valid and important. While there is very little agreement in the professing church as to what, exactly, the gifts of the Spirit *are*, and which gifts are still around today, this will not be an attempt to answer these particular questions definitively. However, we can affirm that *whatever* gifts the Spirit gives to his followers today are *all* valid and important. The Apostle Paul makes this point clearly enough in 1 Corinthians 12:14–26. On this basis alone, it is perfectly reasonable for anyone to raise questions and/or objections when one spiritual gift is elevated above the rest as being the *most* important. To elevate one gift and diminish the rest is sinful; doing so results in disunity and is contrary to the body metaphor that the Apostle Paul is using.[3]

That being said, it is impossible to elevate the spiritual gift of *evangelism* above the rest of the gifts of the Spirit for one major reason: evangelism is

---

2. Col 1:24—2:19.

3. According to the information Paul is presenting in 1 Cor 12–14, the "better" gifts are the ones that edify the most people, not that bring the particular member the most honor or prestige. A good discussion of 1 Cor 12–14 can be found in Hodge, *Exposition*, 237–308.

not a spiritual gift.[4] Therefore, the claim that anyone can elevate *evangelism* above the *other spiritual gifts* is a category mistake.[5] It is not possible to elevate evangelism above other gifts of the Spirit because that would mean that evangelism *is* one of the gifts of the Spirit. But it is not.

As already stated, there is general disagreement as to what the "gifts of the Spirit" really are. Not only is there disagreement in the *number* of the gifts (as a quick survey of different spiritual gifts tests will surely demonstrate), but there are some groups that combine gifts—Are "helps" and "service" the same or are they two different gifts? How about "administration" and "leadership"?—that others would separate. Some groups define gifts differently (is prophecy a gift of *revelation,* or of *proclamation,* or both?). Even more than this, many argue over the validity of certain gifts such as tongues and miracles for the modern church and era.

The most straightforward lists of spiritual gifts are found in Romans 12 and 1 Corinthians 12. Some interpreters point to passages like 1 Corinthians 7:1–9 to include "celibacy" as a spiritual gift. Wherever you happen to fall on these particular issues, you will be hard pressed to find a passage that states *evangelism* is a spiritual gift, no matter how far you extend your parameters. Some claim that this gift is clearly listed in Ephesians 4:11, but look closely: "And He gave some as apostles, and some as prophets, and some as evangelists, and some as pastors and teachers."

In order to view this as a list of spiritual gifts (instead of as *offices*) we must read something into the text; namely, that each of these offices are filled by people who are spiritually gifted with the spiritual gift that corresponds to the office. What I mean is this: since some believe "apostle(ship)" is a spiritual gift, then those with that spiritual gift serve in the office as apostles;[6] likewise for proph*esy* (gift) and proph*ets* (office), evangel*ism* (gift) and evangel*ists* (office), shepherd*ing* (gift) and pastors/shepher*ds* (office), and teach*ing* (gift) and teach*ers* (office). You can even look back to Ephesians 4:7 to see that Christ gave these things listed in 4:11 as special

---

4. I first began wrestling with this idea of evangelism not being a spiritual gift as a result of evangelist Andy Lapins's (www.transfired.org) Search and Rescue School of Evangelism being taught at our local church. Until that time, I had always assumed evangelism was a spiritual gift. After Andy claimed otherwise, I searched the Scriptures and found that he was right—evangelism is not a spiritual gift.

5. A category mistake is a logical error that presents one thing as if it were another type of thing (which it is not).

6. I am not in this camp. I do believe, however, that the apostles were directly chosen by Jesus as a gift to the church; e.g., Luke 6:13; Acts 9:15; 2 Tim 1:1. I believe the office of apostle endures through the apostolic writings (our "New Testament"—which is a tremendous gift by itself), and that no new "apostles" are living today who have the marks of an apostle; 1 Cor 9:1; 2 Cor 12:12.

gifts of grace—which can easily be interpreted as *spiritual gifts*. However, it should be relatively uncontroversial that not everyone with the spiritual gift of *shepherding* is called to fill the office of pastor. It is also true that many who fill the office of pastor are not spiritually gifted as shepherds—they may be gifted as administrators, or leaders, or whatever else. In fact, not all of the apostles were gifted exactly the same. The assumption that the *spiritual gifts* and the *offices* correspond exactly does not hold water scripturally or experientially.

Unlike prophesy, shepherding, and teaching, *evangelism* is nowhere listed as a spiritual gift—which makes the assumption that the office in Ephesians 4:11 of evangelist as being based on a person having the spiritual gift of evangelism a dangerous one. "Evangel*ism*" and "evangel*ists*" are *not* the same things. The first is a verb, the second is a noun. To equate them is to make an interpretive error that will then affect our practice and church structures. Anyone who believes that *evangelism* is a spiritual gift that is given to some individuals (and, more importantly *not* to others) does so with either no textual support or as a result of the serious interpretive error of asserting that *evangelists* = those gifted with the spiritual gift of *evangelism*, which is false. If we grant that evangelists (office) and evangelism (spiritual gift) are *different*, then we have textual support for one (office) and not the other (spiritual gift). Plenty of people are recorded evangelizing in the Bible who were not called *evangelists*.

Outside of Ephesians 4:11 we learn that Philip was an evangelist in Caesarea in Acts 21:8, showing that the early church recognized this office. We must notice that Philip's life and ministry are described earlier in Acts. In Acts 6, he is one of the Seven. In Acts 8, he preaches to the Samaritans and to the Ethiopian eunuch. After the Ethiopian eunuch is baptized, the Holy Spirit snatches Philip away to Azotus and he continues preaching the gospel until he comes to Caesarea. Throughout this detailed description, Philip is never called an "evangelist." Instead, he is simply a representative of what many other regular Christians were doing at the time as they lived as ambassadors for Christ. It is not until we hear of Philip again, some twenty years later, while he is still in Caesarea that he is called "the evangelist." The title is not applied to him while he is travelling, but only after he has settled in Caesarea for decades.

Similarly, Timothy was commanded to "do the work of an evangelist" as part of his ministry in properly ordering the church in Ephesus (2 Tim 4:5). While the exact nature of Timothy's role as a leader in Ephesus is debatable—was he the pastor or was he merely sent there to temporarily oversee the proper ordering of the church which would include raising up leaders?—one thing is beyond dispute: Timothy's call to "do the work of an evangelist" was *not* a call to an itinerant or para-church ministry. Timothy's task from Paul was a call to faithfulness in the work of an evangelist *in the local church at Ephesus*. Timothy was not sent there simply as a missionary. He was sent to an already established local church and told to perform the work of an evangelist (among other things) within that local church context. As Paul instructed this pastor/overseer in the proper ordering of the local church he stressed the internal importance of sound teaching, rebuking error, the Word of God, and also the importance of doing the work of an evangelist. The work of an evangelist is, at least in part, leading the *internal* to the *external*—continuing and contributing to the discipleship process by leading the charge to seek and save the lost through boldly proclaiming the gospel and equipping the body to live as ambassadors for Christ.

It is true that the offices in Ephesians 4:11 are gifts, but they are not the same kind of gifts as *spiritual gifts* are. This is where the main area of disagreement is, and is the *crux interpretum*[7] for our discussion. I believe the text indicates, and therefore I teach, that the items listed in Ephesians 4:11 are not *spiritual gifts* in the same sense that shepherding, teaching, and tongues are. Instead, the Apostle Paul is teaching followers of Christ that these things are gifts to the *church*, not the individual. They are God's design for *governing*, *equipping*, and *leading* his church. This understanding fits the overall context of the subject matter in the entire book of Ephesians much better than a listing of spiritual gifts does.

These offices listed in Ephesians 4:11 are gifts given by Jesus to his church to maintain unity and equip the body of Christ for works of service (see Eph 4:12–16). This is good news, because Paul already told us that "we are His workmanship, created in Christ Jesus for good works, which God prepared beforehand so that we would walk in them" (Eph 2:10). As a gift to the church, Jesus gave officers to equip the body to do just that. If the alternative interpretation of Ephesians 4:11 is true, and "evangelists" are merely those who are gifted with the spiritual gift of evangelism, in what way do they fulfill the purpose for this gifting as outlined in Ephesians 4:12–16?

I have heard many different interpretations of what a "gift of evangelism" entails. All of these are based on personal opinions, not biblical exegesis. These ideas range from enjoying having conversations about Jesus with others to being a "harvester"—that is, a person with the gift of evangelism sees more fruit from their evangelism in the form of conversions than those who are not gifted. *Some plant, some water, but evangelists get to harvest.* We must recognize that these are based purely on speculation, opinion, and/or conjecture because no biblical text(s) actually makes this affirmation.

---

7. That is, the crucial interpretive issue.

If we grant that such ideas are true—that the gift of evangelism is evident in people who like to evangelize or who see a lot of results—then how does this ministry *equip the saints*, which Ephesians 4:12 says evangelists are for? Instead, by equating evangelists with evangelism, we are acting in ways that are contrary to the Scriptures because we are reversing the purpose of the office of evangelist which is to minister *to the saints*! By these non-biblical definitions of evangelism and evangelists, we are attempting to fill the office Jesus designed for evangelists with a ministry *to the lost* instead of *to the saints*. If we maintain Jesus' design, we will recognize that he desires the *saints* to be equipped, for the benefit of the *lost*.[8] Ephesians 4:11–12 plainly states that apostles, prophets, evangelists, pastors and teachers were given by Jesus *for the equipping of the saints*, which will lead to the building up of the body as each part does its work. Therefore, it is impossible that evangelists are expected to merely evangelize, because that completely ignores the purpose of this office by making them primarily ministers to the lost in contrast to other Christians who have an "internally focused" gifting. What's more, if these individuals are gifted with a spiritual gift of evangelism, how can they equip the saints who are not similarly gifted? Teachers do not teach everyone how to *teach* necessarily, but teachers equip the saints in multiple ways. If "evangelists" are those gifted with "evangelism," then in what way can they equip the saints for works of service? That's not their gift!

Properly understanding the purpose of the church will help bring clarity to the purpose of the offices listed in Ephesians 4:11. Only with this understanding can we then truly answer why Fourth Year Ministries, and anyone else for that matter who promotes evangelism, is not unnecessarily exalting this calling for every Christian above God's intended place revealed through his word and Son.

The Apostle Peter gives some explicit instruction for the exercise of spiritual gifts, but it is crucial that we hear loud and clear the purpose for this instruction which is tied to the purpose of the church in general:

> As each one has received a special gift, employ it in serving one another as good stewards of the manifold grace of God. Whoever speaks, is to do so as one who is speaking the utterances of God; whoever serves is to do so as one who is serving by the strength which God supplies; so that in all things God may be glorified through Jesus Christ, to whom belongs the glory and dominion forever and ever. Amen. (1 Pet 4:10–11)

Each individual member of the church is to properly steward their special, individual spiritual gift(s) so that in all things God may be glorified

---

8. John 17:9, 20–21.

through Jesus Christ. This is where so many people are mistaken in their understanding of spiritual gifts and the teaching on the body of Christ. They stop too soon. By focusing on the individual parts and emphasizing the gifts themselves, we are detracting from the more important understanding of the unified body, which is the major point of the metaphor! The offices listed in Ephesians 4:11, on the other hand, exist to *equip* the body to do exactly what Peter is calling for in 1 Peter 4:10–11 (above) and what Paul instructed in Ephesians 2:10 and 4:1. That is why the *offices* are a gift, too: to prepare and equip God's people to fulfill these apostolic commands to the glory of God. Failing to recognize these gifts (offices) in the church, and eliminating them from serving their purpose in equipping the body, will necessarily have a deep impact upon Christ's church and the world. As Christ's church is built up, through the proper working of each individual part, the ability to witness to the world regarding the gospel and glory of God will likewise increase.

Before discussing the importance of the individual parts, Paul emphasized the *unity* of the whole body in 1 Corinthians 12:4–13, and he returns to this theme again in 1 Corinthians 12:27. Paul emphasizes this unity again in Romans 12:4–5. Perhaps most importantly, Paul emphasizes the truth that Christ is the head of the body in Colossians 1:18 and 2:19, and also in Ephesians 5:23.

Now think about this for a minute: when we emphasize the importance of any particular member of the body, we are failing to recognize the importance of our *unity* in Christ. What tends to happen with our disagreements over the importance and/or validity of the individual gifts is that we then separate ourselves into sub-communities that agree with our values and theological conclusions. The result is a dissected body that no longer works in unity and is incapable of doing so—just like a pile of hands, a pile of feet, and a pile of tongues would be unproductive in doing anything that a whole-body could do.

If you think this is crass, how else would you explain the reality that often those who speak in tongues are completely segregated from the rest of the body of Christ? This is just one example, but it should help you see the reality that this is not healthy or helpful for advancing God's mission, even if it is relatively successful in building our mini-kingdoms of denominationalism.

When we contemplate a body we must understand that there is unity of purpose when everything is working properly. Direction for the body comes from the head. When my head wants to go somewhere, it organizes the members of my body into unified action toward that purpose. Of course, each member of my body serves a different function, but every part works toward the same goal or purpose. My toes act in conjunction with my feet, with my legs and torso, my arms, hands, and fingers, even though they all do something different, in bringing my whole body toward the intended goal. When a physical body becomes handicapped in some way—that is, one or more parts of the body are not functioning at full capacity—then the whole body is hindered. It is the same for the body of Christ.[9]

The body metaphor is intended for us to see this same unity in purpose, and to view spiritual gifts as equally important in serving that end, organized by Christ, who is the head. It would be foolish for my toes to criticize my fingers for not fulfilling the same role in driving my car to work. In the same way, it would be foolish for those who are gifted to *serve* to criticize those who are gifted to *teach* in the goal of glorifying God through Christ and proclaiming the gospel to every creature under heaven. I once was envious of my ministry partner and brother in Christ who seems to have much more success in starting conversations with people about the gospel than I do while witnessing on the streets. In my jealousy, my flesh wanted to begin criticizing this brother to find areas that I excel over him. How foolish! When the purpose of the body is being realized, and sinners are hearing the gospel of salvation, should we not celebrate the fact that God is glorified? The Lord used me as a teacher in this particular brother's life, and now he excels in putting many of these principles into practice beyond what I am capable of. Praise God!

Here's where the rubber really meets the road: what is the unity of purpose to which the body of Christ is called? Is glorifying God through Christ not tied to proclaiming his excellencies who has called us out of darkness into marvelous light (1 Pet 2:9–10)? This is the very thing Peter mentioned a few chapters prior to his counsel on spiritual gifts in 1 Peter 4. Is this not *evangelism*? God has revealed his mission and will to his people so that we would participate with him in reconciling the world to himself through Christ as his ambassadors. We do this by proclaiming the gospel of the kingdom to every creature under heaven. The body gets its purpose and marching orders from the head, who is Christ. The head of the church has told us the direction he wants to go and what the ultimate end of human history will be. God has redeemed his people to be a testimony to the world. This is the overarching theme of the Scriptures.

When God saved you, he called you to enter into his work which will ultimately climax on the Day of Christ Jesus, when every knee will bow and every tongue will confess that Jesus Christ is Lord to the glory of God the Father.[10] When God called you, he also gifted you to serve an important

---

9. 1 Cor 12:26.
10. Phil 1:27; 2:2, 9–11. See chap. 2, "God's Mission."

and necessary role within his church.[11] All ambassadors are not equipped or gifted the same.[12] To diminish the entire calling of the church to simply evangelization is to make a mistake of over simplification. Teachers must teach, givers must give, administrators must administrate, servants must serve, and so on. But to what end? And does the fact that my primary gifting is that of a *teacher* eliminate my responsibility to be able to share the gospel faithfully with others? On what grounds can I leave the task of evangelization to others? Because it's not my "gift"? Am I then also absolved of my duty to be hospitable, or to serve, or to give, because these are also not my spiritual gifts? By no means! When we understand our calling as ambassadors to be primary, then the reason for our particular giftedness takes on new purpose and direction.

Having such an understanding sheds new light on how it is that Jesus understood that *unity* in the body would lead to the whole world knowing that Jesus was sent from God:

> I do not ask on behalf of these alone, *but for those also who believe in Me through their word*; that they may all be one; even as You, Father, are in Me and I in You, that they also may be in Us, *so that the world may believe that You sent Me.* The glory which You have given Me I have given to them, that they may be one, just as We are one; I in them and You in Me, *that they may be perfected in unity, so that the world may know that You sent Me,* and loved them, even as You have loved Me. (John 17:20–23, emphasis added)

Jesus prayed for unity because by our unity the whole world will hear the good news of the gospel! It is God's plan to save a people for himself from every tribe, tongue, and nation—those who respond with repentance and faith to the proclamation of the gospel of Christ. This is why Jesus is not only praying for his followers during that first century. Jesus also prayed for those who will believe *through their word*, because they, too, will be transferred from the domain of darkness into the kingdom of light. These new creatures in Christ will (or at least, *should*, if they walk in their calling and live lives worthy of the calling they have received[13]) join in the unified purpose of the body of Christ in evangelizing the entire world to the glory of God, and discipling all those who respond positively to the gospel call to likewise join in this work of God through his people.

---

11. 1 Cor 12:7, 11, 22–25.
12. 1 Cor 12:14–30.
13. Eph 4:1; Col 1:10–14; Phil 1:27. See chap. 9, "Freedom in Christ."

Really, this is the only view of "unity in Christ" that makes sense in leading the whole world to know about Jesus. I have heard it preached and taught that the focus on unity is an *internal* focus and that this internal unity is itself a form of evangelism, but that is not fully accurate. Surely, our unity will be an internal unity, but the world does not drive by our church buildings and poke their heads inside to see if we are "unified." There will not be some magic moment where believers are gathered together inside a church building, holding hands and singing kumbaya, where the community enters *en masse* and falls down on their knees saying, "Brothers, what must we do to be saved? Because you are all in agreement we have come to know that Jesus was sent by God!" It was not until the unified brethren inside the upper room stepped *out* and Peter boldly preached the gospel that the multitude was saved in Acts 2. As these first Christians preached a unified message, everyone who encountered a follower of Christ was confronted with the truth of the genuine gospel. Today, we have myriad versions of professing Christians proclaiming different gospels. Talk about confusing![14]

To believe that people will come to Christ without the church boldly proclaiming the gospel is foolishness and anti-biblical. The world will know that Jesus was sent by God when the body of Christ is unified beyond the *internal* understanding of our call to glorify God through Christ and moves into obedience to the *external* call to go and proclaim the gospel to every creature under heaven, making disciples of all nations. The church will be best equipped and prepared to do this when each part does its work, under the leadership designed by Christ Jesus himself. The gospel is the one unifying truth that all genuine Christians believe in and is the one truth that is the power of God unto salvation for all who believe.[15] "How then will they call on Him in whom they have not believed? How will they believe in Him whom they have not heard? And how will they hear without a preacher? How will they preach unless they are sent?"[16] When the church is equipped, and unified in obeying the call of God, then the world will know.

Your theological belief on if and when there will be a rapture, the number of spiritual gifts or the applicability of them today, the role of women in

---

14. I've encountered some skeptics and atheists who make fun of all these different "flavors" of Christianity each proclaiming to be the only genuine version. On various internet forums I've encountered those who use the tongue-in-cheek phrase "Genuine Christians™" to make fun of those professing Christians who are trying to engage them in conversation. Our disunity is evident, for sure. If Christians were unified on the gospel message, the world would notice because they would be confronted by the genuine gospel consistently and constantly.

15. Rom 1:16; 1 Cor 1:18–24.

16. Rom 10:14–15.

leadership, or the appropriateness of drums being used in a worship service are not the power of God unto salvation for all who believe. Being unified on your particular position on these (and other) theological issues within the confines of your own local fellowship will not result in the world knowing that Jesus was sent from God. A fresh reading of Revelation 2:1–7 is in order if you believe that correct doctrine is the *only* thing that matters. Clearly, correct doctrine matters a great deal—but not if it means we have left our first love and have stopped doing the deeds we did at first. To get all our other doctrine correct and neglect the most important aspect of God's mission is to misunderstand the whole thing. Don't miss that the local church that is being addressed in Revelation 2:1–7 is the church at Ephesus—the church which received Paul's epistle outlining the office of evangelist and which had Timothy as an overseer, tasked with not neglecting the work of an evangelist!

Rallying around minor doctrinal matters results in communities of lost people not knowing or caring about the gospel because our fellowships are irrelevant to them and impotent to effect any change in the community. Those who are *dead* in their trespasses and sins need *life*—which only comes through the gospel. Correct doctrine is for the living, not the spiritually dead. Please understand that I am not trying to disparage any particular denominational beliefs. We've all got some stuff wrong (even though we may not like to admit it). I am not even arguing that these other matters of theology are *un*important. Instead, I am asserting that they are not the *most* important matter of doctrine. By elevating these lesser issues beyond the most important doctrine, in seeking out our own niche, we have collectively wandered away from God's calling and design for his church. This is an understandable result of forgetting the office of evangelist in the local church. When churches are run by pastors and teachers alone, without the external office of evangelist, we will necessarily begin focusing on doctrine to an unhealthy degree.[17]

---

17. I understand this tendency, because I am a pastor and a teacher. If I had my way, I would discuss the Bible all day, every day. While serving in local church ministry, I have seen the difficulty of working together with other local churches that have pastors who hold different opinions on certain (non-salvation) doctrines than I do—especially when the *defensive* mindset is prevalent. On the other hand, I returned recently from a week long witnessing trip in Venice, CA, where our local church participated with another local church of a different denomination, but who also has an evangelist on staff. Our two groups do not agree on everything, but we agree on the gospel. We weren't there to preach ourselves, or our denominations. We preached Christ and him crucified. In our non-witnessing times we had wonderful fellowship, and were able to lovingly discuss some things that we have different perspectives on to the edification of everyone involved in the conversation. As a result of focusing on the truth of first importance, the gospel, we were able to lovingly discuss secondary issues to the edification of the body. We were able to enjoy healthy fellowship, because the body

In light of this reality—that God is going to gain glory through Christ (isn't that what Peter said in 1 Peter 4:10-11?)—we ought to exercise our responsibility faithfully and work out our salvation with fear and trembling, because it is God who is at work in you, both to will and to work for his good pleasure.[18] God has given the church unity in purpose and calling: that we would follow him and allow him to work in and through us for the praise and glory of his name.[19] It is for this reason that God has gifted his people. We ought to use those gifts toward that end. *His* end.

Evangelism is not a spiritual gift. It is really the end *purpose* for each gift! As a teacher in the body of Christ, I employ my gift towards strengthening believers and equipping them to do their part in the church and in the world. In fact, I spend much more time teaching, and preparing to teach, in an average week than I do evangelizing. However, because of the multiplication effect of biblical discipleship, the group I minister to is able to reach multitudes of people each year with the gospel message. And we are a small group! I could never reach that many people on my own, even if I devoted myself to that fully. What I've been blessed to see as the Lord works through my ministry in the gifting he has bestowed upon me for his glory, is that more fruit is produced by the body being the body than could ever be produced if we farm out "evangelism" to some para-church ministry and/or rely solely on crusades and events to reach the masses.[20]

As stewards of the manifest glory of God, each has been given a gift (or gifts) to be employed in the church, under the headship of Christ, for the purpose of glorifying God through Christ to the world and the edification of the body. Everything that we do, whether it is eating or drinking, serving or speaking, is to be done for the glory of God.[21] Related to this, if we think we are not *gifted* for evangelism, we may mistakenly fail to discharge our duties as an ambassador for Christ because of faulty teaching on the purpose

---

was fully functioning—we had the foundation correct, and had evangelists, pastors, and teachers working together in unity on that foundation. As a result of both local churches represented understanding and walking in the *offensive* mindset, our unity was not hindered by such minor disagreements, and we were able to share Christ with thousands of people that week because of our unity. "Oh, when will that time come, when all differences about externals shall be taken away, and we all with one heart, and one mouth glorify our Lord Jesus Christ!" (Whitefield, *Journals*, 132).

18. Phil 2:12-13.

19. See Phil 1:5-6, 11, 27-28, and 2:2 for the emphasis on unity of spirit, mind, and purpose in the gospel leading up to the Day of Christ as the life worthy of our calling as a Christian.

20. That's not to say that we should stop doing massive evangelism crusades; 1 Cor 9:22-23.

21. E.g., Rom 11:36.

of our personal spiritual giftedness. Regardless of your particular gifting, every Christian is called to participate in the evangelism of the whole world through proclaiming the excellencies of him who called you out of darkness into his marvelous light.[22] You may never proclaim the gospel to an assembled multitude—but are you equipped to proclaim the gospel to those in your sphere of influence and those who share your place in time and geographical region? Are you moving beyond simply being equipped to actually walking in obedience to this calling by opening your mouth and sharing the word of life with those who are perishing?

In this light, the offices which are listed in Ephesians 4:11 make even more sense. We have a faith that is revealed from the living God, so there were revelatory offices of Apostles and Prophets that received this faith once and for all[23]—it is not coincidental that Christ's design for his church is being revealed through the Apostle Paul in his letter to the church at Ephesus. It is to this revealed faith that the church must cling and be built from. It is this faith that is the foundation for everything that we do,[24] not the passing winds and waves of doctrine and teaching that continue to roll through the church and seek to get us off course.[25]

Without Christ, our doctrines are worthless—we would still be dead in our trespasses and sins and would perish for our rebellion against the king of heaven.[26] This is why we should not preach ourselves, our denominations, or our favorite teachers.[27] We must preach Christ and him alone.[28] There will not be a theology exam at the end of this life. There will be an examination of our position in Christ. This examination is pass/fail and is not graded on a curve. So much of our modern disunity stems from the same error that was being perpetrated in Corinth, defining ourselves not by Christ alone, but by our favorite teachers and preachers. Our present church culture makes a big deal about being a "Calvinist" or an "Arminian." Was John Calvin crucified for you? Were you baptized in the name of John Wesley?[29]

Thankfully, we are not without Christ. Upon this foundation, Jesus himself has built both primarily external offices (evangelists) and primarily internal offices (pastors and teachers). These offices are designed to work

---

22. See chap. 5, "Ambassadors for Christ."
23. Eph 3:4–5; Jude 1:3.
24. Eph 2:19–22.
25. Eph 4:14.
26. 1 Cor 15:17.
27. 2 Cor 4:5.
28. 1 Cor 2:2; Col 1:28; 1 Pet 2:9.
29. See Paul's discussion in 1 Cor 1:10–31.

together in unity to equip the saints through discipleship training and leading the church out into the world to proclaim the good news of the gospel in fulfillment of the will of God. None of the offices are more important than the other. All are needed in maintaining unity and growing in maturity and love.[30] Evangelists, like pastors, may be differently equipped and gifted by God to serve the needs of their particular local body. It is a mistake of the worst sort to believe that the role of the offices in the church is to do all the ministry as the hired professionals! The evangelist and the pastor both exist to serve the body, equip the body, and lead the body in the task of making disciples of all nations.

We are the body of Christ. We exist to glorify God. We take our marching orders from the head, who is Christ, and he has commanded that we fulfill the great commission: "And Jesus came up and spoke to them, saying, 'All authority has been given to Me in heaven and on earth. Go therefore and make disciples of all the nations, baptizing them in the name of the Father and the Son and the Holy Spirit, teaching them to observe all that I commanded you; and lo, I am with you always, even to the end of the age'" (Matt 28:18–20).

In order to fulfill this commission, our Lord and master has gifted each individually for their part and has given officers to govern his church and ensure that the body is equipped and growing in unity, maturity, and love. Jesus did this because of his care for his people and to fulfill what he promised when he said that he would build his church.[31] In this way, each member is important in fulfilling the overall purpose and mission of the church, which is to evangelize the whole world for the glory of God through his Christ and make disciples of all nations.[32]

To view *evangelism* as a gift given only to some is to misunderstand the entire purpose of the spiritual gifts in general and leads to confusion and disunity amongst the body of Christ. When we separate our spiritual gifts from their intended purpose, we fail to exercise them in love (obedience) for our God[33] and for our brothers and sisters. When we do so, our gifts become about *us* and not about *God* and his glory. Accordingly, we tend

---

30. Eph 4:12–16.

31. Matt 16:18.

32. There is some debate today as to how disciples are made. In the interest of full disclosure, I believe that you can make disciples only of those who are born-again. Therefore, the initial step in "making disciples" involves *going* to the lost and evangelizing, so that those who are converted can be initiated into the community of faith through baptism, and then be discipled (taught to observe). You don't turn a *goat* into a *sheep* by making it act like a sheep. You teach sheep how to be sheep, after the Lord makes them a new creature.

33. See 1 John 5:3.

to clump ourselves together with those who are similarly gifted because we can appreciate each other. It can be difficult to spend a lot of time with others who are gifted differently than us, because they make us uncomfortable and stress things we do not stress. This is why Scripture urges Christians in Ephesians 4:1-3 to make every effort to tolerate one another and to be diligent to maintain our unity of the Spirit. Do you think it is a coincidence that this instruction is found in discussing Christ's design for his church? When we ignore this instruction, we end up where we are now—a divided body that has little tolerance for Christians of different denominations. The world is perishing while we have a church on every corner![34]

In truth, if you belong to Christ then you have been gifted by God to glorify him in the church and in the world. Everything you have been entrusted with in this life, including your spiritual gift(s), are to be stewarded with the singular purpose of glorifying God through Christ. The church exists to proclaim God's glory to the world and to make disciples of all nations. You and your gift (if you are truly a member of the church) are no exception.

Jesus prayed for the unity of his followers in John 17, and it's worth reading again. What he prayed for helps illustrate the truth of my claims above:

> I do not ask on behalf of these alone, but for those also who believe in Me through their word; that they may all be one; even as You, Father, are in Me and I in You, that they also may be in Us, so that the world may believe that You sent Me. The glory which You have given Me I have given to them, that they may be one, just as We are one; I in them and You in Me, that they may be perfected in unity, so that the world may know that You sent Me, and loved them, even as You have loved Me. (John 17:20-23)

May we be unified with our God so that the whole world may know!

It is not a coincidence that immediately after Paul describes that God is able to do abundantly more than all we can ask or think, that he makes this statement:

> Therefore I, the prisoner of the Lord, implore you to walk in a manner worthy of the calling with which you have been called,

---

34. George Whitefield made similar observations when discoursing on Eph 4, "from whence I took occasion to urge on them the necessity of loving one another with a catholic [universal] disinterested love, to be of one heart and one mind, and to join without respect of persons in hastening the Kingdom of our Lord Jesus Christ. I hope God gave a blessing to what was said, for I observed they came constantly afterwards, and was told there was a perfect harmony between them. What infinite mischief have needless divisions occasioned in the Christian world! *Divide et impera*, is the Devil's motto" (Whitefield, *Journals*, 133).

with all humility and gentleness, with patience, showing tolerance for one another in love, being diligent to preserve the unity of the Spirit in the bond of peace. There is one body and one Spirit, just as also you were called in one hope of your calling; one Lord, one faith, one baptism, one God and Father of all who is over all and through all and in all. But to each one of us grace was given according to the measure of Christ's gift. (Eph 4:1–7)

Why do we not experience God doing abundantly more than all we can ask or think today in the American church? Could it be because we have so "improved" upon God's design and plan that we have actually *handicapped* it? We have divided the body of Christ into so many different denominations, how can we possibly claim that we have been diligent to preserve the unity of the Spirit? Are we surprised that a congregation of "hands" and a congregation of "feet" and a congregation of "tongues" make no more impact in our dead world than a literal pile of dismembered body parts would? A unified body working together is amazing. A dismembered body is useless.

Regretfully, much of the professing church today is more concerned with preserving their "brand" and "denominational distinctiveness" than they are in promoting the pure and undiluted gospel of Jesus Christ. Many circles are more interested in promoting certain teachers of the faith than they are in proclaiming to sinners their need for repentance and faith in Jesus Christ who alone can save them from their sin. In addition, we have told Jesus that the gifts he gave *to* his church and *for* his church are no longer necessary. We think we can pick and choose which offices we want to fill and which we want to ignore.[35]

. As the great commission was given to the church by our Lord in Matthew 28:18–20, it was that same risen Lord who gave gifts (Eph 4:7) to the church in the offices listed in Ephesians 4:11. The purpose of the church is to make disciples. The purpose of the offices in the church should work toward that same goal. The church is Jesus' discipleship machine.

The great commission itself is a singular command with three distinct aspects. The commandment is to *make disciples*, and this command requires three related but separate activities: *going, baptizing,* and *teaching*. Since the world is dead in sin and there are none who seek after God,[36] God himself, through his electing love, has lavished his grace upon vessels of mercy throughout history (e.g., Noah, Abraham, Isaac, Jacob, Moses, and Paul) so that the good news of God's saving grace would be proclaimed to the world.

---

35. Or, perhaps, which offices we get to redefine.
36. Rom 3:11.

This is the work that Jesus came to do: to seek and save that which was lost.[37] Jesus has accomplished the work that the Father gave him to do[38] and Jesus now calls his followers to join him in this same work until the Day of Christ Jesus.

> *As You sent Me into the world, I also have sent them into the world.* For their sakes I sanctify Myself, that they themselves also may be sanctified in truth. I do not ask on behalf of these alone, but for those also who believe in Me through their word; that they may all be one; even as You, Father, are in Me and I in You, that they also may be in Us, so that the world may believe that You sent Me. (John 17:18–21, emphasis added)

Jesus prayed that all who would believe through the faithful proclamation of the gospel would be one with the Father, Son, and Holy Spirit in seeking and saving that which is lost, so that the whole world may believe that the Father sent Jesus to redeem a people for himself. The genius of our Lord's design is apparent. He came and did his work and called his first disciples to be unified in it. He prayed for them, knowing that if they were unified in this work, the Holy Spirit would use their faithfulness to accomplish all the Lord's purposes in glorifying his name to the ends of the earth, in drawing people to himself, and in redeeming a people from every tribe, tongue, and nation.

This process is still ongoing. It's a cycle.

Followers of Christ go into the world boldly proclaiming the gospel to every creature under heaven. This gospel, which is the power of God unto salvation for all who believe, does its work in the hearts of people everywhere, either hardening or softening hearts.[39] To those who respond to the gospel call to repent and believe in Jesus, they are initiated into the faith through baptism in the name of the Father, Son, and Holy Spirit as a testimony that they have passed from death to life and are now living under the lordship of Jesus Christ and trusting in him alone for their salvation from the wrath that is to come. All who are baptized begin to be equipped—being taught to obey everything that Jesus commanded, which includes the command to "go" and tell the world the gospel.

---

37. Luke 19:10.
38. John 17:4.
39. E.g., 1 Cor 1:21–31; 2 Cor 2:14–17.

The cycle repeats.

Understanding that this call is for the *church*, and not simply for the *individual*, we can likewise see the further genius in the Lord's giving of offices to govern this process and ensure its success, in addition to gifting the body as he wills; to ensure that his people have everything they need to continue walking in his calling. Instead of relying upon human wisdom, divine revelation was given to Apostles and Prophets. These offices received the faith once for all and we have this revelation recorded in the Scriptures.[40] These sixty six books that we call the Bible, written by Apostles and Prophets, contain the foundation of everything Christians need to know and obey. These writings testify of Jesus and demonstrate that he alone is the Savior. This is why the Apostle Paul describes the work of the church as being built upon this foundation:

> So then you are no longer strangers and aliens, but you are fellow citizens with the saints, and are of God's household, having been built on the foundation of the apostles and prophets, Christ Jesus Himself being the corner stone, in whom the whole building, being fitted together, is growing into a holy temple in the Lord, in whom you also are being built together into a dwelling of God in the Spirit. For this reason I, Paul, the prisoner of Christ Jesus for the sake of you Gentiles—if indeed you have heard of the stewardship of God's grace which was given to me for you; that by revelation there was made known to me the mystery, as I wrote before in brief. By referring to this, when you read you can understand my insight into the mystery of Christ, which in other generations was not made known to the sons of men, as it has now been revealed to His holy apostles and prophets in the

---

40. Jude 1:3.

Spirit; to be specific, that the Gentiles are fellow heirs and fellow members of the body, and fellow partakers of the promise in Christ Jesus through the gospel, of which I was made a minister, according to the gift of God's grace which was given to me according to the working of His power. (Eph 2:19—3:7)

According to the biblical worldview, the present world lies in the power of the devil[41] as a result of human-kind's rebellion against God. Jesus came to initiate and inaugurate the kingdom of God. Jesus promised that he would build his church, and that the church would steadily advance and tear down the gates of the kingdom of hades which is established on this earth.[42] Therefore, in our present age there are two competing kingdoms: the kingdom of light and the kingdom of darkness. The offices of evangelist and pastor and teacher are established to minister to both of these kingdoms and lead the people of God—the church—into fulfilling the great commission to make disciples of all nations, built upon the foundation of the Apostles and Prophets, and upon the gospel of Jesus Christ.

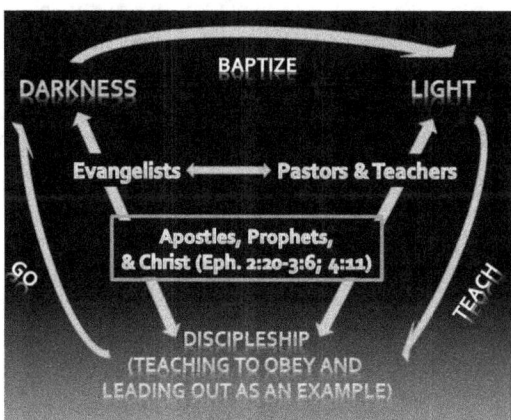

When viewed together, we can see how these offices are a gift from the Lord Jesus to continue the cycle of discipleship for the advance of his kingdom, to the praise and glory of his name.

---

41. E.g., 1 John 5:19.
42. Matt 16:18.

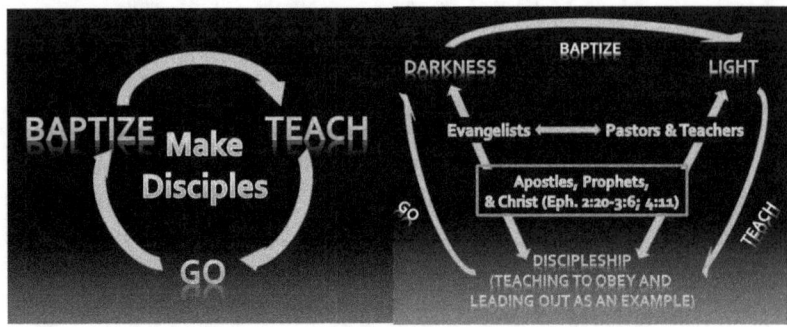

Praise God for his wisdom and for the gifts that he gave!

> And He gave some as apostles, and some as prophets, and some as evangelists, and some as pastors and teachers, for the equipping of the saints for the work of service, to the building up of the body of Christ; until we all attain to the unity of the faith, and of the knowledge of the Son of God, to a mature man, to the measure of the stature which belongs to the fullness of Christ. As a result, we are no longer to be children, tossed here and there by waves and carried about by every wind of doctrine, by the trickery of men, by craftiness in deceitful scheming; but speaking the truth in love, we are to grow up in all aspects into Him who is the head, even Christ, from whom the whole body, being fitted and held together by what every joint supplies, according to the proper working of each individual part, causes the growth of the body for the building up of itself in love. (Eph 4:11–16)

To remove any office from the discipleship machine that is Christ's church is to critically damage the entire organism. Doing so brings additional challenges to unity, maturity, and love within the body of Christ while simultaneously leaving the lost without a witness of the grace of God. Each component must be properly working—the foundation must be in place, because leaving out the word of God or the gospel results in powerless preaching and teaching; the evangelist must be in place, because leaving them out the church forgets the external call to "go" to the lost and plead with them biblically to be reconciled to God and to turn to him in repentance and faith; and the pastor and teacher must be in place, because leaving them out leaves the initiated without proper teaching, care, direction, and instruction. All of these elements should be working together to emphasize the importance that all who are in Christ are new creatures; and as new creatures, we have all received the ministry of reconciliation as ambassadors for Christ.[43] As ambassadors, we must be properly equipped, and we must walk in our calling.

We cannot improve upon Jesus' design for his church. Why would we try? Sadly, the professing church in America has all but forgotten the office of evangelist.[44] This is why we started Fourth Year Ministries in the first place: to raise awareness of the vacancy of the office of evangelist in the local church setting and to raise up, equip, and establish evangelists to fill that vacancy for the glory of God. It has not won us a lot of friends to point out that if this is true, most of the local fellowships in our land have been operating without a critical office that Jesus intended for most of, if not all of, their existence. However, if we have been wrong in the past, does that require that we continue to be wrong moving forward? If we have had a vacant office, should that mean that we refuse to fill it now that we know it is vacant? God's call to the world and to his people is the same as it has always been: repent and trust in Christ. If we have left Jesus out of any part of our church designs, we should repent and trust that he knows better than we do.

Unfortunately, much of our church culture in America reflects the attitude of the Pharisees. We forsake the commandment of God for the (denominational) traditions of men. My heart breaks over the reality of how difficult it is to partner with established local churches in evangelizing the world, or discussing a plan to try and fill the office of evangelist in the local church, because "that's not the way we do things." That is true, but it is answering the wrong question—we know that is not the way you are *currently* conducting ministry, but the question is actually this: *should* you change the way you do things to be in line with what is taught about Christ's church in Ephesians 4:11–16?

Christ's design for his church has been largely forgotten in our current culture and has often been replaced with a "business model" approach that

---

43. 2 Cor 5:6–21.

44. Some local churches have staffed the position of "Outreach Pastor" or some similar title. In many cases, however, this position is responsible for attempting to market the local church and grow the mini-kingdom of the local body they serve. If the job description focuses more on planning and inviting people to events than it does in equipping the saints to faithfully proclaim the gospel, then this is *not* equivalent to filling the office of evangelist as designed by Jesus.

runs the church like a business. While this has been wildly successful in producing "fruit" we can see and measure,[45] it has also taken us further away from the design of our living God, who is the head of the body. Many congregations have forsaken the authority of the Scriptures. Many congregations have strayed from biblical teaching and have substituted false gospels for the true one, or preach a deficient form of Christianity that can be equated with moralism. Virtually every congregation has either ignored the office of evangelist, redefined it to be a "missionary" that is not responsible for *equipping* and *leading* out the people of that same congregation, or has pushed evangelists out into para-church ministry. Shouldn't we be alarmed that our present system of operating the church has required a secondary ministry stream to come alongside (the "para-church" ministry) and help? Did Jesus declare that he would build his church with the help of para-church ministries?[46]

It is true that returning to Christ's design may result in the same types of experiences that Jesus himself and the apostles all faced. Some people will get angry.[47] Many who claim to be his disciples may turn away and grumble, no longer continuing to follow him.[48] Those ministries that continue to distort the gospel and make it "easy" to follow Jesus may continue to grow and grow. If we are afraid of these results—because they are uncomfortable or because they will make it challenging to maintain our present facilities and build our own "mini-kingdoms"—we will continue to walk in our ways and try to improve upon Jesus' design. If we will repent and return to his design,

---

45. Remember the discussion from chap. 8, "Fruit Inspectors."

46. Some may find it ironic that someone who leads a para-church ministry is critiquing para-church ministries! However, Fourth Year Ministries does not believe that we are the answer. The church being the church Jesus designed is the answer. We believe in the power of the church, especially when it is operating at full capacity. Our ministry does not seek to come alongside and help where we think the church is inadequate, but simply to help show the church that she is not operating as designed. Once the office of evangelist is filled, the local church does not need Fourth Year Ministries to come alongside and help any longer. In addition, the staff members of Fourth Year Ministries serve within the local church ministry as a full-time pastor and evangelist, because the church is God's instrument for declaring his glory to the ends of the earth. If we could operate in this role from within the local church alone, we would. Sadly, the defensive mindset of many local churches makes it easier to minister across denominational lines when operating in the para-church ministry instead of the local church ministry. Even still, the ministry model of Fourth Year Ministries would be better described as an eis-church ministry than a para-church ministry, because we seek to work within, not alongside, the church.

47. John 15:18; 2 Tim 3:12.

48. John 6:60–69; Phil 3:17–21; 2 Tim 4:10–16.

we may risk losing some of the tares among the wheat.[49] Yet, might we also see God do abundantly more than all we can ask or imagine through his power which is at work in his church? Isn't that what Paul said God would do in Ephesians 3:20–21 right before describing Jesus' design for his church in 4:1–16?

We must face the reality that we have redesigned the church and deviated from the plans that Christ himself instituted. We have taken upon ourselves authority that was never ours to administer. It is time for us to stand up and confess that the system we have received for operating Christ's church is less than ideal. It is time for us to repent and return to the Lord's design so that he can genuinely have his way in our midst again.

Do you see how this is so much bigger than a question about the size of our congregation or the location we meet? It is a *systemic* question that points to the bigger reality that we have strayed so far from Christ's design that the most we can expect from our congregations now is a moving service from time to time, while the world around us continues to persist in decay and spiritual death.

> Blessed are you when people insult you and persecute you, and falsely say all kinds of evil against you because of Me. Rejoice and be glad, for your reward in heaven is great; for in the same way they persecuted the prophets who were before you. You are the salt of the earth; but if the salt has become tasteless, how can it be made salty again? It is no longer good for anything, except to be thrown out and trampled under foot by men. You are the light of the world. A city set on a hill cannot be hidden; nor does anyone light a lamp and put it under a basket, but on the lampstand, and it gives light to all who are in the house. Let your light shine before men in such a way that they may see your good works, and glorify your Father who is in heaven. (Matt 5:11–16)

I think Jesus was serious about this. Do you? It is true that if you speak out boldly with the gospel of Jesus Christ, people will insult you. Walking by faith, not by sight, says that this is a blessing. I can testify from personal experience that trying to walk in this calling will result in people saying all sorts of things about you that are not true. I would also be lying if I said that this was pleasant. However, Jesus is worth it. Actually, he is worthy of much, *much* more.

It is important to make a clear statement here of what I am *not* saying. I am not saying that I have come up with a new model that you should implement in your church to experience growth. I am not advocating my

---

49. Matt 13:24–30.

personal philosophy or hoping that I can convince you this is right because of my vast personal experience. I am not saying that you should follow *me*. On the contrary, we need to follow Jesus. What I am calling for is for followers of Christ to stop being tossed here and there by every wind of "church growth" strategy and to get back to the design of the head of the church, since he promised he would build his church. We might as well do it his way.[50] We need him. And, we need each other. The body doesn't function correctly unless we all do our part.

Remember when Joshua encountered the Angel of the Lord in Joshua 5?

> Now it came about when Joshua was by Jericho, that he lifted up his eyes and looked, and behold, a man was standing opposite him with his sword drawn in his hand, and Joshua went to him and said to him, "Are you for us or for our adversaries?" He said, "No; rather I indeed come now as captain of the host of the LORD." And Joshua fell on his face to the earth, and bowed down, and said to him, "What has my lord to say to his servant?" (Josh 5:13-14)

If we are going to choose sides, doesn't it make sense to be sure that we are on the Lord's side? He is the Lord, we are his servants. He has told us *what* we are supposed to do and *how* we are supposed to do it. God does not need us to try to improve upon his methods or to suggest alternatives.[51] I would be the first to admit that what God asks us to do is uncomfortable and not what I would choose to do on my own. That is why he told us ahead of time that walking with the Spirit of the living God means doing things contrary to what our flesh would do.[52] This is why we need to be born-again through the grace of God and to be set free in order to walk with him.[53]

I find it hard to come to any other conclusion than much of what we have made the church to be in our culture today is really just an elaborate basket under which we hide our light. How long will God allow us to persist in this state before he takes away our lampstand and raises up the next generation to see if they will be faithful and obedient to his call on their lives?[54]

---

50. Ps 127:1. It is a reality that Jesus is not as concerned about maintaining our facilities and programs as he is about his gospel being proclaimed to the ends of the earth. When we prioritize our programs and facilities above his program, it is no wonder we exclude him from our governing structures.

51. See also 2 Chr 15:1-2.

52. Gal 5:17.

53. Gal 5:1, 13.

54. Esth 4:14.

I don't know about you, but I'd rather not test to see where that line is. God expects fruit. When fruit is not produced, the tree is worth cutting down.[55]

Instead, let us heed the wise and inspired counsel from the Apostle Paul in his epistle to the Ephesians, where he has already been speaking so much about the nature, purpose, and design of the church: "For this reason it says, 'Awake, sleeper, And arise from the dead, And Christ will shine on you.' Therefore be careful how you walk, not as unwise men but as wise, making the most of your time, because the days are evil. So then do not be foolish, but understand what the will of the Lord is" (Eph 5:14–17).

It is time for those who are following Jesus to wake up and to walk wisely according to his revealed will. The church is God's chosen instrument for revealing his glory to the ends of the earth through the faithful proclamation of his gospel. God has designed an offensive church and he has provided everything we need through his abundant grace and power, through equipping his people with spiritual gifts, raising up leaders for the equipping of the body, and empowering each genuine believer with his own abiding presence. What an awesome God we serve!

Get equipped. Obey your king. Glorify your God.

---

55. The parable Jesus told in Luke 13:6–9 was the inspiration for the name of Fourth Year Ministries. Our greatest desire is to be used by God to help reawaken the church to God's original design, so that local churches will bring forth abundant fruit for our master and king. We have been fortunate to witness this become a reality—one local church in particular comes to mind that filled the office of evangelist for the first time and saw more than one hundred professions of faith within the first eight months, which was the fruit of a small group of between five to twenty people taking the call to live as ambassadors for Christ seriously. Praise God!

11

A Theological Tapestry of Field-Preaching

> And the master said to the slave, "Go out into the highways and along the hedges, and compel them to come in, so that my house may be filled."
> (Luke 14:23)

WHY STUDY CHARLES WESLEY?

The author of Hebrews points our attention to the "great cloud of witnesses surrounding us"[1] in order to be an encouragement for followers of Christ to run the race set before them. Hebrews 11 provides a record of some of the aspects of the lives of the saints in this great cloud of witnesses. As a result of this scriptural encouragement to examine the lives of followers of Christ who have gone before us, we will conclude with an examination of a brother in Christ from a previous era: Charles Wesley. This Wesley brother has largely been overshadowed by other key figures in the so-called Great Awakening,[2] which is a shame. In particular, we want to find out what can

---

1. Heb 12:1.

2. Historian Earl Cairns describes the Great Awakening (1726–56) as, "a series of simultaneous, spontaneous, unorganized, rural or village congregational awakenings led by godly pastors such as Jonathan Edwards" (Cairns, *Christianity*, 365).

be gleaned from the life and theology of this faithful brother and his role in expanding the kingdom of God through obedience to our risen king, Jesus. What is particularly enlightening about the life of Charles is the transformation that took place in him as he wrestled with many of the same issues described in the previous chapters.

Focusing on Charles Wesley is instructive because his theology influenced his practice, changing him from a "proper" Anglican clergyman into a bold and effective field-preacher. In describing his initial aversion to the practice of preaching in the open air by George Whitefield, John Wesley stated, "I should have thought the saving of souls *almost a sin* . . . if it had not been done *in a church*."[3] This idea is not all that uncommon today, as it is taboo to discuss religion outside of the acceptable circles and contexts.

Charles's transformation into a bold open air preacher and the responses he received over a large sample size were undeniably biblical. While this may be a strange sounding comment—that someone had "biblical" experiences—the claim is important. For many modern believers, their reading of the biblical text does not match up with their experience of the church. The church described in Acts had an undeniable impact on the surrounding culture and spread with a force[4] that demonstrated the power of God was behind it and coursing through it.

The church in the United States is decidedly and emphatically less powerful. This has less to do with arguments over whether or not the sign gifts (e.g., tongues, healing, prophecy, etc.) are still for the church today, and more to do with the reality that many of the "decisions" we are recording for Christ come with absolutely no evidence of a transformed individual and even less concrete evidence that our communities are being changed for the better. Should we expect that being transferred from death to life[5] would have such trivial observable effects in individuals and communities? Does the biblical record allow such low expectations—even without miraculous signs and wonders? I am compelled to argue that the answer to these questions is an emphatic, "No."

The historical situation of Charles Wesley bears a clear resemblance to the present state of the American church.[6] Despite the major difference

---

3. Collins, *John Wesley*, 103, italics in original. Of course, John Wesley also changed his mind on this and remains the more famous field-preacher between the two Wesley brothers.

4. That "force" was nonviolent. It could not be stopped even when extreme violence was used against it.

5. E.g., Eph 2:5; Col 2:13.

6. Charles's poem entitled "Modern Christianity"—although written more than three centuries ago—is still an appropriate title, as it describes the state of American

of the Church of England being largely *united* under the banner of Anglicanism, and the church in America being largely *divided* under the banner of denominationalism, the reality of pulpits spreading *moralism* instead of the genuine gospel is a fact of both Charles's generation and our own. In addition, Charles lamented the opposition of those who are "Christian-in-name-only,"[7] who believed their society to be "Christian" when really it is not. This, too, is a description of our own time. It can easily be argued that our Christian heritage has influenced our culture, but there is a vast difference between being *Christian* and being *Christianized*. Our current American culture may very well be Christianized, but we are by no means Christian.

Michael Brown pointedly and accurately states,

> as American "believers" we: spend hours watching television but minutes watching in prayer; are hungry for the sports page but have little taste for the Word; spend more money on pet food than on foreign missions; love to feast but hate to fast; welcome God's blessings but are wary of His burdens. Is this what Jesus died for? Is this our "new life" in Him? Stop for a moment and think: Anyone who spends more time playing video games than seeking God in prayer has no right to call Jesus Lord. Anyone who takes delight in today's perverted soap operas is serving another god. Anyone who cannot die to sports for a season is worshiping idols. "If anyone loves this world, the love of the Father is not in him . . . because friendship with the world is hatred toward God" (1 John 2:15; James 4:4). In reality, whose friends are we?[8]

Worldliness has infiltrated the professing church in America and genuine spiritual revival is needed in our day. While genuine revival is a move of God and not of man, it is important to understand that God has declared his purposes for his people to expand his glory and kingdom to the ends of the earth. The church in America is no exception. Hebrews 11 provides a biblical precedent for studying the "cloud of witnesses" in history that have been used as instruments of God in achieving this goal of glorifying God and expanding his kingdom to the ends of the earth. Charles Wesley is one such instrument. In this chapter, quotations from Charles's works have the original spelling, punctuation, and wording left intact. As a result of the

---

Christianity today. See Kimbrough and Beckerlegge, *Unpublished*, 3:198–9.

7. George Whitefield sometimes used the term "almost-Christians" in referring to the same types of experiences and people; see, e.g., Whitefield, *Journals*, 50.

8. Brown, *How Saved*, 1–2.

large number of variations from modern conventions, and the desire for readability, the normal use of *sic* will not be used, in lieu of this more general notice that these deviations are present.[9]

An investigation of Charles Wesley's theology of field-preaching demonstrates that theology is like a tapestry.[10] No doctrine stands on its own; each is related to, affected by, and exerts influence upon other "strands" of related theology. The theological tapestry of Charles Wesley resulted in his being used mightily as an instrument of God for revival and for expanding the kingdom and glory of God in his day. The effects are still felt today—more than 225 years after his death in 1788! Understanding this theology (and even more importantly, being changed by it as Charles was) will be instructive for followers of Christ today in orienting ourselves to likewise be instruments of revival in our own day. If and when God decides to move amongst his people is up to him. His followers are simply commanded to be faithful, ready, and obedient.

Few authors have considered the relevance and impact of field-preaching as it relates to genuine revivals throughout the history of the world. There is a need for further investigation of what happens when preaching in the highways and byways becomes the focus for God's people. It is the claim of this chapter that field-preaching is a critical element in the advance of the kingdom and glory of God, and that any serious study of revival should include this aspect as of primary importance.

Christian bookstores and websites are replete with new resources, methods, and programs that are "guaranteed" to bring results. However, the fruit of such manmade strategies has proven to be short-lived and shallow.[11] Genuine revival will only come about as a result of using God's prescribed methods and means. If you study the Great Awakening, and the men who were used to bring it about, George Whitefield is often credited with being the "innovator of field-preaching." However, this is revisionist history. Whitefield may have been the first to make use of this practice *amongst his contemporaries*, but the Scriptures are filled with field-preachers who all predate Mr. Whitefield.

Charles Spurgeon quipped:

> Now, it can be argued, with small fear of refutation, that open-air preaching is as old as preaching itself. We are at full liberty to believe that Enoch, the seventh from Adam, when he

---

9. For a discussion of the sources used for this chapter, see appendix C.

10. I am indebted to my first theology professor, Dr. John Jelinek, for introducing me to the terminology and concept of "a theological tapestry."

11. For more on this, see Brown, *How Saved*, 43–50.

prophesied, asked for no better pulpit than the hill-side, and that Noah, as a preacher of righteousness, was willing to reason with his contemporaries in the ship-yard wherein his marvelous ark was builded. Certainly, Moses and Joshua found their most convenient place for addressing vast assemblies beneath the unpillared arch of heaven.[12]

Spurgeon lists further examples of field-preachers such as Samuel, Elijah, Jonah, Ezra, Nehemiah, John the Baptist, Jesus, the Apostles, and many others who make up the "great cloud of witnesses" between the first century and his own time. Spurgeon also makes the remarkable claim that "it would be very easy to prove that revivals of religion have usually been accompanied, if not caused, by a considerable amount of preaching out of doors, or in unusual places."[13] This claim is worth its own book and is well beyond the scope of the present chapter. It is certainly true of the revival that occurred, at least in part, as a result of the open air preaching ministries of the Methodists—particularly the best known George Whitefield and the Wesley brothers.

Spurgeon continues to claim that "it is most interesting to observe that congregational singing is sure to revive at the same moment as gospel-preaching. In all ages a Moody has been attended by a Sankey. History repeats itself because like causes are pretty sure to produce like effects."[14] In the case of Charles Wesley, both the hymnist and gospel-preacher are embodied in the same person. It would be poor historical analysis to remember Charles as the "Sankey" to John or Whitefield's "Moody." While broader research would be required to either confirm or deny Spurgeon's sweeping historical claim, he was right on target when describing the Great Awakening. I am inclined to agree with him that like causes produce like effects, which is a reason for hope. This is especially true when considering that like faithfulness to the word of God, and his prescribed methods for expanding his kingdom, would result in like effects of genuine revival, regardless of differing contexts.

As the theology of Charles is investigated, there will be many who simply want to disregard the methods of field-preaching because they are uncomfortable and out of the ordinary for modern Christian experience. Full disclosure: *I am one of them.* My preference would be that none of what follows be true. My personality is that of an extreme introvert. I once was in a situation where we were forced to introduce ourselves and tell a little

12. Spurgeon, *Lectures*, 234.
13. Ibid., 236.
14. Ibid., 238.

bit about ourselves as an ice-breaker, and I followed shortly after a gentleman who described himself as "An extrovert. That means I love people!" My introduction stated, "Unlike our friend, I am an introvert. That means I also love people . . . I just can't stand being around them." I wish I was kidding. In many ways, I admire extroverts. I simply do not enjoy spending any large amount of time with almost anyone—even people that I genuinely like! I am drained by being around people. As a result, starting conversations (especially with people I do not know) is extremely burdensome for me. Being the center of attention, especially doing something like preaching the gospel on a street corner, is the last thing I would choose to do for fun and does not come naturally to me. Nevertheless, we are called to walk by the Spirit, not by the flesh.[15]

Many within the professing church view street corner evangelists and open air preachers as lunatics and fanatics. This is one of the most important reasons for studying Charles in particular. His theological understanding guided his practice and led him through a transition from ministering primarily inside of the "proper church channels" to being a bold open air evangelist. It is perhaps here that our cultural Christianity most closely touches Charles's: we are accustomed to gospel preaching being confined to church buildings, and other structures assembled for that purpose, and may even view anything outside of this normal mode as "a shocking innovation, a sure token of heretical tendencies, and a mark of zeal without knowledge."[16] To be sure, I personally have been accused of all three. However, the Scriptures command Christians not to be conformed to the patterns of this world, but to be transformed by the renewing of our minds.[17] The people of God are not to be influenced by the cultural representation of our Christian faith, but by the biblical standards!

It doesn't matter if our culture has been "Christianized." We must never nullify the commands of God by the traditions of men—even "Christian" men![18] Spurgeon once again struck at the heart of this issue when he wrote, "no sort of defense is needed for preaching out of doors; but it would need very potent arguments to prove that a man had done his duty who has never preached beyond the walls of his meeting-house [church building]. A defense is required rather for services within buildings than for worship outside of them."[19] Building a case for proclaiming the gospel exclusively

15. Gal 5:16–17.
16. Spurgeon, *Lectures*, 254.
17. Rom 12:2.
18. Mark 7:8.
19. Spurgeon, *Lectures*, 254.

within church buildings is essentially a case for hiding our lamp under a basket—albeit, often very elaborately constructed baskets. As Christians, we are instructed not to do this.[20]

The claims and conclusions of this chapter may be difficult to accept because they call for drastic steps for most modern American followers of Christ. There is a tendency in some to elevate the "saints" of the past to heights that the modern Christian cannot attain. Some believe that the likes of Saint Paul and the Wesley brothers are rightly captured on stained glass windows and admired as near superheroes of the faith. But to take the Apostle Paul and Charles Wesley on their own terms, they described themselves as weak and frail. Their power came, not from superhuman abilities, but from a humble submission to their Lord and reliance upon his Spirit to empower them for his service.[21] Charles ministered despite his frail health and attributed his success to the work of God in him, writing in his journal: "My pain and disease increased for ten days, so that there was no hope of my life. But then Jesus touched my hand, and rebuked the fever, and it left me. I had no apprehension of death myself. *It was reported I was dead, and published in the papers*. But God had not finished (O that he had effectually begun) his work in me."[22] A close reading of the heroes of the faith included in Hebrews 11 should immediately discredit the idea that God makes use of "super saints" for big jobs and has little use for the rest of us. On the contrary, God consistently uses broken and sinful people to accomplish his great purposes. It is why he has redeemed us. It's also why God alone receives the glory.[23]

We are no different than Charles Wesley. The same Spirit that lived in him lives in all who have repented of their rebellion and sin and who have put their faith in Jesus as Lord and Savior.[24] The same Spirit which used Charles Wesley to advance the kingdom and glory of God is able to do the same in willing, yielded vessels today. God did not do this through "new" innovations, but through humble and obedient vessels who returned to the "old" methods of God which have been used by the prophets, apostles, and our Lord Jesus himself, to spread the glory and kingdom of God.[25]

One final introductory note should be made on the terminology of "revival" and "field-preaching." First, "revival" is used with different

20. Mark 4:21–23.
21. E.g., 1 Cor 1:27; 2:3; 2 Cor 3:4–6; 12:9–10.
22. Kimbrough and Newport, *Manuscript Journal*, 1:277, emphasis added.
23. E.g., Isa 43:25; 44:21–23.
24. Rom 8:11.
25. 1 Cor 1:21–24.

connotations and qualifications by different authors, so a clarification on exactly what is meant in the present chapter is in order. As revival is discussed here, what is meant is a spiritual stirring or awakening which happens, first in the individual believer, then in the body of Christ, and finally having a deep and lasting impact and expression in the surrounding culture.[26] With this definition in mind, one can see why it is right to study the impact of personal theology first (in this case, Charles Wesley's), then to understand how God can use an individual follower of Christ who is humble and obedient to the means and methods prescribed by God, and finally to see the impact this can have on both the church and the world as a result. If it can happen in Charles, it can happen in us.

Secondly, the term "field-preaching" is not used exclusively for preaching in a literal field—although this is certainly a true example with many historical precedents—but is more loosely defined as any preaching that happens outside of the normal confines of formal religious settings (i.e., outside of a church building or home worship service). Often field-preaching occurs spontaneously and in unexpected places, wherever people congregate. Other examples of field-preaching occur when "proper" channels are impossible to secure, e.g., the crowd is too large to be housed inside the building. If the proclamation is happening out in the open air, this meets the definition of field-preaching as loosely defined here.

CHARLES WESLEY'S THEOLOGY OF FIELD-PREACHING

Charles Wesley's theology of field-preaching is revealed by a rich theological tapestry and will require other theological doctrines being examined as well. One area of theological doctrine that will be conspicuous by its absence in this discussion is Charles's modified Arminianism as compared to the Calvinism of his contemporary, George Whitefield. It may seem necessary to delve into this theological battlefield—especially considering the fact that Charles's view of the unlimited atonement, and conviction that it was essential to offer Christ to all, was a driving force of his evangelistic and field-preaching endeavors. However, it should be carefully noted that both Whitefield and the Wesley brothers devoted much of their lives to preaching in the open air despite their theological differences in this area. Therefore, the particulars of Calvinism vs. Arminianism are purposefully left out of this discussion as they are treated adequately elsewhere. Members of both theological camps believe that the proclamation of the gospel is necessary for

26. This definition of revival is based in part on Kaiser, *Revive Us Again*, 2–18.

salvation. The conclusions reached here should not be accepted or denied as a result of the individual's theological convictions as it relates to the Calvinist/Arminian debate. Studying the Calvinistic George Whitefield's theology and practice would yield virtually identical results and is encouraged.[27]

Charles's personal theology influenced the greater revival in which Charles was a part. Christians today can learn from his example how to properly orient ourselves to spend our lives and to be spent for the praise and glory of our God. Charles wrote, "2. Freely, where'er I would, I went / Thro' Wisdom's pleasant ways, / Happy to spend, & to be spent / In ministering his grace; / I found no want of will, or power, / In love's sweet task employ'd / And put forth, every day & hour, / My utmost strength for God."[28]

Charles Wesley the Anglican

Modern reflections on Charles Wesley often view him first-and-foremost as a hymnist. It is important to recognize that he viewed himself first-and-foremost as an Anglican.[29] As a deeply committed clergyman for the Church of England, Charles Wesley had unity with the established Church constantly on his mind.[30] His refusal to separate from the Church of England as long as the true gospel remained in the Articles and Homilies was recorded by Charles's own hand in his journal regarding a conversation with the Archbishop: "We told him we expected persecution, would abide by the Church till her Articles and Homilies were repealed. He assured us he knew of no design in the governors of the Church to innovate, and neither should there be any innovation while he lived. Avowed justification by faith only, and his joy to see us often as we pleased."[31] While John is included in the "we" from this journal entry, separation became a point of contention between the brothers because of Charles's strong opposition to the ordination of Methodist ministers outside of the proper Anglican channels by John.

John's biblical theology led him to believe that he had just as much authority as anyone to ordain ministers to administer the sacrament of communion. Charles strenuously protested that to ordain Methodist ministers was in effect separation from the Church of England.[32] This contention arose because of the differing priorities of the Wesley brothers, which "Charles

---

27. A great place to start in a study of Whitefield is *George Whitefield's Journals*.
28. Kimbrough and Beckerlegge, *Unpublished*, 2:281.
29. Newport, *Sermons*, 3n1. Cf. Cairns, *Christianity*, 388.
30. Newport, *Sermons*, 14–15.
31. Kimbrough and Newport, *Manuscript Journal*, 1:162.
32. Tyson, *Assist*, 306–22.

summed up... succinctly: '[John's] first object was the Methodists and then the Church; mine was first the Church, and then the Methodists.'"[33] While John sought to do whatever he thought was needed for the spread of Methodism, Charles valued unity with the established Church over pragmatic concerns.

It is important to note that the argument regarding ordination was not over the interpretation of the scriptural authority of John as a biblical *epískopos* to ordain the ministers. The disagreement revolved around the *effects* of these ordinations. Since this was contrary to the orders of Anglicanism, Charles strenuously objected to ordaining clergy outside of the proper Anglican channels because to do so was tantamount to separation from the Church of England (which John denied).[34] Certainly, it could be debated as to which brother was correct—but for the purposes of this chapter it is enough to simply acknowledge the fact of their disagreement and recognize Charles's high commitment to unity with the Church of England, above even John's commitment to the same. John was willing to strain his relationship with the Church of England if it meant the goals of Methodism were advanced. Charles was unwilling to do anything that would cause separation from his Anglican faith unless and until they denied the central tenet of salvation by grace through faith. Charles urged John to lay down his rights and privileges if exercising those rights and privileges would strain unity and hinder the gospel.[35]

The Methodists did eventually separate from the Church of England after both John and Charles died. The new Methodist leadership—who bristled under Charles's opposition to ordination[36]—found it convenient to suppress the memory and work of Charles and instead lifted up the life and works of John.[37]

Charles gives us a glimpse into his theological aversion towards separating from the Church of England in a hymn written as a response to the ordination of ministers by John:

---

33. Newport, *Sermons*, 25.

34. See especially the letters exchanged between the brothers in August and September of 1785, as recorded in Tyson, *Reader*, 433–38.

35. In John's defense, he thought being unable to ordain clergy was a hindrance to the gospel. Both brothers wanted the gospel to advance. John thought the gospel would best advance through the Methodists, Charles thought the gospel would best advance through the Church of England.

36. For some of his hymns that captured his criticism of these ordinations, see especially Tyson, *Reader*, 423–27.

37. Tyson, *Assist*, x–xi.

> 3. Ah! where are all his Promises and Vows / To spend, & to be spent for Sion's Good, / To gather the lost sheep of Israel's house, / The Outcasts bought by his Redeemer's bl[oo]d? / 4. Who won for God the wandring Souls of men, / Subjecting multitudes to Christ's command, / He shuts his eyes, & scatters them again, / And spreads a thous[an]d Sects throughout the land.[38]

Charles saw separation from the Church of England as the seed of "a thousand sects" in America. Charles's theological view resulted in his accurately predicting the results of disunity in producing severe denominationalism in the church in America. It could be argued on the basis of the poetic genre that this was merely hyperbole, but a careful reading of his hymns and poems written as a result of John's ordinations reveal Charles's distinct theological view that this was a scheme of the devil to sow dissension and produce division and schism.[39] If Charles *was* in fact exaggerating for emphasis, he greatly *under*estimated the actual number of denominations that would eventually be formed in the American church.[40]

Although Charles's theology underwent many revisions over the course of his life, his passion for remaining an Anglican never wavered:

> Charles Wesley, for his part in all this, adhered to the original plan. He continued to view Methodism as a renewal movement that functioned best within the bounds of the Anglican communion. He clung valiantly, and stubbornly, to that original vision. At times keeping the movement within the church became Charles's chief ministry among the Methodists. But for all his efforts, the Methodists *would* separate from the Church of England and set up their own church and order of ministry. And it should be no surprise that the lay preachers he battled so long over issues of authority and separation were not prone to sing his praises or canonize his memory. But in the end, Charles got what he wanted most: he lived—and died—in the Church of England.[41]

---

38. Kimbrough and Beckerlegge, *Unpublished*, 3:87.

39. See ibid., 3:79–101.

40. Surely, the present division and amount of denominations cannot be blamed solely on the Methodists!

41. Tyson, *Assist*, 322, italics in original.

Charles Wesley the Preacher

It was this fact of Charles's passionate unity with the Church of England that made his transition into the continued regular use of field-preaching so remarkable. Prior to Charles's evangelical conversion, he took his religious duties very seriously. Trained as an Anglican clergyman, and the founder of the first Holy Club, Charles sought to earn his way to heaven through a "methodical" lifestyle of holiness. This pursuit was apparent by Charles's own words, as he described an encounter he had with the Moravian Peter Böhler:

> He asked me, "Do you hope to be saved?" "Yes." "For what reason do you hope it?" "Because I have used my best endeavours to serve God?" He shook his head, and said no more. I thought him very uncharitable, saying in my heart, "What, are not my endeavours a sufficient ground of hope? Would he rob me of my endeavours? I have nothing else to trust to."[42]

Charles's interaction with Böhler made a deeper impact just two months later as Charles was once again battling a serious illness:

> In the morning Dr. Cockburn came to see me; and a better physician, Peter Böhler, whom God had detained in England for my good. He stood by my bedside, and prayed over me, that now at least I might see the divine intention in this and my late illness. I immediately thought it might be that I should again consider Böhler's doctrine of faith; examine myself whether I was in *the faith*; and if I was not, never cease seeking and longing after it till I attained it.[43]

Charles was serious about this pursuit and realized that he was, in fact, *not* in the faith. A few short weeks after these encounters, Charles laments in his journal, "In the afternoon I seemed deeply sensible of my misery in being without Christ."[44] The following day he made an eye-opening discovery as a result of hearing Luther's commentary on Galatians:

> I marveled that we were so soon, and so entirely, removed from him that called us into the grace of Christ unto another gospel. Who would believe our Church had been founded on this important article of justification by faith alone! I am astonished I should ever think this a new doctrine, especially while our

---

42. Kimbrough and Newport, *Manuscript Journal*, 1:97.
43. Ibid., 1:100, italics in original.
44. Ibid., 1:103.

> Articles and Homilies stand unrepealed, and the key of knowledge is not yet taken away.
>
> From this time I endeavoured to ground as many of our friends as came in this fundamental truth, salvation by faith alone, not an idle, dead faith, but a faith which works by love, and is necessarily productive of all good works and all holiness.[45]

This key discovery for Charles led to his conversion experience less than one week later. It is important to remember that this conversion experience happened *after* Charles had been ordained as an Anglican clergyman, and *after* he returned to England from his troublesome adventure to America as the secretary to James Oglethorpe and to evangelize the natives. His "discovery" of the true gospel as taught in the Anglican Articles and Homilies increased his commitment to the Anglican Church because she taught the truth. At least, she was supposed to.

Up until this point, Charles had preached as a clergyman of the Church of England many times; but always in an official capacity, and in accordance with the worship guidelines of Anglicanism. As his passion for the gospel of salvation by grace through faith expanded, Charles found himself breaking through into unexplored and uncomfortable territory. Charles recorded on May 26, 1738, "In the evening I broke through my own great unwillingness, and at last preached faith in Christ to an accidental visitant."[46] It took only five days after his evangelical conversion to begin challenging some of his convictions as an Anglican clergyman as to the proper avenues to preach the gospel.[47] Charles began being bold in reaching out towards those who may not have expected (or even appreciated!) his "preaching" instead of ministering exclusively to those who did expect to hear him in a religious capacity as a minister.

The content of Charles's message had also shifted for good—from endeavoring for a works based righteousness, to a received righteousness as a result of God's grace through personal faith. Breaking into personal evangelism through proclaiming this doctrine of salvation by grace alone—and not delivering a previously crafted sermon on the importance of personal holiness and pure endeavors for the Lord—was new territory for sure!

In contrast to this quick move into bold personal evangelism, his movement towards open air preaching from the established pulpits of the Anglican Church proceeded a bit more slowly. In an interesting turn

---

45. Ibid., 1:104.

46. Ibid., 1:112.

47. Charles's conversion and subsequent activities bear resemblance to the Apostle Paul's in Acts 9:1–22.

of events, Charles demonstrated more flexibility on this particular break from the norms of Anglicanism than his brother "John—who described his [own] first attempts at field preaching as submitting 'to be more vile.'"[48] That is not to say that Charles's transition was without any difficulty; but the struggle took a different and unexpected course.

Tyson claims:

> like his brother John, Charles was a reluctant evangelist, particularly so when called upon to enter that new mode of preaching, open-air evangelism. Initially, Anglican churches and Methodist societies were the chief locations of his labors; but on June 24, 1739, he "broke down the bridge" and "became desperate" by embarking on that innovation, field preaching; thereafter Charles used streets, fields, and gardens, as well as established churches and Methodist meeting rooms.[49]

Tyson correctly identified patterns and avenues which Charles was sure to adopt. However, his description of Charles as a *reluctant* evangelist, in addition to his beginning date for Charles's shift into open air preaching, is inaccurate. Newport similarly comments that "quite precisely when Charles first engaged in the activity [of field-preaching] is not absolutely clear, but the journal indicates that by 29 May, 1739 he had, somewhat reluctantly, begun to follow in the footsteps of Whitefield."[50]

Reading Charles's journal entry from Newport's tentative proposed starting date (May 29, 1739) indicates that Tyson's date of June 24, 1739, could *not* have been his first foray into the method of field-preaching. Charles records—a full month earlier than Tyson's proposed starting date—that "Franklyn, a farmer, invited me to preach in his field. I did so, to about five hundred, on 'Repent, for the kingdom of heaven is at hand' [Matt. 3:2]. I returned to the house rejoicing."[51] Since Charles has already preached in the open air to a gathering of several hundred people, the "barrier" cannot refer to the mere act of field-preaching itself as Tyson claims.

In fact, Charles notes several instances of preaching in the open air between the dates of May 29 and June 24, 1739. Additionally, there is nothing stated in this journal entry about preaching in Franklyn's field that lends any weight to Newport's claim that Charles was "reluctant" to accept this invitation! Newport's claim of reluctance is lacking in evidence.

48. Tyson, *Reader*, 47.
49. Ibid., 13.
50. Newport, *Sermons*, 39.
51. Kimbrough and Newport, *Manuscript Journal*, 1:174.

A careful reading of Charles's journal seems to indicate that Charles was actually an *eager* evangelist after his evangelical conversion on May 21, 1738. This is the express opposite of both Tyson and Newport's reconstructions of Charles's journey into field-preaching and open air evangelism. As already detailed above, Charles broke through his initial unwillingness to preach his new understanding of faith in Christ (just five days after his conversion) on May 26, 1738, and it is recorded in entry after entry in the *MS Journal* how Charles continued to preach with boldness the "strange doctrine" of salvation by grace through faith in many different modes and differing contexts—with many coming to salvation as a result.[52]

As this evangelistic zeal continued to bubble out of Charles, he made the most of every opportunity. On August 18, 1738, (nine full months prior to the May 29, 1739, date suggested by Newport) Charles records, "at seven we all walked out, were driven by the hard rain to a shed, where we sang and preached to those about us."[53] This "reluctant" evangelist records these events with a seeming zeal, and demonstrates that he took full advantage of the opportunity that he was provided to proclaim the good news of the gospel—here turning a shelter from the elements into a pulpit from which he proclaimed the good news of Christ to everyone who happened to be nearby and were likewise seeking refuge from the storm.

It could be argued that this event of preaching in the shed does not fully constitute a move towards field-preaching, but was yet a further example of Charles's personal evangelism, which frequently took place outside of church buildings and meeting-houses, in places like carriages and homes.[54] If this case is discounted as such, then another possibility exists for Charles's first field-preaching event on Sunday, October 29, 1738, where he "preached with strength at St George's, then at Ironmongers' Almshouses, and at night expounded Rom. 5 to a large audience in the Minories."[55]

Both Newport and Tyson note the shift in Wesley's language used to describe his own preaching activity in his journal from "preached" to "expounded" as he moved increasingly towards using *ex tempore* methods in lieu of his former manuscripted sermons.[56] In the journal entry for October 29, 1738, above, we see both terms being used by Charles. Charles preached

---

52. See ibid., 1:106–80.

53. Ibid., 1:144.

54. This objection would be nitpicking, since the evangelistic proclamation is clearly happening in accordance with the working definition of "field-preaching." To disqualify this example one would need to place a limit to the number of people that must be present to hear the proclamation which would necessarily be arbitrary.

55. Kimbrough and Newport, *Manuscript Journal*, 1:151.

56. See Newport, *Sermons*, 34–37, and also Tyson, *Reader*, 15–20.

from his prepared sermon manuscript on 1 John 3:14[57] at both St. George's and Ironmongers,' then ventured into the streets at night to "expound" (or preach *ex tempore*) the gospel in the open air of the Minories, which "is a street that runs north from the Tower to Aldgate."[58] This appears to be an even more clear-cut example of field-preaching, seven months before the earlier date proposed by Newport of May 29, 1739.

Charles Wesley had been preaching regularly in the open air for seven to nine months prior to the dates cited by Tyson and Newport supposedly "breaking through the barrier." Failing to understand this will cause our understanding of Charles to be skewed even further and will lead to improper conclusions about his struggle. To properly understand Charles's struggle with preaching in the open air, it is helpful to read the full sentence from the *MS Journal* which Tyson quoted above, because it was written the day before (on June 23, 1739) his proposed starting date for Charles's "reluctant" use of the means of field-preaching and reads, "My inward conflict continued. Perceived it was the fear of man; and that, by preaching in the field next Sunday, as George Whitefield urges me, I shall break down the bridge and become desperate. Retired, and prayed for particular direction, offering up my friends, my liberty, my life, for Christ's sake and the gospel's."[59] On the following day (June 24, 1739), Charles does preach to a gathering of nearly ten thousand people and recounts that "my load was gone, and all my doubts and scruples. God shone upon my path, and I knew this was his will concerning me."[60] If his inward conflict was not about the decision to make use of the fields for the first time—which is impossible, since Charles had preached under similar circumstances regularly for months—as Tyson claims, then what was it?

A better understanding of this struggle is that it is the opposition from his fellow clergymen in the Church of England that was causing his conflict. Charles demonstrated from the very earliest stages after his conversion experience that he was not reluctant to proclaim the good news to any and all, across diverse contexts. In fact, as a clergyman who was already well-versed in the Scriptures, Charles had a clear understanding that opposition and persecution would come. He argued this with a man named Mr. Chapman, who "insisted that there is no need of our being persecuted now. I told him I was of a different judgment, and believed every doctrine of God must have

---

57. Kimbrough and Newport, *Manuscript Journal*, 1:151nn110–11. See also Newport, *Sermons*, 132.

58. Kimbrough and Newport, *Manuscript Journal*, 1:151n112.

59. Ibid., 1:179.

60. Ibid., 1:180.

these two marks: 1) meeting all the opposition of men and devils, 2) triumphing over all."[61] What Charles did *not* expect was the hostility from his fellow clergymen, as he did not say he expected the doctrine to meet "all the opposition of men and devils *and churchmen.*"

Charles notes a meeting he and his brother John had with the Bishop of London on October 20, 1738, in response to complaints about their preaching of salvation by grace through faith alone. On November 12, 1738, Charles notes that "Mr Piers refused me his pulpit, through fear of man, pretending tenderness to his flock. I plainly told him, if he so rejected my testimony, I would come to see him no more."[62]

The opposition within the Church of England continued to grow. Charles found himself answering objections and accusations on a more regular basis from among his fellow clergymen. This opposition from his fellow Anglicans caused Charles to move in a new direction when "a Quaker sent me a pressing invitation to preach at Thaxted. I scrupled preaching in another's parish, till I had been refused the church. Many Quakers, and near seven hundred others, attended, while I declared in the highways, 'The Scripture hath concluded all under sin' [Gal. 3:22]."[63] Not only was Charles willing to preach in the open air, but he was even willing to accept invitations to preach in the pulpits of Dissenters prior to Tyson's later date for his first field-preaching experience—a move which was very close to separation from the Anglican Church! Charles's own language—describing his preaching in the pulpit of Dissenters as "declaring in the highways"—indicates that *he* considered this event an example of field-preaching, according to our definition.

As a dedicated Anglican, this was no small deviation and meets the criteria of what Spurgeon said of preaching in "unusual" places. Charles detested the idea of separation from the Church of England. Yet, when he was denied the ability to preach the genuine gospel from the pulpits of the Church, he took whatever opportunity was offered him—even in the pulpits of Dissenters. While Charles was faithful to the Church of England, he was *more* faithful to the gospel.

Keeping this context in mind, it is most sensible to understand the "inward conflict" to which Charles was referring was not about making use of the "innovation" of field-preaching for the first time as urged by Whitefield (as Tyson suggests). Instead, the conflict revolved around the difficult position that a commitment to the genuine gospel had put him in as an

---

61. Ibid., 1:140.
62. Ibid., 1:152.
63. Ibid., 1:175.

Anglican: he was being accused by his own clergymen and denied the use of pulpits within the Church of England at an increasing rate, and was now even being threatened with excommunication if he continued. The prayer that Charles recorded on June 23, 1739, offered up everything for the sake of Christ and his gospel. As a result, Charles found peace in the reality that opposition would not only come from the world, and devil, but also from within the ranks of the professing church. His unwavering loyalty to the Church of England could be misunderstood and even called "stubborn," but his loyalty was *really* to the gospel that the Articles and Homilies proclaimed.

As Charles maintained from the beginning, unless and until the Articles and Homilies were repealed, he would remain in the Church of England as long as it was in his power to do so. Nothing else mattered. Even when those from among his own fellow clergymen turned their backs on him and closed their pulpits, Charles came to understand that he was not the one who was preaching separation—they were, by their shutting out the true gospel!

My proposed understanding of the source of Charles's "inward conflict"—as opposed to Tyson and Newport's claim that Charles was reluctant to use the innovation of field-preaching—is further bolstered by understanding the events which happened earlier in that same week that Tyson cites. Charles recorded a conversation with John Potter, the Archbishop of Canterbury, on Tuesday, June 19, 1739:

> His Grace expressly forbade him to let any of us preach in his church—charged us with breach of the canon. I mentioned the Bishop of London's authorizing my forcible exclusion. He would not hear me, said he did not dispute. He asked me what call I had. I answered, "A dispensation of the gospel is committed to me" [1 Cor. 9:17]. "That is, to St Paul. But I do not dispute, and will not proceed to excommunication yet." "Your Grace has taught me in your book of church government, that a man unjustly excommunicated is not thereby cut off from communion with Christ." "Of that I am the judge." I asked him, if Mr Whitefield's success was not a spiritual sign, and sufficient proof of his call; recommended Gamaliel's advice. He dismissed us—Piers, with kind professions; me, with all the marks of his displeasure.
>
> I felt nothing in my heart but peace. Prayed and sang at Bray's. But some hours after, at West's, sank down in great heaviness and discouragement.[64]

---

64. Ibid., 1:178–79.

As an avowed Anglican, it is not surprising to see that Charles expressed a "great heaviness and discouragement" as a result of his being threatened with excommunication. It is only four days (and two journal entries) later in which Charles refers to his "inward conflict" and seeks to take Whitefield's advice in preaching anyway. After considering the evidence, it is clear that Tyson is mistaken in his understanding of this being Charles's first use of the means of field-preaching, nor is it evidence of his *reluctance* as an open air evangelist.

Instead, it is to be preferred that Charles's shift towards evangelism, even in the use of open air preaching, was actually rather easy and quick. Whatever reluctance could be pointed to was not in the *initial* use of these controversial methods, but in their *continued* use after raising opposition from his own beloved Church! As an ardent Anglican, Charles did not take this opposition lightly. However, as he expressed very clearly, his truest allegiance was to Jesus Christ and his gospel of salvation by grace through faith. Therefore, Charles was unwilling to leave the Church of England *as long as her Articles and Homilies* remained. If, however, the gospel was removed from the official teaching of the Anglican confession, it is safe to say that Charles would not have remained in her communion. Charles was also willing to be excommunicated from the Anglican Church for his commitment to the biblical gospel.

With this understanding, we can once again see that his peace came from offering his entire self "for Christ's sake and the gospel's."[65] This produced an allegiance to the Church of England as long as they officially embraced the same gospel. This was a turning point in the ministry of Charles, because he no longer viewed opposition from nominal Anglicans or nominal Christians as a problem. Instead, Charles incorporated evangelizing and confronting them as part of his ministry.

In one sermon, Charles

> preached at the Green, on the strong man armed [Luke 11:21], and disturbed him in his palace.... I took occasion to show the degeneracy of our modern Pharisees.... And yet these men cry out, "The Church, the Church!" when they will not hear the Church themselves; but despise her authority, trample upon her orders, teach contrary to her Articles and Homilies, and break her canons.[66]

This is strong language from an avowed Anglican! In another journal entry, Charles records an encounter he had with a different clergyman of the

---

65. Ibid., 1:179.
66. Ibid., 1:217.

Church of England who was preaching false doctrine that was out of line with the genuine gospel. In this instance, Charles "stayed and mildly told the preacher he had been misinformed. 'No,' he answered, 'it was all the truth.' 'Sir,' said I, 'if you believe what you preach, you believe a lie.' 'You are a liar,' he replied, and I put him in mind of the great day, testified my good will, and left him for the congregation."[67]

Charles's example is instructive. He demonstrates the proper response for followers of Christ who are faced with the cost of true discipleship. As I reflect on my own conversion to Christ, I recall a similar evangelical zeal to tell the world about my Lord who saved me from my sins. Suffice to say, most people were not nearly as excited to hear about my faith as I was to tell them! I was slightly discouraged by the lack of enthusiasm I found in others, but this was expected for me since I was a vocal opponent of Christianity for a period of time prior to my conversion. I was well aware of the types of opposition I experienced since I had acted similarly in the recent past.

What I was less prepared for was the attitude of those *within* the professing church as a response to my zeal for proclaiming the good news wherever I went. I can recall telling some fellow church members on a Sunday about a discussion I had with a gentleman about Christ while I was in line at the supermarket earlier in the week. They looked at me like I was crazy for bothering people with "religion" while they are minding their own business and trying to buy groceries! I wish I could say that my initial response was as committed as Charles's. Instead, I demonstrated a decidedly less mature response in conforming myself to the "acceptable" patterns of my church culture. *Don't talk to people in the supermarket about Jesus. Just drink your coffee and raise your hands during worship!*

Feel free to conduct your own experiment—next time you are fellowshipping with your Christian friends, encourage them to preach the gospel with you wherever you go. How will they respond? How would you respond?

Charles could have responded differently to the rebuke, persecution, and threat of excommunication from Church of England authorities. He could have gone back to preaching "holiness"—not as the fruit of salvation, but as a path towards salvation—with little opposition from his colleagues. Thankfully, Charles remained steadfast to the true gospel, knowing that any other gospel is really no gospel at all.[68] His understanding of what it means to be a Christian was more than simply acknowledging or accepting God's grace by coming to Christ. For Charles, being a Christian also included a commitment to *follow* Christ until the end. It is my opinion that many of

---

67. Ibid., 2:358.
68. Gal 1:8–9.

the shortcomings in the American church today are a result of failing to understand that our gospel call is more than simply come and believe. More accurately the call of the gospel is come, believe, and *follow*. In his sermon on Titus 3:8, Charles indicates that "these two, receiving Christ and walking in him, or faith and obedience, comprehend the whole duty of a Christian and are, and must continue, for ever, inseparable."[69] To fail to walk in obedience to Christ's commands—to spread his glory and kingdom to the ends of the earth—is a mark of false Christians, in Charles's view.

No matter the opposition he faced, Charles viewed his calling as a Christian (not as an Anglican or as a Methodist) to spread the news of the gospel, because this is the mission for all true Christians. Charles commented on Acts 11:26, "3. Thus may we still improve / The precious time of rest, / And preach the Saviour's love / That all with pardon blest / May know, & imitate the Lamb / And truly bear the Christian Name."[70] Charles incorporated opposition from nominal Christians into his theological tapestry, understanding that his call to preach was not just for those *outside* of the professing church but also to those *within*—to show them what a true follower of Christ looks like.[71]

As a result, it should not be surprising to hear Charles claim after his health no longer permitted his itinerant preaching ministry that "God, having graciously laid His hand upon my body, and *disabled me for the principle work of the ministry*, has thereby given me an unexpected occasion of writing the following hymns."[72] Charles clearly understood preaching to be the principle work of the ministry—not hymn writing. He was thankful for the opportunity to devote himself to his lyrical writing *after* his time as a dedicated preacher of the gospel concluded. To simply remember Charles as a hymn writer today is to commemorate a caricature of the real Charles Wesley. Yes, he wrote hymns; but even in his hymns he expressed his understanding that "3. We live to make the Saviour known, / And bring his gifts and blessings down / On those who Christ obey; / Joyful in this to persevere, / For all a pastor's business here / Is but to preach and pray."[73]

To understand Charles's theology of preaching we must understand that he was "an evangelical preacher whose interest was in conversion and

---

69. Newport, *Sermons*, 164.

70. Kimbrough and Beckerlegge, *Unpublished*, 2:346.

71. See, e.g., "Call of the First *Sound* Methodist Preachers," in Kimbrough and Beckerlegge, *Unpublished*, 3:59–60.

72. Tyson, *Reader*, 377, italics added for emphasis. Charles remarked that the "true use of music" was to catch the ear of people, so that they may hear the gospel; see Kimbrough and Newport, *Manuscript Journal*, 2:456.

73. Kimbrough and Beckerlegge, *Unpublished*, 2:307.

the sustaining of faith as it was practiced in the early Methodist societies."[74] As a result, "he ought not to be seen in the context of the academic establishment of his day, but rather in that of heart-felt revivalist religion."[75] This is not to say that Charles was against academic pursuits. However, he did not view Christianity as a set of propositions to merely be understood. Therefore, his preaching was not composed simply of rigorous logical argumentation intended to win converts through sheer force of reason. The modern church would do well to understand that the command to make disciples includes "teaching to obey"—which goes beyond teaching to understand.

Newport includes six shorthand sermons in his collection and argues that "these six sermons, then, have a real claim to being the heart of the surviving homiletic corpus."[76] After a careful reading I am inclined to agree with Newport's claim that these "give a picture of a man with an overriding message: Christ and him crucified."[77] As Charles continued to proclaim Jesus, he no longer needed to prepare sermon manuscripts. He began *expounding* more than *preaching*[78] because of his familiarity with the gospel and his ease at proclaiming it, he "could preach 'Christ and Him crucified' from virtually any Bible text."[79]

Charles wanted to faithfully communicate the gospel message and was less interested in being "prepared" or "practiced" in his delivery, in a formal sense. Charles's theological view had shifted to believing that the *content* of the message was more important than the outline, illustrations, and mannerisms! Charles did not put any faith in his ability to produce genuine converts, but gave all the credit and glory to God: "2. Thou, Lord, dost still the fruit produce, / When sinners listen to the news / of reconciling grace; / Thou only dost prepare the heart, / Doer of all the work Thou art, / Worthy of all the praise."[80]

Building upon the theological foundation of God doing the work through the faithfulness of the message proclaimed, it is understandable that Charles forsook the need for carefully preparing and editing sermon manuscripts and practicing their delivery for the more free "method of selecting a sermon text by opening the Bible and picking a passage at random" which "became rather common for Charles, and it is reported with a degree

---

74. Newport, *Sermons*, 43.
75. Ibid.
76. Ibid., 73.
77. Ibid., 76.
78. See discussion of this shift above.
79. Tyson, *Reader*, 19.
80. Kimbrough and Beckerlegge, *Unpublished*, 2:318.

of regularity in his terse journal entries."[81] For some, this method may be seen as lazy or ill-advised—but Charles was well-versed in the content and message of the Scriptures. According to Newport, "it is true, as Baker notes, that few knew the Bible as well as Charles, and his knowledge of the Scriptures made the business of *ex tempore* preaching less of a hazardous occupation for him than it might have been for most others. However, he did encourage others to adopt the practice."[82]

For the reader who is familiar with Methodist history, it may be surprising that Charles would encourage other preachers to use *ex tempore* methods, especially considering how much trouble he caused for some of the lay preachers commissioned under John:

> John often added to their ranks, and Charles frequently fired them as quickly as John hired them. As Charles confided to John Bennet, in a manuscript letter dated August 11, 1751, "A friend of ours [John Wesley] (without God's counsel) made a preacher of a tailor. I with God's help shall make a tailor of him again." Over the years, as the lay preachers clamored for more and more rights and authority in the Methodist movement (such as the authority to administer the Lord's Supper), Charles Wesley assumed the role of reproving them and striving to keep them in the proper role for unordained laymen.[83]

This was a complicated issue—as ordination, administering sacraments, and preaching the gospel were intertwined. As a good Anglican, Charles held a high view of the clergy and their function; particularly in administering the sacrament. While Charles's theology of the sacraments is beyond the scope of this chapter, it is essential to note that he did believe in some form of sacramental grace—not grace *for* salvation, but grace for keeping the believer firmly in the faith. The "use of the means of grace" (as Charles called it) was important for Charles's ecclesiology and so he had a clear distinction between *ordaining clergy* and *the commission* for all Christians to preach the gospel. Charles was not against "lay preaching *per se*, but against poorly qualified and ill-suited lay preachers practicing the homiletic art."[84] *Preaching* for Charles was serious business: "2. 'Tis not for Jesus' messengers / Partitions of estates to make, / The burthen of external

---

81. Tyson, *Reader*, 16.
82. Newport, *Sermons*, 36.
83. Tyson, *Assist*, 81–82.
84. Newport, *Sermons*, 370.

cares, / The needful charge let others take, / True ministers of Christ the Lord / Should only live to preach his word."[85]

We must not read our own understanding of these terms into Charles's, or else we will misunderstand his position. Charles believed every Christian had a responsibility to preach the gospel to the lost. Such preaching we would more likely term "evangelism"—a practice which happened outside of the walls of church buildings. On the other hand, he fought valiantly to keep ill-equipped preachers and teachers from filling the pulpits as ordained ministers. Such ill-equipped ministers often hindered the call to the church to live as ambassadors for Christ, since they were often the ones who refused Charles the use of the pulpit and objected to the open air preaching methods.

According to Charles, for those who are serious about faithfully proclaiming the full gospel message and who are committed to following the Lord Jesus with their whole heart, soul, mind, and strength, proclamation of the gospel is their call: "2. Women, & men, & children too / By powerful godliness / The general observations drew, / And shew'd the truth of grace. / O that we all might preach & live, / Like them, the gospel-word, / And force the heathen to receive / Our dear redeeming Lord!"[86] What does it mean to be serious for the Lord? Charles explains, "1. Fresh fatigue for Jesus' sake / Is an apostle's rest; / Happy who his zeal partake, / His successors confess'd! / They with joy renounce their ease, / Themselves in everything deny, / Sinners for their Lord to seize, / And Jesus glorify."[87]

Charles was a driven man. He believed that all Christians should be likewise driven to serve the Lord in this life: "1. Man, sinful man, to labour born, / And urg'd by the divine command, / Till, dust he doth to dust return, / Idle on earth shoud never stand; / But still his six days' work pursue, / And do what God appoints to do."[88] Charles believed that submission to the divine decrees and will is a great privilege for the Christian, and urged that: "1. With readiness and lowly fear / We come, O God! to serve thy will, / Sentenc'd to toil incessant here, / And then to rest on Sion's hill. / But while thy justice we obey / O let thy love point out our way."[89]

Since Charles viewed the Christian's primary work as preaching, it is easy to understand why "at the height of his ministry, [Charles] was

---

85. Kimbrough and Beckerlegge, *Unpublished*, 2:137.
86. Ibid., 2:317.
87. Ibid., 2:401.
88. Ibid., 3:426.
89. Ibid., 3:427.

preaching as often as four times a day in as many different towns and villages"[90] and why he also "encouraged lay ministry."[91] Charles preached an entire message on how the laity should be involved in the broader evangelical task of proclaiming Christ, and publishing his kingdom and glory to the ends of the earth.[92]

If God does the work through the message proclaimed, then God's people ought to obey him and proclaim his message! Charles makes this point clear in his sermon on Romans 3:23–25 saying, "Would to God, my brethren, the following words were applicable to us all, 'I have confidence in you through the Lord that ye will be none otherwise minded!' Would to God that everyone who hath not made shipwreck of the faith would avow and preach and publish it upon the housetop. Suffer ye the word of exhortation from the least and meanest of your brethren."[93] Charles sees in the Scriptures a universal call to Christians to glorify God through their proclaiming from the rooftops the good news of the kingdom of God and of the Christ.

Since the message itself is the power of God and the wisdom of God,[94] Charles encouraged faithfulness to the biblical mandate that we "be determined not to know or preach anything save Jesus Christ and him crucified. Preach the gospel in simplicity. Insist on justification by faith only, even by faith in the blood of Jesus, that only name given under heaven whereby we may be saved else I call holy writ to record against you this day!"[95] God is serious about this call. So was Charles. The church today would do well to heed this exhortation and preach the gospel in simplicity and boldness—without hindering it by mingling our denominational distinctives, our personal preferences, and our pet doctrines along with it. The Lord must be our banner.[96] Our unity is in the pure gospel.

According to Charles's theology of preaching, it is the proclaimed word by the people of God in faithfulness that expands the kingdom and glory of God and that effects the conversion of sinners to saints. In order to see revival and the church continue to grow, then the church must take this task of preaching the gospel seriously:

90. Tyson, *Assist*, viii.
91. Newport, *Sermons*, 20.
92. See sermon 22 on Prov 11:30, recorded in ibid., 369–79.
93. Ibid., 207.
94. Rom 1:16; 1 Cor 1:18–25.
95. Newport, *Sermons*, 209.
96. Exod 17:15.

> 1. If Thou the word bestow, / If Thou the preachers bless, / Thy church will always grow, / Thy witnesses increase, / And help'd by every obstacle / Thy gospel over all prevail. / 2. Didst Thou not give the seed / We in thy name have sown, / And send us forth indeed, / To make thy goodness known? / Give then multiplied success, / And let the world our Lord confess.[97]

God has given us the word and the mission. Are we being faithful today? It is the curse of our age that we often try to improve upon the methods of God, thinking that we can come up with a better method than what he has prescribed. God is not looking for us to reinvent the wheel or to build a better mousetrap. God is calling us to proclaim his glory to the ends of the earth!

Charles Wesley's Theology of Prayer

As Charles understood the message to be God's, he also recognized the power and plan had to come from God as well. While it may be better to preach *anywhere* than *nowhere*, Charles still emphasized the need for striving in private prayer to keep in step with God's will and to remain reliant upon him for direction. As the body of Christ, we are literally participating in God's mission which he has begun and will bring unto completion for his names' sake.[98] As a result, Charles viewed prayer as a sacrifice of our life to God: "2. Thine Unction we partake, / Thy threefold office share, / Our souls to God give back / In sacrificial prayer, / Make known thy Father's will to man / And sufferers in thy kingdom reign."[99]

Closely related to this theology of preaching is Charles's theology of prayer. Even prior to his evangelical conversion, Charles placed a strong emphasis on personal prayer. The rigorously ordered life of the Methodists included devoted times of prayer in the daily schedule. After his evangelical conversion, Charles's theology of prayer shifted from being one of his religious duties to being of primary importance in finding success in his call and ministry. Without pressing in to God in fervent personal prayer, Charles believed that the Christian could wander from God.[100] Charles believed that prayer keeps you tethered to the Lord, and is where he gives his direction and power for successful ministry.

---

97. Kimbrough and Beckerlegge, *Unpublished*, 2:349.
98. See chap. 2, "God's Mission."
99. Kimbrough and Beckerlegge, *Unpublished*, 2:339.
100. E.g., "And always dread th'apostate's doom / And watch, and pray, till Jesus come!" (ibid., 2:152).

Early in Charles's field-preaching career he would proclaim the word seemingly wherever he was. As part of his convictions—which will become even clearer in the investigation of his theology of the kingdom below—Charles expected hostility towards his message and called it "the blessing of opposition."[101] As his ministry progressed, Charles certainly encountered his fair share of this "blessing." Over time, his theology matured to understand the importance of following the lead of the Holy Spirit, remarking: "I cannot help observing from what passed yesterday that we ought to wait upon God for direction when and where to preach, much more than we do. A false courage, which is fear of shame, may otherwise betray us into unnecessary dangers."[102] This waiting upon the Lord to discern and hear his will is done through prayer.

When God's will is discerned through fervent prayer, Charles understood that he was safe in God's will. This was expressed after reflection on a hostile event, which he described in his journal entry on March 14, 1744: "The news was soon spread through the town, and drew many to the place, who expressed their compassion by wishing all our necks had been broke. I preached out of the town, in weariness and painfulness. The Lord was our strong consolation. Never did I more clearly see that not a hair of our head can fall to the ground, without our heavenly Father."[103]

A separate inquiry could rightly be made into Charles's theology of the Spirit ("pneumatology"), but for the present chapter it is sufficient to see that Charles relied on the Holy Spirit both for *power* and *direction* in his preaching ministry. Both were the result of devoting himself to prayer. Without prayer, Charles saw the Christian as disconnected from the Holy Spirit's power, and direction, and was therefore walking in the flesh. Charles's theology of prayer demonstrates that he viewed the best *preparation* for proclamation of the gospel (beyond knowing the basic content of the gospel message) was a devotion to private prayer. In this light, his comments quoted above about the business of a pastor being just to "preach and pray" makes even more sense from his perspective.

The Word & the Spirit

Charles certainly had a high view of the written word of God and sought to live his life in obedience to this revelation. It is the written word that teaches the importance of being in humble submission to the Spirit (who

---

101. Kimbrough and Newport, *Manuscript Journal*, 1:177.
102. Ibid., 2:386–87.
103. Ibid., 2:395.

will never lead us in contradiction to what is written), which is why Charles could state his ambition that "I shall with simple faith receive, / And by the Word & Spirit live."[104] For Charles, studying the Bible is the source for understanding the content of the written word, and devoted prayer is the source for discerning the Spirit's will for the individual believer in applying these universal truths. It is not enough to simply preach the word, because Charles's theology informed him that to preach according to our own will was still sin! This may seem like a strange claim, but disobedience to God's direction can make even seemingly "holy" actions sinful.[105] For example, if God is commanding you to be the instrument of salvation to your neighbor, yet you are disobeying that command because it is more comfortable to stay inside the comfort of your own home and read your Bible, this is still disobedience and sin.

If Christ is Lord (and he is!), then we should submit our will to his: "Not as his inclination leads, / But by the order of his Lord, / The minister of Christ proceeds, / And propagates the gospel-word, / And spreads the power of reigning love, / Which lifts our souls to thrones above."[106] How can we discern our specific marching orders within the broader evangelical task? Charles tells us to pray: "Who minister the gospel-word, / And truly fast unto the Lord, / And seek his face in prayer, / To them He doth unfold his mind, / (Whate'er he hath for each design'd), / And all his will declare."[107]

Charles's theology continues to point back to a high view of the Lordship of Christ and of his sovereignty. The proper Christian response is to *submit* and *obey*. The aim of this Spirit-led and empowered preaching was to bring about the conversion of sinners through presenting them with the gospel message—which included boldly proclaiming that God has commanded them to turn from their rebellion (repent) and place their faith in Christ to be saved from the wrath that is rightly due to them for their wickedness:

> 1. We, Jesus, have heard Thy wonderful fame, / The power of thy word To sinners proclaim, / With hearty thanksgiving Acknowledge thy grace, / The living, the living Should publish thy praise. / 2. Our spirits were dead And buried in sin; / But waken'd & freed From death we have been; / The true Resurrection We found in our graves: / And Jesus' affection Whole multitudes saves. / 3. Come then at his call Our Jesus to meet! / His wonders

---

104. Kimbrough and Beckerlegge, *Unpublished*, 2:18.
105. Christianity is not moralism. See chaps. 3 & 5, and appendix A.
106. Kimbrough and Beckerlegge, *Unpublished*, 2:25.
107. Ibid., 2:349.

on all He waits to repeat: / The proofs of his favour Ye all shall receive, / And friends of your Saviour And witnesses live.[108]

According to Charles's theological understanding, God has saved individuals by his grace and called them into his service to further publish the good news of salvation by grace through faith in Christ, being led and empowered by the indwelling Holy Spirit. The aim of this leading and empowering act of God in the lives of redeemed individuals is to bring about further conversions and thus repeat the cycle of individuals "Made willing to repent, believe, / And live thy witnesses."[109]

The Kingdom of God

Related to Charles's doctrine of conversion is his theology of the kingdom of God. It is essential to maintain a proper focus when exploring this particular thread, because it is easy to get off track. There are at least three separate facets to Charles's theology of the kingdom, but only two of these facets will be considered in any detail below. With the goal of better understanding Charles's theology of field-preaching, we are necessarily most interested in the theology of the kingdom as it relates to this present world. Therefore, the theology of the kingdom in an eschatological sense (that is, the future and coming kingdom in its fullness) will not be considered. Instead, we will focus on the theology of the kingdom in relation to the kingdom within the individual and then spiritual warfare, as expressed by Charles.

The Kingdom Within

Charles had an understanding based on his reading of the biblical text that the present world lies in the power of the devil and is ruled by him.[110] This understanding is not pervasive in the Christian world and is certainly not without controversy in some circles. To claim that the devil has authority over this world is borderline blasphemous to some, yet the Scriptures plainly state this to be the case in 1 John 5:19. Despite the possible objections, this genuinely biblical worldview is essential for understanding the general brokenness of the world in which we live and it answers most directly the so-called problem of human suffering.[111]

108. Ibid., 2:253.
109. Ibid., 2:231.
110. E.g., 2 Cor 4:4; 1 Pet 5:8; 1 John 5:19.
111. Philosophers and skeptics have shifted recently from continuing to call this

The argument asserts that a deity of the biblical description cannot exist because an all-powerful, all-knowing, and all-benevolent God would do something about the suffering present in the world. The presence of suffering implies that any god that may exist is unable to eliminate suffering (and, therefore, not all-powerful), wants to help but can't figure out how to eliminate it (and, therefore, not all-knowing), or is not willing to eliminate it (and, therefore, not all-benevolent). Of course, this philosophical "problem" fails to take the biblical God at his word and makes him out to be a liar. The Bible indicates that the present world has been handed over to Satan (who seeks only to steal, kill, and destroy) and that the rebellious human race has been sold into bondage to sin and death under the rule of this tyrannical spiritual dictator as a result of God's curse upon his creation for our rebellion. Yikes!

The Bible further describes what God has done to release these captives and set them free—God became a man in the person of Jesus Christ to fulfill the Scriptures and lay down his own life, taking the full burden of sin upon himself, and bearing the penalty of the full wrath of God being poured out upon him, so that all who repent of their foolish rebellion and trust in the completed work of Jesus through his death, burial, resurrection, and exaltation in fulfillment of the Scriptures can be saved from the wrath that is to come. In this worldview, God is not *unable* to help humans, nor is he *unwilling*—but God has done it in a way that isn't oriented to bring comfort to rebels, but to bring glory to his own name. God *has* done something about human suffering. Many reject his solution because they are waiting for God to serve them and make their rebellion more comfortable.

We deserve wrath. The world could be much worse than it is. To see what the devil does when given the opportunity, simply read Job 1–2. The fact that such terrible circumstances do not befall every living person is evidence of the restraining hand of God despite the world's continued and persistent rebellion against him. These themes, and particularly Charles's theological understanding of this reality, will become even more apparent when his evangelistic methods are considered.

As it pertains to the kingdom, Charles understood that the converted sinner has been transferred *out* of the domain of darkness and kingdom of the devil and *into* the kingdom of light under the Lord of life, Jesus Christ. This conversion and transfer of domains gives the believer the hope of a

---

the problem of *evil* because of the potentially sticky situation that is raised by claiming in their premises the existence of evil as an objective thing, which then implies a standard of good that is similarly objective. The problem of *suffering* is more subjective and eliminates this potential concession of an objective good, while still essentially arguing for the same thing as the original problem of evil.

future spent in the presence of the Lord (the eschatological kingdom of heaven), but also has a very real *present* reality beginning at the moment of conversion: "From knowing *now* your Sins forgiven, / From tasting *here* the Joys of Heaven!"[112] This genuine conversion experience and gift of salvation goes beyond an intellectual understanding and assent, in Charles's view, to being a real receiving of the kingdom of God *into* the believer.

It is clear that Charles had both a *positive* and *negative* conception of salvation. The positive aspect emphasized being reconciled to God and united with him in the present life through receiving his kingdom and Holy Spirit into the life of the believer. The negative aspect was the avoidance of hell. Both of these benefits are good, but one is positive in the sense that you "get" a relationship with God and privileges as a citizen of heaven, and the other is negative in the sense that you "don't get" what you deserve in the form of everlasting, conscious torment for your sins in the Lake of Fire.

This inward reception of the kingdom of God should begin to transform the individual from the inside out, producing a growth of Christlikeness in response to the redemptive and transformative grace of God. By understanding this high view of God's grace, it helps us to view Charles's continued preaching regarding the importance of holiness in the proper perspective. After his evangelical conversion, Charles no longer viewed religious endeavors as a means of earning salvation. However, the evidence of the transforming grace of God in the life of an individual *must* be present according to his theological understanding; lest the confession of faith not match the reality of the kingdom and Spirit of God now dwelling inside of the person. For Charles, it was impossible to think that a conversion had in fact taken place if there was no tangible fruit of their conversion in the form of increased holiness and devotion to Christ.

Charles expressed this truth in dealing with those who profess saving faith in Christ, saying, "I neither reject nor receive their saying, but require their fruits and bid them go on."[113] While this may seem judgmental to some, this conviction was derived from his theological understanding that a conversion from death to life, and from darkness to light, would be tangible and evident. Charles confronted those who had no visible signs of conversion out of his love for them (not from judgmental pride) because he firmly believed that "to tell one in darkness he has faith is to keep him in darkness still, or to make him trust in a false light, a faith that stands in the words of men, not in the power of God."[114]

---

112. Tyson, *Reader*, 229, emphasis in original.
113. Kimbrough and Newport, *Manuscript Journal*, 2:353.
114. Ibid., 2:350–51.

Sinners who are in bondage to the devil are often not aware of their plight as their chains and shackles are of an inward sort to sin and rebellion. These chains are not felt on the outward members of the body as literal bonds would be. Charles believed the scriptural declaration that these prisoners of the kingdom of darkness need to hear the proclaimed word, because the gospel is the power of God for salvation.[115] For Charles, the reality of the kingdom of God being received inside the individual meant that they were truly able to be set free from the tyranny to sin. One of Charles's most well-known and studied convictions is his theology of Christian perfection. This doctrine was a byproduct of his view on the kingdom within.

Charles believed in a relationship of "sanctification with resignation of spirit (or self-will), which became an important theme in Charles's later work."[116] As the believer resigned himself more to the lordship of Christ, and rested in the kingdom of God within, they likewise experienced greater freedom to be led by the Spirit and from the tyranny of sin. In this way, the kingdom of God within was like leaven inside of the believer, which Charles expressed in a short hymn on Matthew 13:33 ("The kingdom of heaven is like unto leaven"): "That heavenly principle within, / Doth it at once its power exert, / At once root out the seed of sin, / And spread perfection through the heart? / No; but a gradual life it sends, / Diffuse through the faithful soul, / To actions, words, and thoughts extends, / And slowly sanctifies the whole."[117] Charles looked forward to more freedom from the inward tyranny to sin as a result of God's kingdom spreading deeper into his own soul. He taught that all believers should likewise seek and experience this reality. For Charles, this theology of Christian perfection was "one of 'the two great truths of the everlasting Gospel' (the other being 'universal redemption')."[118] Charles firmly believed and preached that Christians should be free in spirit and *truth*, not in spirit and *theory*.

In this view, the individual believer still has a responsibility to strive to continue in submission to the Lord so that the kingdom would spread within (*and* without as a response to their Spirit-led and empowered proclamation). Newport notes, "As a study of the later sermons indicates, Charles never lost this insistence that the Christian must strive to be perfect or that it is the duty of the believer to seek out and do God's will, and it would be inaccurate to suggest simply that a works-based righteousness was replaced

---

115. Rom 1:16. This does not necessarily exclude the written word as a form of "proclamation."

116. Tyson, *Reader*, 392.

117. Ibid., 463.

118. Ibid., 360.

by a Christ-based righteousness following"[119] his evangelical conversion. To continue to die to self and submit to our Lord is one of the great Christian privileges; and it demands serious and devoted attention.[120] Charles also viewed the claim to having attained perfection as proof of the opposite. To make such a declaration was itself a prideful act, and "following Jesus' parable he concludes that sanctification must be hid in the field of one's life rather than being pridefully flaunted."[121]

Spiritual Warfare

Charles believed the kingdom of darkness was established on the earth. He believed that the faithful proclamation of the gospel is the vehicle through which sinners are converted, redeemed, and transferred into the kingdom of heaven. Understanding this, we are better able to understand his theological views of preaching as an act of spiritual warfare and how it expands the kingdom of God by releasing prisoners from the kingdom of darkness. Charles viewed the proclamation of the gospel by the Christian as performing an act of aggression against the kingdom of darkness! Charles believed in an *offensive* church.[122]

Charles wrote in his journal once after preaching, "We are now come to close quarters with the enemy, who threatens hard to drive us out of his kingdom."[123] Despite this fearsome foe, Charles was not deterred because his theology convinced him that above all else, the enemy has been defeated through the cross. While the devil still prowls around, roaring and seeking to devour, he knows his time is short. Charles was driven by his theological convictions to continue preaching the good news of the gospel of the kingdom and was not surprised to be opposed everywhere he went, saying, "I marvel not that Satan should fight for his kingdom—it begins to shake in this place."[124]

---

119. Newport, *Sermons*, 59.

120. The Apostle Paul likewise affirmed this theological paradox of hard work on behalf of the believer and the grace of God working simultaneously in 1 Cor 15:10 and Phil 2:12–13. Similarly, the Calvinistic Whitefield wrote, "desired their prayers to God for me that I might now more devote myself to my blessed Master's service, and study daily to purify my corrupt nature, that I might be made an instrument under Him of winning their souls to God" (Whitefield, *Journals*, 163).

121. Tyson, *Reader*, 377.

122. Similarly, George Whitefield wrote, "By the help of God, I will still go on to attack the devil in his strongest holds" (Whitefield, *Journals*, 315).

123. Kimbrough and Newport, *Manuscript Journal*, 2:511.

124. Ibid., 2:365.

A Theology of Evangelism

The final strand of Charles Wesley's theological tapestry to consider is in relation to evangelism. While related to proclamation, Charles's evangelistic style goes beyond simply expounding the gospel from the biblical text, but also applies principles of his theological understanding in his methodology. Charles was much more influenced by his theological convictions than he was by the mores and manners of a sinful and dead society. Therefore, his methods were tailored to cut directly to the heart of the matter without beating around the bush.

In understanding the natural state of man, Charles describes working hard "to convince [the sinner] of unbelief (our first point with all)."[125] The most straight-forward method that Charles made use of often was to ask "that rude question, 'Do you deserve to be damned?'"[126] While the modern Christian may find this methodology to be quite unpleasant, Charles was under no conviction that being "polite" was better than being faithful to his theological convictions.[127] The Scriptures declare that all are shut up under sin and rightfully deserving of wrath and condemnation. Therefore, Charles's question is not meant to be rude and offensive (although it was often taken as such). This question was intended to serve as a diagnostic of the spiritual state of the person he was speaking with.

I am a Christian. As a follower of Jesus I have no misgivings about the depth of my personal depravity, my sin, and of my complete need for a Savior. I understand that even on my *best* day I deserve to be damned for my sinfulness. My need for a savior is not relegated to simply needing to be saved from my previous sins. I need a savior every moment.[128] So do you. This is why we take refuge in Jesus, not coming out for even a moment, since salvation is *in* Christ alone.[129] Charles, likewise, professed the same:

> In the coach to London I preached faith in Christ. A lady was extremely offended, avowed her own merits in plain terms, asked if I was not a Methodist, threatened to beat me. I declared I deserved nothing but hell; so did she, and must confess it before she could have a title to heaven. This was most intolerable to

---

125. Ibid., 1:147.

126. Ibid.

127. Whitefield railed against "polite preachers" in his journal; see, e.g., Whitefield, *Journals*, 237, 247, 300–301.

128. Whitefield likewise notes, "Whatever foreseen fitness for salvation others may talk of and glory in, I disclaim any such thing. If I trace myself from my cradle to my manhood, I can see nothing in me but a fitness to be damned" (ibid., 38).

129. E.g., Pss 2:12; 34:22; Eph 2:1–10.

her. The others were less offended, began to listen, asked where I preached.[130]

If Charles asked me this question I would not be offended. I would answer plainly, "Yes." The mere fact of offense at the question served as proof to Charles that the person he was speaking with was separated from God, did not believe the testimony of God, and was still dead in their trespasses and sins. It is important to keep in mind that Charles himself once responded in the same fashion as the woman in the coach above did when confronted by Peter Böhler—he appealed to his own merits. The person who trusts in their merits is not trusting in Christ. If any would hope to be saved by Christ, they must first confess that they are deserving of God's wrath and condemnation for their rebellion against him.

When confronted with someone who denied their desert of condemnation, Charles "laboured hard to convince her she deserved hell."[131] Charles's theological understanding once again guided his practice, as he followed the methodology prescribed primarily through the canonical writings of the Apostle Paul regarding the proper use of the law.[132] In brief, Charles understood the purpose of the law and commandments to be used to demonstrate to the sinner that they are, in fact, in violation of God's righteous decrees and in active rebellion against him. As such, they are worthy of God's wrath and hell.[133] Following the theological conviction that God resists the proud and gives grace to the humble,[134] Charles prescribed a healthy dose of law to those who denied they are deserving of damnation, and who proclaimed their own goodness and merit. By showing them their true status before a holy God, they can understand their need to be reconciled to God, and then be led to seek that reconciliation through Christ.[135]

Charles described his own methodology clearly in his journal from Monday, September 3, 1739: "Preached at the Brick-yard, to upwards of five thousand, from 1 Corinthians 6:9. I marvelled at their taking it so patiently, when I showed them they were all adulterers, thieves, idolaters, etc."[136] The observant interpreter will notice that these explicit categories are included in the passage (1 Cor 6:9–10) and are also violations of the Ten Command-

---

130. Kimbrough and Newport, *Manuscript Journal*, 1:141.

131. Ibid., 1:132.

132. E.g., Rom 3:20; 7:7; 1 Tim 1:8–11.

133. Prov 20:2; Ps 68:21.

134. Jas 4:6; Ps 34:22.

135. Job 4:17–21; 9:1–12; 25:4; Prov 20:9; Rom 3:9–31; 2 Cor 5:11–21; 1 Tim 2:5–6; Heb 2:17; 1 John 2:1–2; 4:10.

136. Kimbrough and Newport, *Manuscript Journal*, 1:193.

ments (the seventh, eighth, and first/second respectively).[137] When someone is humbled by the law of God, and sees their true state of depravity, then Charles happily and freely gives them the grace of the gospel.[138]

Charles was sometimes surprised by encountering individuals who were already humbled by their sin and unworthiness of salvation. In one such evangelistic encounter, Charles records that he "attended Mr Piers to a poor old woman whom he could never prevail upon to go to church. Expected we should be called to preach the law, but found her ready for the gospel, and glad to exchange her merits for Christ's."[139] Most people are unaware of their guilt before God because we are good at justifying our rebellion and we suppress the truth in our unrighteousness.[140] Others are aware and simply do not know how to receive forgiveness. As a result, Charles often started with that "rude question" to diagnose the spiritual state and labored to convince those who were not in Christ of their unbelief.[141] He then proceeded to apply law and/or grace as necessary.

Despite the distaste that many modern Christians may feel towards such methods, it is critical to realize that Charles, too, recognized that these methods were potentially offensive. Yet, faithfulness was his goal; the stakes are too high to rely on human reasoning instead of God's revealed will.[142] Despite our best intentions, humans are often wrong and come to faulty conclusions. Charles knew that hell is real and a terrible fate. His love compelled him to speak the truth in love, even though many found it offensive. Many Christians today would prefer to never even potentially offend anyone. At the funerals of friends, loved ones, and acquaintances, many try to convince themselves that everything probably worked out okay. I've gone to many funerals where the minister preached on the goodness of the deceased as the foundation for their eternal hope. On the contrary, Jesus taught that there are none good but God.[143] At the funeral for my own grandfather,

---

137. For anyone interested in studying the method of using the law to bring about conviction as revealed in the Scriptures, I encourage you to study the Way of the Master methodology as taught by Ray Comfort. He has written many books and provides others resources for free on the internet at www.livingwaters.com. You can also check out www.transfired.org.

138. The best example of this preaching style and methodology in the extant sermons is in Newport, *Sermons*, 238–58 on John 8:1–11. This sermon is well worth reading in its entirety.

139. Kimbrough and Newport, *Manuscript Journal*, 1:123–24.

140. Luke 16:15; Rom 1:18.

141. Kimbrough and Newport, *Manuscript Journal*, 1:147.

142. Prov 14:12.

143. Luke 18:19.

the priest stressed over and over my grandfather's striving to live by the beatitudes (found in Matt 5:1–12), being careful to hedge his comments saying, "Of course, no one is perfect, and he did not keep them *perfectly*. But he tried! Every day, he tried his best." Sadly, if we only read to the end of this same chapter, Jesus states plainly in Matthew 5:48, "Therefore you are to be perfect, as your heavenly Father is perfect." Trusting in our own merits and best effort is the broad path to destruction.[144] Comments that are intended to comfort us about those who were "good, decent people" should send a chill down our spine if we are biblically aware and understand the teaching of Scripture. The *loving* thing to do is to warn people beforehand that the road they are travelling is not headed where they think it is.

Once, Charles "called on a friend, near death yet unprepared for it, and faithfully, not fashionably, told him his condition."[145] It was not fashionable in his day, nor is it in ours. The truth remains that without Christ, a man is dead in his trespasses and sins, and without hope in the world.[146] It is true that many of our modern evangelism strategies are much more appealing to the flesh and often remove the offense of the cross. In doing so, they likewise remove the power.

Are we ashamed of the gospel today? Charles was not. The Lord was pleased to sweep many into the kingdom, and pour out his grace and love, through Charles's willingness to be faithful (rather than fashionable) in presenting the gospel. God's methods, in God's timing and power, are the only way to bring lasting results and advance the kingdom—both without and within.

WEAVING IT ALL TOGETHER

After briefly examining each of these various theological strands,[147] a picture emerges of Charles's theology of field-preaching. The decision to make

---

144. I often meet people who believe they will be rewarded for "trying their best" when they are judged by God. However, this is wishful thinking. Effort is important, but so are results. It is a plain truth that often people try their very best and fail anyway. I remember a high school art assignment, which required a self-portrait to be painted. I tried my very best. The end product, despite my best efforts, received a "C"—which was generous! God judges our righteousness, not our effort. Ambassadors for Christ must be equipped to lovingly demonstrate this reality to people for their own benefit. See also Luke 17:7–10.

145. Kimbrough and Newport, *Manuscript Journal*, 2:381.

146. Eph 2:12–13.

147. Many more examples from Charles's writings could be cited for each of these, as these themes are pervasive throughout all of his extant materials.

such extensive use of open air evangelism follows from these individual doctrines, in addition to Charles's understanding that the Christian will be judged at the end of their life—not for salvation, but for their stewardship of the gospel in this life:

> 1. When we before our Judge appear / The day shall all our lives reveal, / How we employ'd our substance here, / Our time, and intellect, and will; / What gain'd we by the heavenly trade, / How many souls we won for God, / What use of all his graces made, / What use of Jesus, and his blood. / 2. But O, what answer at the throne / Will that unfaithful pastor give, / Who call'd his Master's goods his own, / And for his God refus'd to live, / Who dar'd his talents misemploy, / In sloth, and luxury, and pride, / Nor fear'd to stumble and destroy / The souls for whom his Saviour died.[148]

In order to make the biggest impact for Christ and his kingdom—and since the aim of preaching the gospel is the conversion of sinners[149]—Charles would naturally find himself going where the sinners are. This included preaching the gospel both inside and out of the walls of church buildings, to convert those far from God (whether they call themselves Christians or not), and to encourage those who are redeemed to join in the mission of God in advancing the kingdom and glory of God to the ends of the earth.

As individuals are converted through faithful gospel preaching, societies and communities will also likewise be changed for the better. When the church—not the formal structures of 501(c)3 ecclesiastical organizations, but the body of redeemed people of God—expands, then the impact will necessarily be felt in the surrounding culture. It is not a surprise to see genuine and lasting revival flow from Charles's commitment to living out his theology.

When field-preaching and the offensive nature of the church are forgotten, the kingdom of darkness remains undisturbed. As a result, revival ends, and the church gradually becomes irrelevant and impotent in the culture. It happened in Charles's day and it has happened in our own. When Whitefield opened the flood gates by rediscovering the practice of field-preaching—which was picked up by John, Charles, and many other preachers throughout the Methodist movement—genuine and deep revival was the result. If we are willing to learn from the past, are we also willing to rediscover the practice of proclaiming the gospel where the sinners are,

---

148. Kimbrough and Beckerlegge, *Unpublished*, 2:175.

149. For more discussion of preaching with the aim of conversion, see Spurgeon, *Lectures*, 336–48.

instead of hoping they will come to us? Moving towards filling the office of evangelist—to protect the gospel, to equip the saints, and to lead the outward charge—in our local churches will be a good first step in remedying this malady.

As Charles embraced his calling and sought his Lord in prayer, relying on God for direction and power, he preached the full gospel in faithfulness using the prescribed methods of the Scriptures. Charles was unconcerned about trying to conform to the ways of the world. Our culture loudly and aggressively preaches *tolerance*, in addition to a subjective morality where virtually anything goes—except, of course, discussing religion outside of "proper channels!" Our society tells us that it is impolite to talk about religion. It tells us you should never try to cram your ideas down someone else's throat; all while forcing their idea of tolerance upon followers of Christ. The genuine gospel message has very little to do with "our ideas"—it is the message of the risen king!

Our culture is sick and dying. The church has the cure. Many may not like our message, but it is life and peace to all who accept it. The church cannot keep silent while the world perishes! The patient may not like the cure, but the physician is not rude who tells them the truth.

As Charles said, "But let the world smile or frown, my work goes on."[150] As a result, his theological tapestry created a sail which caught the winds of revival and allowed Charles to be used mightily as an instrument of God for expanding the kingdom and glory of God. This theology, when put into practice by Charles, resulted in a deep and lasting impact on him, the church, and the world.

Examining Charles Wesley, particularly in relation to his theology of field-preaching, has shed new light on the previous (and popular) misconceptions of him. The testimony of his sermons, journal, letters, hymns, and poems testify that he was much more than simply the hymnist of the Methodist movement! Charles was a bold, powerful, enthusiastic, and *eager* preacher of the gospel of Christ.

Charles was not satisfied—as many modern theologians are—to simply let his theology become a matter of intellectual exercise. It was not enough to *affirm* the unlimited atonement.[151] His conviction actually drove him into the highways and byways to preach Christ to all that he could. God gave him breath; he used it to praise and proclaim God's glory. We need not agree with Charles on the extent of the atonement to share his urgency.

---

150. Kimbrough and Newport, *Manuscript Journal*, 2:341.

151. A theological strand that was intentionally ignored due to being both controversial and also adequately covered elsewhere.

All Christians can hopefully agree that the Apostle Paul's encouragement is binding for us today: "We proclaim Him, admonishing *every man* and teaching *every man* with all wisdom, so that we may present *every man* complete in Christ" (Col 1:28, emphasis added).

Charles's theology is also instructive because we have the luxury of seeing its results in history. Charles was not convinced to spend his life and to be spent because of his particular historical occasion. He did so because this is the will of God for his people at all times, and in all places. Charles mocks the idea that the world is "Christian" and chides those who use this as an excuse for being slothful with their stewardship of the gospel. His message in his own day should still speak to our own in attempting to awaken those who take upon themselves the Christian name and seek to live lives of comfort and ease while the world is perishing around them.[152]

I believe that the Scriptures teach that God is willing to revive his people again—not because we deserve it, but for his names' sake. The life and theology of Charles Wesley are indicative of the impact that God can make through the use of yielded individuals who no longer submit themselves as slaves of unrighteousness but rather as slaves of righteousness.[153] By following the example of the "cloud of witnesses," we too can see revival in our day. It is not going to happen if we continue to invent our own methods of revival. The prophets consistently called the people of God to return to him. Will we hear their voice in our time? If we desire to see revival, we must return to God with our whole heart, soul, mind, and strength. This starts with seeking his face in prayer. It should end with boldly declaring God's goodness and glory to a world that desperately needs him.

Spurgeon sums up this matter saying, "Not only must *something* be done to evangelize the millions, but *everything* must be done, and perhaps amid variety of effort the best thing would be discovered. 'If by any means I may save some' must be our motto, and this must urge us onward to go forth into the highways and hedges and compel them to come in. Brethren, I speak as unto wise men, consider what I say."[154] God has given us his message and his methods. Will we lay down our desire to be *editors* of the gospel and submit ourselves to be ambassadors for his kingdom? Are we prepared to crash the gates of hades and to set the captives free? Revival starts in the individual and necessarily impacts the church and the world. Both Charles and John were raised in the same family. Both yielded themselves to their God; and "from this household would come a religious revival to shake

---

152. Jas 5:1–6.
153. Rom 6:12–14.
154. Spurgeon, *Lectures*, 253, italics in original.

England and the New World."[155] By following their faithful example and walking in our calling as an *offensive* church, revival could likewise come to your house and once again shake the world.

---

155. Tyson, *Reader*, 3.

12

Afterword

Behold, I send you out as sheep in the midst of wolves; so be shrewd as serpents and innocent as doves. (Matt 10:16)

I've been asked (more than once), "So, do you think everyone has to quit their jobs and just preach on street corners all day, every day?" Usually those asking the question are surprised to hear that my answer is, "No." I'll admit that my teaching and perspective on these things makes that a reasonable question. I understand why people might think that's what I'm saying. But I'm not.

I don't think that at all.

However, I do dwell on the question: What if every born-again Christian was equipped to share the gospel in *any* and *every* context? If this were the case, we may be surprised to find that there are many more "opportunities" to share the gospel than we ever imagined. I can't help but find it humorous when I hear Christians say that they are praying for "opportunities" to share the gospel, and for God to open a door for their evangelism. He already has! God has given us his word, he has commanded us to preach the gospel to every creature under heaven, he has given us breath and mouths, and he has given them ears. What more do we need? What more could we possibly be waiting for?

Sometimes people cover their fleshly-desires with language that stresses "waiting on the Holy Spirit"—but this is just a "churchy" way to sound good in our disobedience. The Scriptures have declared that we are to tell the whole world the gospel; therefore, we do not have to be told a second time! When we "pray" about such things, really we are demanding that God tell us the same thing again. You do not need to pray about whether or not you should be faithful to your spouse. You do not need to pray about whether or not you should get drunk this Friday evening. You do not need to pray to hear if the Lord wants you to steal, kill, or lie. The Bible tells us the plain answer to these things. Of course we should pray; but our "prayers" cannot be an excuse for continuing to walk in the flesh because we are not "hearing" from the Lord on matters that he has *already* plainly expressed his will in the Scriptures!

The church—every genuine member—must be equipped and ready. Presently, we're not. For the glory of our Lord and Savior, we must prepare our minds for action and get equipped.[1] Spurgeon said:

> What can one man do alone? What can he not do with an army of enthusiasts around him? Contemplate at the outset the possibility of having a church of soul-winners. Do not succumb to the usual idea that we can only gather a few useful workers, and that the rest of the community must inevitably be a dead weight: it may possibly so happen, but do not set out with that notion or it will be verified. The usual need not be the universal; better things are possible than anything yet attained; set your aim high and spare no effort to reach it. Labour to gather a church alive for Jesus, every member energetic to the full, and the whole in incessant activity for the salvation of men.[2]

Quite frankly, I emphasize the scriptural truths you read about in this book because they are being forgotten, not because they are the only truths. You have to remember, I'm not an evangelist. I'm a pastor. That means that I tend to focus on doctrine and the internal needs of the body as part of my call and spiritual gifting. I emphasize *this* doctrine, because it helps unify the body of Christ in our purpose. I desire a strong, edified body of Christ (as a pastor and a teacher), because a strong, healthy body is better equipped to fulfill the task before us than a sickly, dismembered body is. I desire this, because it glorifies our God and is in line with his revealed will.

---

1. 1 Pet 1:10—2:3.

2. Spurgeon, *Lectures*, 347. This is contrary to the mindset that I've encountered from many different leaders in churches (both pastors and elders), who are content with a few such workers and who desire not to trouble the rest of the congregation. My view is much closer to Spurgeon's and Charles Wesley's, who quipped: "I laboured to trouble the careless, as well as comfort the troubled, hearts" (Kimbrough and Newport, *Manuscript Journal*, 2:446).

AFTERWORD

If you want to sit and have a theological discussion on election or the end times, I'm game. We just can't let it distract us from actually sharing the gospel with the world. George Whitefield wrote, "Let a man go to the grammar school of faith and repentance, before he goes to the university of election and predestination. A bare head-knowledge of sound words availeth nothing. I am quite tired of Christless talkers. From such may I ever turn away. Amen."[3] I don't want to be a Christless talker, or a Christian who has a bare head-knowledge of doctrine, but who doesn't put these things into practice . . . do you? That's why we need to operate according to Jesus' design for his church as defined in Ephesians 4:11–16.

We have to be equipped as ambassadors for Christ, first and foremost. We must understand the gospel and its implications. Then, we must actually *live* in accordance with those implications. These are primary, and they relate to every member of the body. Every single member of Christ's church is called as an ambassador, has been given the ministry of reconciliation, and is only in that position because of the gospel being shared with them.[4] After we are equipped, we can move on to contemplating the deeper things of God. Understanding our call as ambassadors *first* allows us to be equipped to serve in our secondary ministries more fruitfully. These secondary ministries are myriad—things like giving, serving, music, teaching, etc. I can't express to you how awesome it is to hear Christians testify that they are *living* for the first time when they begin embracing their call as ambassadors, and who are walking *with Jesus* in the ministry of reconciliation. I also can't express how burdensome it is to hear Christians bickering with each other about which ministry is most important—children's ministry, prayer ministry, women's ministry, pot-luck ministry, whatever—while the world perishes around them and *no one cares to reach out to them.*

Countless pastors are burned out with needless meetings about secondary matters; all the while the primary work of the church is forgotten and neglected. My heart breaks over this. O, how I wish that pastors could experience the joy of shepherding a flock that is offensive, not defensive! So many of the typical burdens fall away when the focus is no longer maintaining our pet programs and preserving our niche, but in expanding the kingdom of God in power and unity with our living God, and with our brothers and sisters in Christ.

The modern church has flipped this model on its head. Most of the time, we feed into the idea that people should not share the gospel until they have all the answers and understand all the doctrines, if they are ever to

---

3. Whitefield, *Journals*, 491.
4. 1 Cor 15:1–5; 2 Cor 5:11–21.

evangelize at all. As a result, I meet people all the time on the street who can clearly explain their denominational creeds, and can explain all the reasons why they don't associate with other denominations, yet are stumped when asked to explain the gospel or why Jesus, who lived two thousand years ago, is able to save sinners from hell. It is shocking how many professing Christians I meet who cannot explain the gospel or answer me when I ask, "What does some guy who lived so long ago in a place far, far away have to do with *me*." This scenario plays out time and time again, with professing church goers from every local church around![5]

When properly equipped, we are free to follow our Lord Jesus, through the Holy Spirit, in whatever sphere he has called us to. It's possible that Jesus is calling you to quit your job. It's more likely that he wants to you be his ambassador *where you work, live, and play*. As the Scriptures say, we must be wise as serpents and innocent as doves. This does not give us authority to change the message or define our own ministry assignments. Instead, it calls for responsibility on behalf of the properly equipped ambassador to exercise wisdom in walking in their individual calling. It calls for faithfulness in doing the good works he has prepared in advance for us to do.[6]

Our calling as the church is not passive and it is not defensive. It is the opposite. God's church is called to walk in his will and power as an aggressive and offensive entity. We are called to be gate crashers of the kingdom of darkness and heralds of the gospel of the kingdom of God and his Christ. Are you on board?

Get equipped. Obey your king. Glorify your God.

---

5. Certainly, some local churches seem to churn out more confused members regarding the gospel than others.

6. 1 Cor 7:20–24; Eph 2:10; Titus 2:11–15.

Appendix A
Judgment According to Deeds

A common question regarding biblical theology is: How do you reconcile the teaching on salvation by grace through faith alone with passages that seem to indicate judgment for salvation based on good versus bad deeds? Is this a contradiction?

The link between faith and deeds is real in the Scriptures. In fact, deeds are (at least in part) a good test of whether or not you are actually a Christian! However, there are some passages in the Bible that, on the surface, seem to teach contradictory conclusions regarding how the judgment will be decided for individuals standing before the throne of God. Teaching that emphasizes the reality of salvation being a free gift of God by his grace through faith alone, apart from any deeds done by the individual, can be found in passages like John 3:16; Romans 6:23; Ephesians 2:1–10; and Titus 3:4–7. But what about what Jesus taught in John 5:28–29? "Do not marvel at this; for an hour is coming, in which all who are in the tombs will hear His voice, and will come forth; those who did the good deeds to a resurrection of life, those who committed the evil deeds to a resurrection of judgment."

These words of Jesus (see also Matt 25:31–46) seem to indicate that the judgment for *salvation* (not stewardship and not rewards) is based on the doing of good and/or the doing of evil. So, is this a contradiction? Does this mean we should throw out the passages which teach that salvation is *not* by works? Should we attempt to begin working for our salvation?

The answer is simple. No.

Does this mean that we are going to do some interpretive gymnastics to try and explain away the fact that Jesus meant something *different* than what he actually said?

No, we're not going to do that either.

Jesus' teaching illuminates a broader theme in the Scriptures that means exactly what it says. It is still easily misunderstood because we have redefined the terms. We then bring our new meaning to the text, which is what causes the confusion. To understand what Jesus is saying, we must base our understanding on the meaning he intends, not what we have imposed upon the text! In order to properly interpret, we must take biblical terms on their own. We will make mistakes if we impose our own meanings. Defining terms is always important, because people often mean different things even when using the same terms. A clear example is when people discuss "Jesus"—what is meant by this term is radically different if you are a Muslim, a Jew, an Atheist, a Jehovah's Witness, or a biblical Christian.

Before proceeding any further, I need to make a disclaimer: I am about to make a case that people are judged based on their works for salvation. Before you burn me at the stake as a heretic, understand that this is exactly what Jesus said in John 5:28–29. If you stick with me until the end of the explanation, you should see that everything Jesus said is perfectly in line with the understanding that salvation is a gift of God, received by the individual by grace through faith. Even after arguing this claim, I will still affirm that salvation is *not* of works lest any man should boast (Eph 2:8–9). I know that sounds contradictory now, but it isn't.

One of the biggest and most influential lies that has abounded since the beginning of the church—and has endured to the present age—is the preaching and teaching of *moralism* instead of the genuine gospel. The reason that this is so dangerous and insidious is that moralism can be preached very easily from the Bible. Even worse, moralism has pervaded much of our language, thinking, and culture to the point that genuine biblical counsel on what is "good" and what is "bad" is completely ignored—often because of ignorance and biblical illiteracy.[1]

If we understand the difference between moralism and the biblical ideal of obedience to the Father, then we can understand what Jesus was teaching in John 5:28–29. Consider these words from Jesus:

1. Not everyone who says to Me, "Lord, Lord," will enter the kingdom of heaven, but he who does the will of My Father who is in heaven will enter. Many will say to Me on that day, "Lord, Lord, did we not prophesy in Your name, and in Your name cast out demons, and in Your name perform many miracles?" And then I will declare to them, "I never knew you; Depart from me, you who practice lawlessness." Therefore everyone who hears these words of Mine and acts on them, may be compared to a wise man who built his house on the rock. And the rain fell, and the floods came, and the winds blew and slammed

---

1. For a discussion of this difference and an example using a son's "moral" disobedience to his father, see chap. 5.

against that house; and yet it did not fall, for it had been founded on the rock. Everyone who hears these words of Mine and does not act on them, will be like a foolish man who built his house on the sand. The rain fell, and the floods came, and the winds blew and slammed against that house; and it fell—and great was its fall. (Matt 7:21-27)

2. For whoever does the will of My Father who is in heaven, he is My brother and sister and mother. (Matt 12:50)

3. Jesus said to them, "My food is to do the will of Him who sent Me and to accomplish His work." (John 4:34)

The fallen nature of humanity is inherited from our rebellious ancestor, Adam. It has been passed to every generation. In Adam, all have been sold into bondage to rebellion against the king of the universe. This rebellion infects every action, which is why God looks upon his creation and makes the following judgments. Prior to flooding the world: "Then the LORD saw that the wickedness of man was great on the earth, and that every intent of the thoughts of his heart was only evil continually" (Gen 6:5).

After the flood, God promised to withhold his wrath *despite* the following reality: "The LORD smelled the soothing aroma; and the LORD said to Himself, 'I will never again curse the ground on account of man, for the intent of man's heart is evil from his youth; and I will never again destroy every living thing, as I have done'" (Gen 8:21).

In the flood, God judged his creation for their rebellion because, according to his standard, *every* intent of the human heart is *only* evil *all* the time (cf. Gen 6:5 in the NIV). This is why the prophet Isaiah could write the following: "For all of us have become like one who is unclean, / And all our righteous deeds are like a filthy garment; / And all of us wither like a leaf, / And our iniquities, like the wind, take us away" (Isa 64:6). The imagery that the prophet is appealing to is often lost on the modern reader since we do not encounter those who are "unclean" in this same sense. According to the Mosaic Law, a person could become unclean for various reasons (e.g., touching a corpse) and when the person was unclean, their "uncleanness" could be transferred to others (e.g., Hag 2:11-14). The state of being "unclean" is infectious and it taints everything it comes into contact with. Therefore, Isaiah is teaching (just like Haggai claims in Haggai 2:14) that our rebellious nature, inherited from Adam, infects all of our deeds and renders even our *best* moral acts (according to human judgment) as filthy, unclean rags before a holy and righteous God.

This is the poverty of moralism. To tell someone who is unclean that they can perform "righteous acts" is a serious error. They cannot. Their very nature as a rebel makes it impossible for anything they do to be considered "good" in the sight of God. David wrote under the inspiration of the Holy Spirit (quoted by the Apostle Paul in Rom 3:10–12):

> The fool has said in his heart, "There is no God." / They are corrupt, they have committed abominable deeds; / There is no one who does good. / The LORD has looked down from heaven upon the sons of men / To see if there are any who understand, / Who seek after God. / They have all turned aside, together they have become corrupt; / There is no one who does good, not even one. (Ps 14:1–3)

Similarly, the author of Hebrews stated clearly: "And without faith it is impossible to please Him, for he who comes to God must believe that He is and that He is a rewarder of those who seek Him" (Heb 11:6). So, what does this all mean? It means that unless a person is born-again through repentance and faith in Christ, they cannot do anything "good" in the sight of God. It makes no difference how other human beings judge our deeds— apart from Christ we can do nothing "good" in God's sight.

This was exactly what Jesus taught:

1. I am the vine, you are the branches; he who abides in Me and I in him, he bears much fruit, for apart from Me you can do nothing. If anyone does not abide in Me, he is thrown away as a branch and dries up; and they gather them, and cast them into the fire and they are burned. (John 15:5–6)

2. And Jesus said to him, "Why do you call Me good? No one is good except God alone." (Mark 10:18; Luke 18:19)

The Scriptures teach that because of the rebellion of humanity, no one is capable of doing *anything* good in the sight of God on their own. The best examples we can point to—e.g., Gandhi or the Buddha—are all completely *un*righteous in the sight of God. Not "mostly good, but still falling short." Completely unrighteous. This is not how most people (even professing Christians) think about, or view, the world. Even so, it is the picture the Bible presents regarding humanity.

For this reason, moralism is deadly. You cannot tell an unclean person that they can do "good" because their very nature as unclean spoils everything they think, touch, and do![2] This is also why the good news of the gospel is so good.

Jesus is able to make the unclean clean!

---

2. Prov 20:9.

> For if the blood of goats and bulls and the ashes of a heifer sprinkling those who have been defiled sanctify for the cleansing of the flesh, how much more will the blood of Christ, who through the eternal Spirit offered Himself without blemish to God, cleanse your conscience from dead works to serve the living God? For this reason He is the mediator of a new covenant, so that, since a death has taken place for the redemption of the transgressions that were committed under the first covenant, those who have been called may receive the promise of the eternal inheritance. (Heb 9:13–15)

This is the heart of Jesus' lesson on the tree and its fruit. Bad trees cannot produce anything other than bad fruit. In order to make good fruit, you must first make the tree good. Jesus said in Mark 12:33, "Either make the tree good and its fruit good, or make the tree bad and its fruit bad; for the tree is known by its fruit." Apply this teaching to human nature and we can understand why we must be born-again. Our nature must be transformed from "corrupt" before anything good can be produced by us.

1. For as in Adam all die, so also in Christ all will be made alive. (1 Cor 15:22)
2. Therefore if anyone is in Christ, he is a new creature; the old things passed away; behold, new things have come. (2 Cor 5:17)

Salvation from sin must be entirely based upon the free grace of God, because nothing we could ever do in our corrupt nature would be able to earn salvation. We are incapable of transforming our natures from *unclean* to *clean*. Although it is impossible for us, it is not impossible for God.

1. When the disciples heard this, they were very astonished and said, "Then who can be saved?" And looking at them Jesus said to them, "With people this is impossible, but with God all things are possible." (Matt 19:25–26)
2. For by grace you have been saved through faith; and that not of yourselves, it is the gift of God; not as a result of works, so that no one may boast. (Eph 2:8–9)

And look at what we've been saved to do, according to the very next verse (2:10) in Ephesians: "For we are His workmanship, created in Christ Jesus for good works, which God prepared beforehand so that we would walk in them."

Interesting.

For those whom God has saved by his grace, he has transformed our nature,[3] saved us by his own power and mercy,[4] and adopted us into his family as his children so that we are no longer children of the devil.[5] As God's kids, he has specifically prepared good works in advance for each of us to do[6] and doing these works is supposed to be the result ("the fruit") of our salvation.[7] This brings us back to the tree illustration above and the difference between moralism and biblical Christianity.

Our Father has given us specific things to do. He expects us to do them! What God doesn't want us to do is live disobedient and rebellious lives, while covering our rebellion with "moralism." We must not neglect the flip-side of this teaching and the reality of the tree bearing fruit metaphor that Jesus used. Many people profess to be Christians with their mouths, but does the fruit of their life match their confession? This is a fair question and cannot be quickly passed over. The Apostle Paul had some pointed words regarding the fruit of some professing believers' lives when writing to Titus (1:16): "They profess to know God, but by their deeds they deny Him, being detestable and disobedient and worthless for any good deed."

Imagine you are standing in the middle of an orchard, and in the distance you see a fruit tree. As you begin walking toward this fruit tree, you see hanging on its limbs big, beautiful oranges. As you continue to walk closer, you also notice that nailed to the trunk of the tree is a small sign. Once close enough you read the sign which simply states: "This is an apple tree."

Do you believe the sign, or do you believe the fruit?

If you're smart, you believe the fruit. Yet, in our culture many have believed that they are "Christian" because they have labeled themselves as such. Putting a cross necklace on or sitting in a church doesn't make someone a Christian. When some people want to examine the fruit, often this is met with accusations of legalism and works-based-righteousness. If the fruit of our lives does not match our confession, then the Bible indicates that we should question the reality of our conversion.[8] Putting a sign on an orange tree that says it's an apple tree doesn't change its nature. Similarly, sitting in a church doesn't make someone a born-again follower of Jesus.[9]

---

3. 2 Cor 5:17.
4. Eph 2:8–9, Titus 3:5–7.
5. Gal 3:26; 1 John 3:10.
6. Eph 2:10.
7. E.g., 2 Cor 5:18–21; Titus 3:8; Rom 6:1–7.
8. Matt 3:8; 2 Cor 13:5; 1 John 1:1—5:21.
9. John 3:3.

According to Scripture, nothing is inherently "good" on its own, aside from obeying the will of the Father. I understand that this is a controversial statement. People may object saying, what about passages like Isaiah 1:16-17, which commands God's people to learn to "do good" by such things as seeking justice, reproving the ruthless, defending widows, and pleading for the cause of orphans? Plucked out of the greater biblical context, passages like this—and there are others—seem to indicate that certain deeds are inherently righteous. However, when considering the greater biblical context we can understand that certain deeds serve as indicators that we are, or are not, walking in God's will.

A prominent example is found in Galatians 5:19-21, which lists certain deeds that make it evident that the person is not walking with the Spirit of the living God. Isaiah 1:16-17 (and passages like it) serves a similar purpose, but from the opposite angle. It can be true that if you are *not* doing things like seeking justice, clothing the naked, feeding the poor, and defending orphans, then you are similarly not walking in the Spirit. However, the reverse is *not* necessarily true—that is, if you are abstaining from drunkenness and sexual immorality, and if you are working in a soup kitchen and seeking justice for the oppressed, this does not guarantee that you are walking in God's will.[10] A helpful example should illustrate the logical mistake that is being made:

1. All turtles are animals. *True.*
2. All animals are turtles. *False.*

In the same way:

1. Walking in God's will is abstaining from drunkenness and seeking justice. *True.*
2. Abstaining from drunkenness and seeking justice is walking in God's will. *Possibly false.*

After all, many atheists, secular humanists, and worshippers of false religions do these same types of things as part of their idolatry. Yet, the Bible clearly teaches that none of these other paths leads to salvation and boldly declares, despite the prevalence of what many would call "good deeds" being done by those who do not follow Christ, that there are *none* good but God.

---

10. In Gal 2:1-9, the Apostle Paul describes an encounter he had with the other Apostles when he laid his gospel before them. They recognized Paul's gospel as a genuine revelation from God for the Gentiles and extended the right hand of fellowship to Paul, putting apostolic approval on Paul's ministry. In 2:10, Paul records, "They only asked us to remember the poor—the very thing I also was eager to do." Paul was encouraged to remember the poor *while* ministering the gospel, not *instead of* ministering the gospel.

When we do these same types of activities, with wrong motives, we are performing them in rebellion against God, which is a violation of the first and greatest commandment! Our impure motives taint the activities and make them wicked in God's sight.[11]

Reading my Bible can be disobedience if he has prepared in advance that I speak the truth in love to my neighbor instead. This is why the New Testament so emphasizes walking with the Holy Spirit instead of moralism—although pulpits across this nation seem to emphasize moralism over walking with the Spirit!

1. So then, brethren, we are under obligation, not to the flesh, to live according to the flesh—for if you are living according to the flesh, you must die; but if by the Spirit you are putting to death the deeds of the body, you will live. For all who are being led by the Spirit of God, these are sons of God. (Rom 8:12-14)

2. Now those who belong to Christ Jesus have crucified the flesh with its passions and desires. If we live by the Spirit, let us also walk by the Spirit. (Gal 5:24-25)

As we bring this all together, now we can make sense of what Jesus said in John 5:28-29. The common idea that someday our works will be judged on some cosmic scale—that those whose "good deeds" outweigh their "bad deeds" will go to heaven and the rest will go to hell—is completely wrong and inadequate. Look very carefully at what Jesus said again in John 5:28-29: "Do not marvel at this; for an hour is coming, in which all who are in the tombs will hear His voice, and will come forth; those who did the good deeds to a resurrection of life, those who committed the evil deeds to a resurrection of judgment."

Jesus' description says nothing of one type of deed *outweighing* the other. Instead, Jesus states plainly that those who did *good* deeds will go to the resurrection of life and those who did *evil* deeds will go to a resurrection of judgment. Based on the testimony of the Bible, outside of Christ not a single person will have even one good deed on their record. Not one! No matter how virtuous or "good" *we* may judge someone to be, unless they have been born-again they are *incapable* of producing any good fruit because their fallen nature taints *every single thing they think, say, and do.* If we go back to the tree illustration—with apples representing good deeds and oranges representing evil deeds—the judgment for orange trees requires that they produce some apples. Unfortunately, they can't. All the orange tree can offer is oranges. While the quality and quantity each orange tree may

---

11. Prov 16:2; 21:2.

offer is different, there will *never* be any apples. Conversely, every apple tree is accepted—regardless of whether there is only one apple or a billion found in its branches.

Remember God's description of humanity from Genesis 6:5—every intent of the heart is only evil all the time.

For those who have been transformed and renewed by the regeneration of the Holy Spirit, they are called to walk in good deeds prepared in advance for them to do. Each time we obey God rather than our flesh, our new nature actually produces genuinely "good fruit"! This does not mean that our works result in our salvation. Instead, our salvation results in genuine good works. God transforms the redeemed into a new creature—to maintain the illustration from the parable, God changes the orange tree into an apple tree. When the judgment comes, those who have done "good deeds" (even one!) will go to the resurrection of life! Since those who have been saved have been transformed by the grace of God, they cannot boast about their works because everything *good* that they've done has been worked by God in and through them. They produce *apples* because God changed their nature. And, if we're honest, some of the fruit they produce is still rotten.[12]

The freedom we have as children of God allows for moments of obedience and disobedience to God's will for us as his children.[13] When we abide in Christ and obey him, we produce genuinely good fruit which will endure for eternal life. When we disobey, God disciplines us as sons and daughters in order to bring about the fruit of righteousness in our lives.[14]

With this understanding we can see that the teaching of Scripture is unified and not at all contradictory. The Apostle Paul gives us a beautiful picture which should drive home the importance of our stewardship of the grace of God in this life:

> According to the grace of God which was given to me, like a wise master builder I laid a foundation, and another is building on it. But each man must be careful how he builds on it. For no man can lay a foundation other than the one which is laid, which is Jesus Christ. Now if any man builds on the foundation with gold, silver, precious stones, wood, hay, straw, each man's work will become evident; for the day will show it because it is to be revealed with fire, and the fire itself will test the quality of each man's work. If any man's work which he has built on it remains, he will receive a reward. If any man's work is burned up,

---

12. 1 Pet 2:16.
13. Rom 6:12–14.
14. Heb 12:4–11.

he will suffer loss; but he himself will be saved, yet so as through fire. (1 Cor 3:10–15)

The foundation of Christ is first necessary (salvation by grace through faith alone). Upon this foundation, we build with works that will endure (through obeying our Father) through the judgment and ones that will not (when we disobey our Father). Yet, the person themselves *will be saved* because even one good work is enough for salvation.

Therefore they said to Him, "What shall we do, so that we may work the works of God?" Jesus answered and said to them, "This is the work of God, that you believe in Him whom He has sent."[15]

Believe in Jesus! Turn to the Lord and be saved, all you ends of the earth![16]

Knowing that this is true, hear the word of the Lord all you, his children:

1. As obedient children, do not be conformed to the former lusts which were yours in your ignorance, but like the Holy One who called you, be holy yourselves also in all your behavior; because it is written, "You shall be holy, for I am holy." If you address as Father the One who impartially judges according to each one's work, conduct yourselves in fear during the time of your stay on earth; knowing that you were not redeemed with perishable things like silver or gold from your futile way of life inherited from your forefathers, but with precious blood, as of a lamb unblemished and spotless, the blood of Christ. (1 Pet 1:14–19)

2. Therefore, my brethren, you also were made to die to the Law through the body of Christ, so that you might be joined to another, to Him who was raised from the dead, in order that we might bear fruit for God. For while we were in the flesh, the sinful passions, which were aroused by the Law, were at work in the members of our body to bear fruit for death. But now we have been released from the Law, having died to that by which we were bound, so that we serve in newness of the Spirit and not in oldness of the letter. (Rom 7:4–6)

3. For this reason also, since the day we heard of it, we have not ceased to pray for you and to ask that you may be filled with the knowledge of His will in all spiritual wisdom and understanding, so that you will walk in a manner worthy of the Lord, to please Him in all respects, bearing fruit in every good work and increasing in the knowledge of

---

15. John 6:28–29.
16. Isa 45:22.

God; strengthened with all power, according to His glorious might, for the attaining of all steadfastness and patience; joyously giving thanks to the Father, who has qualified us to share in the inheritance of the saints in Light. For He rescued us from the domain of darkness, and transferred us to the kingdom of His beloved Son, in whom we have redemption, the forgiveness of sins. (Col 1:9–14)

Amen.

Appendix B
Servants & Stewards

The Apostle Paul is someone who understood the surpassing value of knowing Christ and the cost associated with dying to self so that Christ might live through him.[1] Sometimes Christians look at the men and women whose lives are recorded in the Bible and view them as "super saints"—people whose images are rightly captured on stained glass windows and whose sacrificial service to the King of kings is beyond the grasp of "normal" Christians.

This is not how the Apostle Paul viewed his own ministry. Twice in his first letter to the Christians in Corinth, Paul urged them to be imitators of him.[2] Paul actually went further than this, writing that this instruction of imitating him and his conduct is not only for the church at Corinth, but is something that he teaches everywhere he goes! "Therefore I exhort you, be imitators of me. For this reason I have sent to you Timothy, who is my beloved and faithful child in the Lord, and he will remind you of my ways which are in Christ, just as I teach everywhere in every church."[3]

Paul travelled around preaching the gospel and planting churches. It is interesting to study his missionary journeys in Acts because he planted fewer churches than many people realize. Paul recognized that genuine churches—fellowships of born-again followers of Jesus Christ—are potent. When the church operates as Jesus intends, you don't need a different church on every corner.[4] Paul included in his teaching *everywhere and in*

---

1. Gal 2:20.

2. 1 Cor 4:16; 11:1. For more statements of this type, see also Eph 5:1; 1 Thess 1:6; 2:14; 2 Thess 3:7-9; Heb 6:12, 13:7; and 3 John 1:11.

3. 1 Cor 4:16-17.

4. Today, we have churches on virtually every corner and yet, our impact is decidedly less potent than the churches Paul planted. It continues to be my claim that the lack of power stems from our straying from Jesus' design for his church, outlined in

every church about what it means to follow Christ. He urged these disciples to imitate his own ways in Christ. To view Paul's life as one which is out of reach for the common Christian is completely *contrary* to the teaching of the Apostle himself!

What's worse, this type of attitude on behalf of the "normal" Christian is often veiled in modesty. This attitude actually has a false teaching as its foundation which views the Christian walk as something *we* do as opposed to something that *God has done and will continue to do*.[5] When we say that our walk cannot be like Paul's, we are not being modest and humble. Instead, we are insulting the grace of God. In reality, we are insisting that God is not able to do in us what he has done in our brothers and sisters before us. Our problem is not an *inability* to be like Paul and these "super saints." Our real problem is an unwillingness to die to self so that Christ might live through us.

In Paul's letter to these Christians in Corinth, he expressed his heart and method for dying to self, and allowing the grace of God and Christ in him to act powerfully for the advance of the glory of God. Paul did not view himself as a super saint. Paul viewed himself as a servant and as a steward. To go a step further, he wanted everyone to regard him—and his fellow Christians—in the same way: "Let a man regard us in this manner, as servants of Christ and stewards of the mysteries of God" (1 Cor 4:1).

Just like you and your walk with Christ, everyone had an opinion of Paul and his walk. Some liked what he was doing. Others did not. But Paul was unconcerned about others' views and judgments of him and his conduct.[6] He instructed Christians not to be deceived about themselves, either. To our own master we stand and fall.[7] Therefore, God's opinion of us is the only one that matters.[8]

Are you concerned with the opinions of others? Or are you consumed with pleasing the God who loved you and redeemed you with the precious blood of Christ?[9]

If you are a Christian, and you understand that you are no longer your own, but that you have been purchased with a costly price for God and his glory, then you are called to imitate Paul's ways in Christ. You, too, should identify yourself as a servant of Christ and as a steward of the mysteries of

---

Ephesians 4:11–16.

5. Gal 3:1–3.
6. 1 Cor 4:3.
7. Rom 14:4.
8. 2 Cor 5:9–10.
9. 1 Cor 6:19–20; Rev 5:9.

God. And if that's you, then this applies to you: "In this case, moreover, it is required of stewards that one be found trustworthy."[10]

The concept of being a servant and a steward is not common to much of what passes for Christianity in North America. Yet, the Scriptures have been delivered to us from the living God who reigns as a righteous king and whose kingdom extends over all the kingdoms of the earth.[11] This revelation from the living God and creator of all things is what we are to steward for the praise and glory of his name.

Unfortunately, many who profess Christ are negligent in their responsibility and are ignorant of the content of the Scriptures. They are more concerned with other matters.[12] As a result, we often fail to discharge our duty as servants and stewards.

Our God is not a wishy-washy God. He has taken great care to reveal himself and his plan through the Bible and through his Son.[13] Our task as servants and stewards is to know and understand this revelation from God so that we may walk according to God's good will and pleasure. It is *not* our task to pick and choose which portions of Scripture to obey and emphasize (and to ignore the rest), nor is it our task to go beyond what is written.

"Now these things, brethren, I have figuratively applied to myself and Apollos for your sakes, so that in us you may learn not to exceed what is written, so that no one of you will become arrogant in behalf of one against the other. For who regards you as superior? What do you have that you did not receive? And if you did receive it, why do you boast as if you had not received it?" (1 Cor 4:6–7)

As followers of Christ, we serve the same master. Our allegiance is not to our denomination or our culture. Our allegiance is to Christ. As such, we who have been purchased by the blood of Christ are not enemies of each other. We are brothers and sisters in the family of God! Yet, most of the fighting I hear of between professing believers is speculation on theological implications that go well beyond that which is written, or which relies on human reasoning, as we try and connect some of the same dots (but do so differently).

Going beyond what is written happens all the time—often because Christians have no idea what *is* written, because we don't take the time to diligently read and understand what the Scriptures say. I've heard all the excuses:

10. 1 Cor 4:2.
11. Ps 103:19.
12. Rom 8:1–14; Col 3:2; Phil 3:18–19; 2 Tim 4:10; 1 John 2:15–17.
13. Heb 1:1–2.

I don't have time.

I'm very busy.

You don't understand . . . with my job, I simply can't read my Bible every day.

What much of modern Christianity has forgotten (or, simply never been taught) is that if you are a Christian, your job is first and foremost to be both *a servant of Christ and a steward of the mysteries of God as his ambassador.* Whatever *other* tasks and responsibilities God has given to you, you are to exercise in subordination to your primary calling as a servant and steward; not the other way around! "Whatever you do, do your work heartily, as for the Lord rather than for men, knowing that from the Lord you will receive the reward of the inheritance. It is the Lord Christ whom you serve."[14]

I repeat: our problem is not an *inability* to be like Paul and these "super saints," but really an unwillingness to die to self that Christ might live through us. As Paul was writing to these believers in Corinth, he was addressing a bad strain of teaching that was influencing them and encouraging them to be comfortable—to even look down upon his own sacrificial service for the Lord. Paul had no problem pointing out the contrast:

> For, I think, God has exhibited us apostles last of all, as men condemned to death; because we have become a spectacle to the world, both to angels and to men. We are fools for Christ's sake, but you are prudent in Christ; we are weak, but you are strong; you are distinguished, but we are without honor. To this present hour we are both hungry and thirsty, and are poorly clothed, and are roughly treated, and are homeless; and we toil, working with our own hands; when we are reviled, we bless; when we are persecuted, we endure; when we are slandered, we try to conciliate; we have become as the scum of the world, the dregs of all things, even until now. (1 Cor 4:9–13)

In our present, North American context, it sure seems like Paul's description of the Corinthian state is much better than his own! These believers are prudent, strong, distinguished, and comfortable. Yet, Paul does not commend them in this. Instead, Paul tells them to be like him and the other apostles! He even points out that their current view of themselves could be considered shameful. "I do not write these things to shame you, but to admonish you as my beloved children. For if you were to have countless tutors

---

14. Col 3:23–24.

in Christ, yet you would not have many fathers, for in Christ Jesus I became your father through the gospel. Therefore I exhort you, be imitators of me."[15]

Imitators of Paul—the one who is a spectacle to the world, a fool for the sake of Christ, weak, without honor, hungry and thirsty, poorly clothed, roughly treated, and homeless. A hard worker who blesses when reviled, endures when persecuted, and tries to reconcile when slandered. Scum and dregs. *Imitate this.*

Paul's language is vivid. When Paul says he is the scum[16] of the world he is using language that equates himself to being the filth that is scoured off of a dirty dish and thrown away—the filth that must be cleansed so that the valuable part remains and becomes more useful once the worthless part is eliminated. As the "scum of the world," Paul is painting a clear picture of the value others put on him and his ministry—they think the world would be better off without him! Continuing the vivid picture, Paul says he is the dregs[17] of all things, which is a word that carries a similar range of meaning to scum, but meant something very particular to the Corinthians. In nearby Athens, they attempted to pacify the Greek god Poseidon each year by taking the worst criminal they had, and flinging them into the sea as a propitiatory offering. It was hoped that this offering would help to avert any public disasters by appeasing the god. By calling himself the "dregs of all things," Paul is similarly declaring that the world thinks his best use would be to be sacrificed for the good of the world. Paul is emphatically pointing to himself as being viewed as the lowest, vilest, and most worthless of all things—everyone would be better off without him. *Imitate this.*

The call to abundant life in Christ is really a call to death. Death to self. Death to the flesh. Death to the world. Death to these, so that Christ might live *in* and *through* us. Much of what passes for Christianity these days is just *talk*. We talk the talk, but Paul walked the walk. He taught everywhere in every church that this walk is for all who claim to follow Christ—not just the "super saints."

On our own, and in our strength, this is impossible. But praise God for his amazing grace and power which is so readily available to all who call on him and who rest in him! "But I will come to you soon, if the Lord wills, and I shall find out, not the words of those who are arrogant but their power. For the kingdom of God does not consist in words but in power."[18]

---

15. 1 Cor 4:14–16.
16. Gk: *perikathármata*.
17. Gk: *perípsēma*.
18. 1 Cor 4:19–20.

If the grace of God is active in your life, then the same power that made a weak and fearful man like Paul a powerful servant and steward of the mysteries of God is active in you!

> And when I came to you, brethren, I did not come with superiority of speech or of wisdom, proclaiming to you the testimony of God. For I determined to know nothing among you except Jesus Christ, and Him crucified. I was with you in weakness and in fear and in much trembling, and my message and my preaching were not in persuasive words of wisdom, but in demonstration of the Spirit and of power, so that your faith would not rest on the wisdom of men, but on the power of God. (1 Cor 2:1–5)

It is a testimony to the powerful grace of God at work in and through Paul, that history remembers him as an imposing and "strong" historical figure. Paul was transformed by the power of the gospel. He proclaimed those same truths as a faithful steward. His message was not his own. What he received he passed on.[19] As a servant of Christ, the grace and power of God worked actively and powerfully in his life because he was willing to die to self and submit himself to the living God. The power and strength for his ministry sprang forth from this willingness.[20] As a result God was glorified through Paul's weakness.

> And He has said to me, "My grace is sufficient for you, for power is perfected in weakness." Most gladly, therefore, I will rather boast about my weaknesses, so that the power of Christ may dwell in me. Therefore I am well content with weaknesses, with insults, with distresses, with persecutions, with difficulties, for Christ's sake; for when I am weak, then I am strong. (2 Cor 12:9–10)

Is God's grace sufficient for you? Are you willing to die to self, that Christ might live through you? Are you willing to suffer the loss of all things so that you might gain Christ? Are you doing what is necessary to be a faithful servant and steward of the mysteries of God? Are you walking in your call as an ambassador for Christ?

If you are a follower of Christ, it is required that you be found trustworthy.[21]

He is worthy of nothing less.

---

19. 1 Cor 15:1–10.
20. 1 Cor 15:10; Phil 2:12–13.
21. 1 Cor 4:2.

Appendix C
Source Discussion

Chapter 11 focuses on the life, ministry, and theology of Charles Wesley. In doing research on Charles, I was somewhat selective on the sources that were used with a purpose. The following explanation is supplied for completeness and clarity.

One of the leading authorities on the life of Charles Wesley, and a leader in the recent emergence of scholarly investigation into the life and works of this "other Wesley,"[1] is John Tyson. He notes that "most people who are acquainted with the work of Charles Wesley rightly think of his hymns as his most enduring legacy and contribution to contemporary Christian life."[2] Certainly, Charles Wesley was a prolific hymn writer and "the numerical calculation of Charles's hymns runs from a high of 9,000 down to a low of 3,000 . . . The median estimate reaches about 7,300 hymns."[3] Of these thousands of poetical selections, "he published some 4,600 poems and hymns" while living, "and another 3,000 were published posthumously."[4]

Commenting on the reasons for the varied estimates of Charles's lyrical output, Tyson notes that one of the major issues is "the general question of authorship. Was a particular hymn composed by John or Charles? Since the brothers seemed to have had a gentlemen's agreement about not designating the composer of the separate hymns, the inquirer is faced by what Frank Baker has aptly called 'the vexed problem of joint authorship.'"[5] As a result of this particular issue of uncertainty as to which poetical works are exclusively the work of Charles in these jointly published works, as well as

1. Tyson, *Assist Me to Proclaim*, vii.
2. Ibid.
3. Tyson, *Reader*, 21.
4. Kimbrough and Beckerlegge, *Unpublished*, 1:11.
5. Tyson, *Reader*, 20–21.

the problem of knowing exactly where the editorial hand of John has entered into Charles's compositions even when Charles *is* identified as the sole author, I chose to largely ignore these previously published works attributed to Charles Wesley in order to restrict us to the poetic selections that *undoubtedly* belong to Charles and are free from the editorial hand of another.

I'm particularly thankful for the excellent work of S. T. Kimbrough Jr. and Oliver A. Beckerlegge for publishing *The Unpublished Poetry of Charles Wesley* in three volumes. The completion of these volumes (published in 1988, 1990, and 1992 respectively) has attempted to "publish the unpublished Charles Wesley lyrical corpus which is vital to literary, historical, theological and biblical studies, as well as to the life of the church."[6] As a result of these efforts, further insight into the editorial hand of Charles himself can be identified.

In volume 2 of the *Unpublished Poetry of Charles Wesley: Hymns and Poems on Holy Scripture*, Kimbrough comments after a comparison of these unpublished documents to previously published works that "one sees clearly in the poems of this volume how Wesley continued to appropriate and rework poetry he had written earlier or already published."[7] Further examples demonstrate that Charles did not consistently publish his complete compositions, but rather "he randomly published portions of poems, e.g. two verses of a six verse poem, with no explanation."[8] As a result, even some of Charles's most popular published works have been published in their complete form for the first time in Kimbrough and Beckerlegge's volumes.

With such a large array of poetic selections to choose from, the previously unpublished materials as included in the works of Kimbrough and Beckerlegge have received the largest amount of attention for this chapter. Some may object to limiting the scope of the investigation of the poetic corpus to these selections, arguing that this will provide an inadequate picture of the theological views of Charles. However, this potential shortcoming is overshadowed by the following two considerations.

First, the purpose of this research is an investigation of *Charles's* theological views. It is not an inquiry into a distinctive *Methodist* or even *Wesleyan* theology. As such, removing any potential mingling from the better known Wesley brother is advantageous in this pursuit, no matter how slight that influence from John may be. Secondly, to truly examine Charles on his own terms, I am not as interested in what he edited for public consumption and use as I am in his genuine personal thoughts, attitudes, and views as it

---

6. Kimbrough and Beckerlegge, *Unpublished*, 1:11.
7. Ibid., 2:8.
8. Ibid.

relates to particular theological doctrines. It could be argued that the works which are edited and published are the best representation of an individual's personal views; but this is merely conjecture. It could likewise be argued on the same conjectural grounds that the *unpublished* works are a better representation of the true views precisely because they are *not* edited for public consumption.

As a result of the scholarly work of Kimbrough and Beckerlegge, it is apparent that Charles continued to work on at least some of his lyrical works after they had been published. Therefore, the conclusion that the body of poetic works which were published during Charles's lifetime is the *best* representation of his theological views is untenable.

Regardless of the potential objection(s) to limiting the view of Charles's works to those which are undoubtedly his sole composition and in their fullest and unedited[9] form, it is worth noting that there is nothing in the published works that will contradict the conclusions and claims of this narrower focus. Nothing has been discovered in these previously unpublished works that would contradict the previous understandings of Charles's major theological views. On the contrary, what has resulted is a greater fullness in expressing these views through gaining a more complete glimpse into the mind of this important leader in the Methodist movement and the Great Awakening.

It may also be objected by some that the lyrical nature of these works makes them unsuitable for theological consideration. After all, these are poetic compositions and not rightly understood as theological treatises. Newport states that "it is worth noting in passing, however, that it is quite possible, as Rattenbury has suggested, that some of Charles's hymns carry in poetic form the theological weight of his (now lost) expositions and sermons."[10] The appropriateness of considering the "lyrical theology" of hymns and other poetic compositions is currently gaining more attention in the academic setting, being led by Kimbrough.[11] The view taken in chapter 11 is that these lyrical selections do in fact carry significant weight in understanding the particular theological views of Charles—they give a glimpse into his passions and pursuits as a minister of the gospel.

---

9. By "unedited" I simply mean "for publication." Charles clearly edited and revised some of these works and his editorial hand can be seen and is noted in the critical editions. However, they were not edited for publication, which would cause other deletions and changes to be made to suit the particular circumstances and occasion for publishing the materials.

10. Newport, *Sermons*, 65.

11. See Kimbrough, *Lyrical Theology*, 23–41 for an overview of this emerging arena of academic inquiry as it relates to the theology of hymns and other poetic works.

Although arguably best known as a hymn-writer in the present day, this was not how Charles was best known in his own time. Newport points out that "such a divide is fairly typical in Methodist scholarship; one studies John's theology, but Charles's hymns. Charles is seen largely as a poet, not as a theologian."[12] This understanding, however, is unfortunate and incomplete. While Charles's hymn writing was certainly prolific and many of these writings have endured into present hymn books, his brother John "reportedly spoke of Charles's poetic abilities as his 'least.'"[13] As a preacher and itinerant minister, Charles left a wealth of other extant documents and resources to consider. Therefore, to simply study the lyrical compositions of Charles for their musical and/or poetic character would be incomplete. In addition to the hymns and poems, these other extant sources available must be considered to further examine the value of Charles's expressed theology.

As an itinerant preacher, Charles travelled and preached extensively. The extant sermons as compiled in Newport's *Sermons of Charles Wesley: A Critical Edition with Introduction and Notes* is rightly included in this investigation to gain an understanding of Charles's distinctive theological views. Newport's work gives excellent insight into the reason for the lack of extant sermon material despite Charles's extensive preaching career. Newport also helps to distinguish between those sermons which originated from Charles, those which were copied from his brother John's manuscripts (with edits from Charles's hand that are representative of those views exclusive to Charles) which demonstrate a shared theology between the brothers, those sermons which represent the important theological shift after Charles's "evangelical conversion" and personal Pentecost on May 21, 1738,[14] and finally, those sermons which are of contested authorship which are attributed to Charles. In keeping with the goal of identifying a distinctive theology of Charles, and an examination of his life in particular as he puts this theology into practice, those sermons of "doubtful" or "disputed" character have been eliminated from consideration without any real fear of substance being lost.

Another primary source which provides a wealth of information regarding Charles's perspective and theology is in the recent manuscript journal publication by Kimbrough and Newport. The importance of this updated and critical edition of the manuscript journal cannot be overstated and was "dedicated to one of the most pressing needs, as regards primary texts, for future study of Charles Wesley—to provide a *complete, accurate,*

---

12. Newport, *Sermons*, 48n1.
13. Ibid., 28.
14. Kimbrough and Newport, *Manuscript Journal*, 1:106–8.

and *accessible* edition of his manuscript journal."[15] Comparing Kimbrough and Newport's edition to the previous available editions (namely, the editions by Telford and Jackson) demonstrates the significant shortcomings of these previous works. For any serious inquiry of the events and perspective of Charles Wesley's life from March 1736 to November 1756, these two volumes by Kimbrough and Newport are indispensable.[16]

A final area of primary documentation that forms the foundation for this study are letters and correspondence to and from Charles, in addition to letters and correspondence between his contemporaries. These primary sources help to fill out some details, especially in the cases of eye witness testimony of some of Charles's *ex tempore* preaching style,[17] of which no documentation exists beyond these testimonials since they were preached without a sermon manuscript ever having been written. At present, there is a need for a resource that compiles the extant letters of Charles Wesley to eliminate the difficulty in accessing these documents.[18] For the purposes of the present study, letters and correspondence as recorded in the manuscript journal, Newport's collection of sermons, and the works previously cited by Tyson will form the main source of these writings for consideration.

While the lack of a complete source of extant letters at present is not ideal, the wealth of other sources makes it virtually impossible to think that any of these yet-to-be-published materials would contradict any of the findings discussed here. On the contrary, it is expected that these additional resources will add credibility to the conclusions reached.

---

15. Ibid., 1: xviii, italics in original.

16. For a fuller discussion and explanation for why this updated edition was needed, see ibid., 1:xxiv–xxxi.

17. E.g., Newport, *Sermons*, 29–31. One interesting anecdote for those who see the pictures of Charles Wesley and get the idea that he was stiff or lifeless in his preaching style, "there is other evidence to suggest that Charles may sometimes have put more energy into his sermons than was good for him. Indeed, he once got himself so worked up while delivering a sermon on Psalm 23 that he bled from the nose for some time afterwards" (ibid., 29).

18. The forthcoming Kenneth G.C. Newport and Gareth Lloyd, eds., *Letters of Charles Wesley*, promises to make significant strides in filling this need.

Bibliography

Bahnsen, Greg L., et al. *Five Views on Law and Gospel*. Grand Rapids: Zondervan ,1996.
Baker, Frank. *Charles Wesley, as Revealed by His Letters*. London: Epworth, 1948.
———. *Charles Wesley's Verse*. London: Epworth, 1988.
———, ed. *Representative Verse of Charles Wesley*. London: Epworth, 1962.
———, ed. *Letters*. Works of John Wesley 25–26. Oxford: Clarendon, 1980.
Bauer, Walter, et al. *Greek-English Lexicon of the New Testament and Other Early Christian Literature*. 3rd ed. Chicago: University of Chicago Press, 1961.
Berger, Teresa. *Theology in Hymns? A Study of the Relationship of Doxology and Theology according to a Collection of Hymns for the Use of the People Called Methodists (1780)*. Nashville: Kingswood, 1995.
Brailsford, Mabel Richmond. *A Tale of Two Brothers*. London: Hart-Davis, 1954.
Brown, Michael L. *The Rude Awakening: How Saved Are We?* Shippensburg, PA: Destiny Image, 1990.
Cairns, Earl E. *Christianity through the Centuries: A History of the Christian Church*. 3rd ed. Grand Rapids: Zondervan, 1996.
Carson, D. A. *A Call to Spiritual Reformation: Priorities from Paul and His Prayers*. Grand Rapids: Baker, 1992.
Church, Leslie F. "Charles Wesley—the Man." *London Quarterly and Holborn Review* 182 (1957) 247–53.
Collins, Kenneth J. *John Wesley: A Theological Journey*. Nashville: Abingdon, 2003.
Doughty, W. L. "Charles Wesley, Preacher." *London Quarterly and Holborn Review* 182 (1957) 263–67.
Gilbert, Greg. *What Is the Gospel?* Wheaton, IL: Crossway, 2010.
Gill, Frederick. *Charles Wesley, the First Methodist*. Nashville: Abingdon, 1964.
Heitzenrater, Richard P. *Wesley and the People Called Methodists*. Nashville: Abingdon, 1995.
Hodge, Charles. *An Exposition of the First Epistle to the Corinthians*. Grand Rapids: Eerdmans, 1969.
Jones, D. M. *Charles Wesley, a Study*. London: Epworth, n.d.
Kaiser, Walter C., Jr. *Revive Us Again: Biblical Insights for Encouraging Spiritual Renewal*. Nashville: Broadman & Holman, 1999.
Kimbrough, S. T. *Charles Wesley: Poet and Theologian*. Nashville: Kingswood, 1992.
———. *The Lyrical Theology of Charles Wesley: A Reader*. Eugene, OR: Cascade, 2011.
Kimbrough, S. T., and Oliver A. Beckerlegge, eds. *The Unpublished Poetry of Charles Wesley*. 3 vols. Nashville: Kingswood, 1988–1992.

Kimbrough, S. T., and Kenneth G. C. Newport. *The Manuscript Journal of the Reverend Charles Wesley, M.A.* 2 vols. Nashville: Kingswood, 2007–2008.

Koukl, Gregory. *Tactics: A Game Plan for Discussing Your Christian Convictions.* Grand Rapids: Zondervan, 2009.

Moreland, J. P. *Love Your God with All Your Mind: The Role of Reason in the Life of the Soul.* Colorado Springs: NavPress, 1997.

Newport, Kenneth G. C. *The Sermons of Charles Wesley: A Critical Edition, with Introduction and Notes.* Oxford: Oxford University Press, 2001.

Newport, Kenneth G. C., and Ted A. Campbell, eds. *Charles Wesley: Life, Literature and Legacy.* Peterborough: Epworth, 2007.

Newport, Kenneth G. C., and Gareth Lloyd, eds. *The Letters of Charles Wesley: A Critical Edition with Introduction and Notes.* 2 vols. Oxford University Press, 2013–.

Osborn, George. *The Poetical Works of John and Charles Wesley Together with the Poems of Charles Wesley Not Before Published.* London: Wesleyan-Methodist Conference Office, 1868–1872.

Packer, J. I. *Evangelism and the Sovereignty of God.* Downers Grove: InterVarsity, 1991.

Payne, Karl I. *Spiritual Warfare: Christians, Demonization, and Deliverance.* Washington, DC: WND, 2011.

Rattenbury, J. Ernest. *The Evangelical Doctrines of Charles Wesley's Hymns.* London: Epworth, 1954.

Spurgeon, C. H. *Lectures to My Students: Complete and Unabridged.* Grand Rapids: Zondervan, 1954.

Tyson, John R. *Assist Me to Proclaim: The Life and Hymns of Charles Wesley.* Grand Rapids: Eerdmans, 2007.

———, ed. *Charles Wesley: A Reader.* Oxford: Oxford University Press, 2000.

Wallace, Charles. *Susanna Wesley: The Complete Writings.* New York: Oxford University Press, 1997.

Wallace, Daniel B. *Greek Grammar beyond the Basics: An Exegetical Syntax of the New Testament.* Grand Rapids: Zondervan, 1996.

Ward, William Reginald, and Richard P. Heitzenrater, eds. *Journal and Diaries.* 7 vols. Works of John Wesley 23. Nashville: Abingdon, 1988–2003.

Washer, Paul. *The Gospel's Power and Message.* Grand Rapids: Reformation Heritage, 2012.

Whitefield, George. *George Whitefield's Journals.* Edinburgh: Banner of Truth, 1998.

Wiseman, Frederick Luke. *Charles Wesley: Evangelist and Poet.* New York: Abingdon, 1932.

Wright, Christopher J. H. *The Mission of God: Unlocking the Bible's Grand Narrative.* Downers Grove: IVP Academic, 2006.

www.ingramcontent.com/pod-product-compliance
Lightning Source LLC
Chambersburg PA
CBHW070305230426
43664CB00014B/2638